Suspicion of Money Laundering

In the Crossfire of International Due Diligence Obligations

Liechtenstein – Austria – Germany – Switzerland

By Professionals – for Professionals

Hypo Investment Bank (Liechtenstein) AG

Principality of Liechtenstein
Vaduz, January 2006

Vienna · Graz 2006

Bibliographical information from Deutsche Bibliothek

Deutsche Bibliothek records this publication in the German
national bibliography; detailed bibliographical data can be retrieved on the Internet at
http://dnb.ddb.de.

All rights reserved.

Publication in Belgium:
ISBN 90-5095-555-X
Intersentia N.V.
Groenstraat 31
B-2640 Mortsel (Antwerpen)
Phone: ++32 3 680 15 50, Fax: ++32 3 658 71 21

Publication in Austria:
ISBN 3-7083-0389-X
Neuer Wissenschaftlicher Verlag GmbH
Argentinierstraße 42/6, A-1040 Vienna
Tel.: ++43 1 535 61 03-24, Fax: ++43 1 535 61 03-25
e-mail: office@nwv.at

Geidorfgürtel 20, A-8010 Graz
e-mail: office@nwv.at

www.nwv.at

© NWV Neuer Wissenschaftlicher Verlag, Vienna · Graz 2006

English translation: Alexandra Cox, Global Translations
Printing: Széchenyi Nyomda Kft., H-9024 Györ

Hypo Investment Bank (Liechtenstein) AG

Hypo Investment Bank (Liechtenstein) AG has been active as a private bank in Liechtenstein for seven years and is already well established. Managing more than one billion Swiss francs, the bank is a subsidiary of Vorarlberger Landes- und Hypothekenbank AG.

The institute enjoys an AAA rating.

The focus of its business activity is a comprehensive investments advisory service for wealthy families and institutional investors. The bank's highly qualified employee structure, organised according to language regions with German, English, Italian, Russian and Turkish, provides a particular level of customer proximity.

The number of staff was 29 as of January 2006.

A project of
Hypo Investment Bank (Liechtenstein) AG

Contributors

Dr. Andreas INSAM (initiator, contributor and project manager)
Specialist areas: Change in Russia, amnesty
   supported by MMMag. Franz Glatzl

Dr. Joachim KAETZLER (contributor)
Specialist areas: Supranational and German law

Dr. Erek NUENER (contributor)
Specialist area: Liechtensteinian law
   supported by Dr. Christa Burschowsky

Mag. Johannes TRENKWALDER, LL.M (contributor)
   Co-contributor: Mag. Wendelin Ettmayer
Specialist area: Austrian law

Dr. Peter BOSSHARD (contributor)
Specialist area: Swiss law

Dr. Wilfried Ludwig WEH (contributor)
Specialist area: Money laundering and fundamental rights

DDr. V. Vladislav MUDRYCH (contributor)
Specialist area: Russian law (guest commentary)

Illustrations: Dipl.-Ing. Johannes Türtscher

Our thanks also extend to <u>Dr. Harald Jung</u>, partner at CMS Hasche Sigle, member of the CMS Executive Committee and advisor to Hypo Investment Bank (Liechtenstein) AG, without whose assistance this work would not have appeared in its present form.

Table of Contents

Editor's Preface 13
Foreword 17

**I. Banks Between Due Diligence and
Money Laundering** 21

  **A. Combating Money Laundering at the International and
European Level** 23

    1. Introduction: What is money laundering, and how does it
work? 25

      1.1. What is understood by "money laundering"? 25

      1.2. Basic concepts of how money laundering works 26

      1.3. Dimensions of global money laundering
and damage 28

    2. Money laundering in the awareness of state and
financial system 31

      2.1. State measures 31

      2.2. Supranational developments: major international
regulations for combating money laundering 33

      2.3. Self-imposed obligations of the "Wolfsberg" banks .. 43

      2.4. Outlook 46

    3. The currently internationally customary bank measures
in the combat against money laundering 48

      3.1. Obligations of the banks 48

      3.2. Banks as "police deputies"? 50

      3.3 The search for the needle in the haystack – which
possibly is not even there 50

Table of Contents

    4. International standards on customer due diligence: from KYC to "politically exposed persons" 51

        4.1. History of the KYC approach / History of PEP regulations 52

        4.2. The scope of application of regulations concerning PEPs 61

        4.3. Individual risk benchmarks as a solution? 65

    5. Practical organisation and form of PEP inspection by institutions 66

        5.1. Scoring systems for establishing the degree of risk of a transaction or business relationship 67

        5.2. PEP identification via "blacklists" 68

        5.3. Consequences of PEP identification 68

    6. Deficiencies and implementation problems when applying inspection programmes 69

    7. Outlook 72

B. Combating Money Laundering in Liechtenstein 75

    1. Liechtenstein in general 77

        1.1. History of the Principality of Liechtenstein 77

        1.2. Liechtenstein's foreign policy 79

    2 The decisive legal stipulations for combating money laundering in the Principality of Liechtenstein 81

        2.1. Introduction 81

        2.2. Criminal law coverage of money laundering in the Principality of Liechtenstein 84

        2.3. The due diligence act 96

    3. Legal assistance 121

3.1.	General	121
3.2.	Law concerning international legal assistance in criminal cases (legal assistance act (RHG))	122
3.3.	No legal assistance in fiscal matters	135

C. Combating Money Laundering in Austria 137

1. Legal context 139
   - 1.1. Legal sources 139
   - 1.2. Statistics 140
   - 1.3. Term of money laundering 141
2. §§ 39ff. Austrian banking act (BWG) 148
   - 2.1. The obligations standardised for banking and financial institutions in §§ 39ff. Austrian banking act (BWG) 149
   - 2.2. Digression: damage compensation 169
   - 2.3. Banking secrecy and data protection 173
3. Money laundering in Austrian lawyer regulations (RAO) .. 173
   - 3.1. Due diligence obligation 174
   - 3.2. Duties to identify 175
   - 3.3. Organisational obligations 176
   - 3.4. Duties to report 176
   - 3.5. Duties to inform 178
   - 3.6. Duties to retain 178
   - 3.7. Legal consequences of a breach 178
   - 3.8. Damage compensation 178
4. Politically exposed persons – PEPs 179

D. Combating Money Laundering in Germany ... 183

1. Legal context / transposition of international measures into national law ... 185
   1.1. The facts of money laundering ... 185
   1.2. The German money laundering act (GwG) ... 191
   1.3. Administrative practice: Announcements from the German Federal Financial Supervisory Authority (BaFin) ... 195
   1.4. The Federal Financial Supervisory Authority letter of 10th August 2000 concerning corruption and misappropriation of state assets ... 201
   1.5. Overlaps with tax laws and so-called "automated account querying" ... 204

2. Sanctions and risks for banking institutions and bank employees ... 206
   2.1. Risks for banking institutions ... 207
   2.2. Risks of culpability for acting bank employees ... 208
   2.3. Criminal law risks for the agents of the bank and the money laundering consultant ... 212

3. Difficulties when dealing with PEPs in Germany: obligation to contract, data protection and bank secrecy .. 215

4. Business or not – The tightrope between business interests and the general public interest ... 218

5. Conclusions: Risk models as decision aids ... 220

E. Combating Money Laundering in Switzerland ... 223

1. About the term ... 225

2. Evolutionary history ... 225

3. Regulation and self-regulation 226

4. Success 226

5. Legal context... 227
   5.1. Regulations concerning money laundering in the Swiss criminal code (StGB) 227
   5.2. Money laundering act with ordinances 228
   5.3. Self-regulation 232
   5.4. International regulations 233

6. Practical organisation by institutions............................... 234
   6.1. Banks.. 234
   6.2. Lawyers 237

7. Conflicts 238
   7.1. Banking secrecy 238
   7.2. Professional secrecy 238
   7.3. Data protection 238
   7.4. Legal assistance, particularly in tax matters 239

8. Weak points or room to manoeuvre?.............................. 239

9. A question of reputation 240

F. Money Laundering Law and Fundamental Rights 243

1. The Council of the European Union............................... 245

2. European Convention for the Protection of Human Rights and Fundamental Freedoms................................ 246

3. European Community law... 250

4. Data protection directive 255

5. International organisations 260

6. National fundamental rights guarantees 260

7. Money laundering and fundamental rights 261

8. Legal resources against anti-money laundering 264

9. The duty of discretion of liberal professions 268

10. Closing remarks 269

II. The "Ivanov" Case Study – In the Crossfire of Due Diligence Obligations 271

A. Reputation – The Underestimated Factor 273

B. "Boris Ivanov" 281

1. Making contact 283

2. Red Flags / enhanced due diligence 284

3. Course of the business relationship / close monitoring 286

4. New information / Ivanov's tax problems 287

C. Questions to be Analysed 289

D. The "Ivanov" Puzzle is Solved 293

1. "Boris Ivanov" according to Liechtenstein's legal position 295

2. "Boris Ivanov" according to Austria's legal position 299

3. "Boris Ivanov" according to Germany's legal position 302

4. "Boris Ivanov" according to Switzerland's legal position .. 305

5. Summarising comparison of the solutions 308
    5.1. Handling of "privatisation cases" 308
    5.2. Moment of submitting a suspicious transaction report 309
    5.3. Notions concerning corporate liability law 310
    5.4. Expression of the bank customer's rights 310
    5.5. Conclusion 312

E. A Question of Statistics 313

1. Principality of Liechtenstein 315
2. Austria 316
3. Germany 317
4. Switzerland 318
5. Duty of diligence and success rates 320

III. Russia Undergoing Change – Solutions Required .. 325

A. Amnesty – Bridge to Tax Honesty 329

1. General remarks about the term 331
2. Amnesty on capital – tax amnesty 332
    2.1. Germany 2004/05 333
    2.2. Italy 2002/03 337
3. Success factors 342
4. Amnesty in Russia? 343
    4.1. Capital amnesty 344
    4.2. Personal amnesty 346

Table of Contents

    4.3. Realistic and economic appraisal 346

    4.4. Recommendation 349

B. Russia's Tax Situation – An Outline of Reforms 353

C. Tax Chaos: Optimisation, not Maximisation 359

D. Examples Concerning Capital Flight and Tax Evasion... 365

Closing Remarks 369

Annexe – Further Sources of Information 371

Editor's Preface

"HYPO VADUZ INVESTIGATES"

Dr. Andreas INSAM

Dr. Andreas Insam, born 1957, is an Austrian citizen. After completing a degree in business studies and obtaining his doctorate as Dr. rer. soc. oec. he worked as an assistant at the Institute for Mathematics and Statistics at the University of Innsbruck. He joined the LGT-Bank in Liechtenstein AG as an assistant to the management in June 1983. Following a trainee programme in London he switched to the Bank in Liechtenstein (Frankfurt) GmbH in 1986, where he was responsible for Institutional Sales as a member of the Board of Management from 1991. Dr. Insam moved to Vorarlberger Landes- und Hypothekenbank AG, Bregenz, in 1993. In 1998 the Austrian financial group commissioned Mr. Insam with setting up Hypo Investment Bank (Liechtenstein) AG, Vaduz. The institution has been under his management since business commenced; he is the spokesman for the Board of Management. A financial specialist, he has been a member of the board of management of the Liechtenstein Bankers' Association since March 2004. Dr. Insam has been imparting his specialist knowledge in his regular role as a lecturer at the Leopold-Franzens University, Innsbruck, since 1994.

In addition to various supervisory board mandates, he is chairman of the board of the non-profit IMPULSE private foundation[1], which invests ethically and ecologically.

---

1 http://www.impulse-stiftung.com

Every year, Hypo Investment Bank (Liechtenstein) AG (HIB) takes up a current topic that is distilled and presented to a broad public audience. Following surveys from previous years ("Lottery winnings – an onslaught of luck" *Lottogewinn - Überfall des Glücks*, "Tax-optimised residence" *Steueroptimierter Wohnsitz* and "MBA - putting savings to wise use" *MBA - Sparstrümpfe sinnvoll einsetzen*), which all met with lively interest, with the EU expanding to the east HIB decided to link a highly bank-specific area of expertise with "Europe's new neighbour", Russia.

"Money laundering" – this catchword usually generates heightened interest among the general public. Criminals laundering their illicit gains through shady banks and living like kings – or at least this is the cliché that exists in the imagination of simple citizens or the massively influential daily gutter press. HIB now shows which counter-measures have been and are being taken at an international level, illustrates the close interplay between legislation and the banks bound by it, and documents international efforts using the example of a case with public appeal. Only a very few people know that due diligence also affects innocent persons – particularly so-called politically exposed persons (PEP's), i.e. individuals in the limelight – to a strong extent, which is why PEP's are paid particular attention in the present publication.

Our renowned experts clearly explain the current legislative status against the background of the international smokescreen of supranational legislative standards and agreements[2] as well as from the point of view of Liechtenstein[3] and the immediate neighbour states of Austria[4], Germany[5] and Switzerland[6].
The reader is guided into the topic via a comprehendible glossary of terms and an introductory explanation of how money laundering works. There then follows a description of legislation, while separate thoughts about the human rights conformity of money laundering regulations[7] form the conclusion of the broadly informative first part.

---

2   See p.23
3   See p.75
4   See p.137
5   See p.183
6   See p.223
7   See p.243

Editor's Preface

In the second part of the publication you will encounter a practical case study[8] from Eastern Europe. In view of its not yet fully developed local institutions and due to its intensifying capital relations with the former Eastern bloc, Russia presents itself as an exemplary case for a clear examination of due diligence in particular.

Under the motto *"HIB INVESTIGATES"* our experts tell you how a PEP – of Russian nationality in the case study – would be checked for money laundering by the banks in conformity with the law in the respective state territory and how the case would be judged according to all legislative regulations.

"Know Your Customer", known by the abbreviation KYC, applies to a particular extent to PEP's – our substantiated clarification of stipulated KYC principles in the four-country comparison using the example of the striking "Ivanov" case shows the efforts of all concerned to refute the high-life cliché.

In addition to its real-life depiction of daily due diligence and the case study, HIB provides a complementary section on combating money laundering. In the light of the recent Yukos case concerning the Russian natural gas giant of the same name, it appears appropriate to take a closer look at the "eastern giant". The continuingly problematic change[9] from a superpower with a communist planned economy into a democratically capitalist federation requires solutions. Could an amnesty – referring to recent amnesties in Germany and Italy – finally put an end to the oft-discussed privatisation process and restore the many billion euros of annual flight capital urgently needed by the Russian market? HIB permits itself to estimate the potential consequences of an amnesty ruling in Russia and puts forward concrete suggestions concerning its form. Alongside this, our Russia expert deals with potential further measures to reform Russian tax legislation[10], without which, he argues, an amnesty ruling does not appear possible.

The aim of this year's survey is to enable a somewhat different insight into the Liechtenstein banking business. Efforts by

---

8   See p.271
9   See p.325
10 See p.259

Liechtenstein's financial sector, too often kept in the background, to create the greatest possible transparency while at the same time preserving its customers' interest, give the public the opportunity to look beyond their own field of vision and see the bigger picture from the truncated reports in the daily press. At the same time, the survey presents up-to-date information about Europe's big new neighbour and hazards a glimpse at its (economic) future.

The overall reflection familiarises the reader with the coalescence of international capital and financial markets by providing highly practically oriented access. In the process, potential investors and their environment – using the example of the Eastern European case study – are brought into touch with the dynamic financial centre of Liechtenstein and the neighbouring states or their current legislative situation, respectively. Thoughts about Russia's domestic problems and suggestions for coping with these complete the survey.

An understanding of "due diligence" and the latest trends in the field of combating money laundering will no longer be foreign concepts for the reader in future.

"CARRY OUT YOUR OWN INVESTIGATIONS!"

Andreas Insam
CEO, Hypo Investment Bank (Liechtenstein) AG

Foreword

by the Liechtenstein Bankers' Association

Michael C. Lauber

Michael C. Lauber, born 1965, is a Swiss citizen. A lawyer, he was active as an examining judge in the Swiss canton of Bern after completing his studies. In autumn 1993 he switched to the management of the criminal investigation department of the canton of Bern, where he was responsible for Special Search 1. In 1995 he took over the management of the central Organised Crime office at the Swiss Federal Police Bureau in Bern and was responsible for implementing combative measures, in particular against Russian Organised Crime and money laundering. In this connection he was commissioned to set up the Swiss registry for money laundering. Following a brief period as an independent lawyer in Zurich, Michael Lauber was commissioned by the Liechtenstein government with the setting up and management of the Liechtenstein registry for money laundering (FIU). During this time he was also particularly responsible for managing the secretariat of the Liechtenstein task force for combating the financing of terrorism and managed Liechtenstein's delegation to the European Council's anti-money laundering committee (MONEYVAL). He also acted as an evaluator for the International Monetary Fund and the World Bank for Oman and Luxembourg, for the European Council for Cyprus and Monaco and for the FATF for Russia. Michael Lauber has been CEO of the Liechtenstein Bankers' Association since 2004.

Those were the days, the 1990s. The world was still neatly categorised then; it was still clear what was good, and what was bad. Domestic security was still disassociated from external security and combating money laundering was generally recognised as a high complex matter. The appropriate instruments and means were still provided by the state; and the opinion predominated that repressive measures could primarily call a halt to this abuse of our financial systems.

Today, however, it is a different story. With the focus on prevention, account has been taken of the understanding that repression alone cannot prevent the global and interlinked problem of money laundering. Today, it is a matter of course that every serious financial intermediary follows the internationally standardised and interwoven "KYC" regulations. This is a good thing and ultimately encourages financial market participants to deliver good quality services.

A broader understanding of prevention has gained ground at least since September 11th, 2001, but the approach varies. Lists containing the names of presumed terrorists are the most widely known products in this process. Apart from the technical problems when implementing these measures - which can be summed up under the term "name and shame" - a basic observation can be made:

A financial market is considerably ordered on trust: trust in the participants and their integrity and trust in the liberal system forming its basis. Intervention measures must therefore be predictable, simple and strict. Intervention measures that encourage basic mistrust, thus rendering the abuse systematic, bring uncertainty. Ultimately, therefore, the abuse is not combated, but abusive machinations are covered up.

In other words:
If the global combating of money laundering and the financing of terrorism is going to be successful, and it needs to be, then it must be restricted to the essential and carefully thought out. Global standards are important. Yet every culture must also be allowed to take its individual experiences in combating money laundering and the financing of terrorism as the basis.

Forward by the Liechtenstein Bankers' Association

It is a dangerous illusion to believe that the financial sector and the authorities are able to eliminate these phenomena independently of each other. Rather, it requires a combined and, above all, focused effort.

Prevention is of central importance; real prevention leads to the maintenance and enhancement of the reputation, not only of individual institutions, but also of financial centres. Reputation management as the common interest of every financial market participant and every financial centre must be placed at the focus of the combat against money laundering and the financing of terrorism.

The present survey is a contribution to greater understanding of this problem. I hope it gains the readership and interest of many.

Michael Lauber
CEO of the Liechtenstein Bankers' Association

I.
Banks Between Due Diligence and Money Laundering

giving particular consideration to
politically exposed persons (PEPs)

Liechtenstein – Austria – Germany – Switzerland

"One can never be careful enough"

A.
Combating Money Laundering at the International and European Level

Dr. Joachim KAETZLER

Joachim Kaetzler is a lawyer at CMS Hasche Sigle in the field of Banking and Finance in Frankfurt.

After reading law and English at the University of Augsburg, he gained his doctorate in the field of international criminal law. He was employed under the criminal law professorship of Prof. Joachim Herrmann from 1993 until 2000. From 2000 until 2001 he was the spokesman for the Bavarian State Association of the Protective Union for Securities Ownership (DSW). He has been a lawyer at CMS Hasche Sigle since 2001, first in Munich, and in Frankfurt since 2003. His specialist areas there are in the fields of finance, banking watchdog regulations, money laundering prevention and Securities Litigation.

In addition to his career, he has been a member of Transparency International (German Chapter) e.V. since 1999, where he is responsible for the area of money laundering prevention. Besides numerous publications on the topic of money laundering, he regularly makes guest speeches at many renowned universities around the world.

1. Introduction: What is money laundering, and how does it work?

Before shedding light on the particular correlations between money laundering and persons in the public interest, we first need to outline the multilayered term of money laundering in closer detail and highlight essential formalities. Since the particular intention of the following report is to discuss in detail the problem of dealing with politically exposed persons in the area of conflict between the interests of the customer, of the bank and of the general public, in compliance with their interests, the explanations concerning the general backgrounds are naturally restricted to the issues that are relevant to this subject.

1.1. What is understood by "money laundering"?

Whoever mentions "money laundering" is generally referring to a criminal's activity in purposefully feeding proceeds arising from serious or organised crimes into commerce in order to give them the appearance of legitimacy following transit through the circular flow. The reason for these activities – which from the criminal's point of view are costly and frequently not without risk – is the criminal's fear of the state's opportunities to intervene and attempt to siphon off the illegally gotten gains using the methods of seizure, confiscation, taxation or wealth penalties.

The more often the illegally gotten assets have transited the regular circular flow, the less the criminal needs to fear that the state will be able to conclusively attribute an asset to an actual crime. If the state authorities (or the victims of the crime) do not manage to provide this proof, the criminal is able to use his illegally gotten gains for his own interests. The state's apparatus for siphoning off proceeds can accordingly, to a certain extent, be understood as a "motivating force" for the money launderer; the more comprehensive the state's opportunities to intervene and siphon off proceeds are, the more likely it is that the criminal will find it necessary to move the illegal assets. The more often he is obliged to move them, the higher are the chances, in turn, for the state's bodies to discover and confiscate the illegal assets[13].

The term money laundering has now become an established feature of international discussion; to be precise, not only are cash and deposit money affected, of course, but also securities, receivables, valuable objects (e.g. precious stones) or commodities, which are purposefully smuggled through legal and illegal commerce in order to conceal their criminal origins.

1.2. Basic concepts of how money laundering works

There is no generally valid basic technical concept for money laundering. The methods are manifold and vary in complexity. Illegal proceeds from street dealings in drugs or arms, for example, typically arise as cash at first and are simply laundered via the direct purchase and sale of goods. Assets that move exclusively within the criminal milieu or a grey area are naturally difficult to trace; conclusive attribution to an actual crime is, in addition, rarely possible. However, as soon as the perpetrator brings the assets into the regulated circular flow - pays cash into a bank account, for example - there are opportunities for the state to intervene.

Money laundering from organised economic crime, on the other hand, takes place according to far more complex patterns. Nowadays, different financial instruments are often used in this connection; it is not uncommon for the illegal assets to cross national borders during the process.

For decades, the basic pattern of money laundering was typically explained on the basis of three phases which reappeared, often staggered and interwoven, at least in part behind every money laundering scheme in a differing form and at different times. Traditional definitions in respect of the functioning of money laundering are therefore based on the following three-tiered model:

---

13 Compare also recommendation No. 7 of the OECD / FATF of 1990

1. **Placement:** In the first phase, a criminal attempts to accommodate the illegally gotten assets in the formal financial system in order to then be able to move them.
2. **Layering:** In the second phase, incriminated and legally acquired assets are typically mixed, illegal assets are sent out of the country, or the origin of the incriminated assets is obliterated by some other means. Tangible assets frequently change their physical condition during this second phase, are exchanged, or used for real or imaginary services in return.
3. **Integration:** In the third phase, on the other hand, the criminal attempts to re-feed the variously laundered assets into the legal circular flow, for example by investing them or, (as the original drug money-based ideal would have it), using them to acquire luxury objects such as villas or cars.

In this way of thinking, which nowadays appears to be almost "romantic" but is still in general use, one of the essential deficiencies in modern anti-money laundering efforts can clearly be seen: whereas a three-phase conceptual approach is thoroughly appropriate for tainted assets (which may arise from drug crime, for example), modes of thinking of this kind misjudge the fact that fully legally acquired assets are not infrequently already present in formal banking systems and only become, and then possibly only partially, incriminated assets during the subsequent period. This primarily applies to criminal offences such as insider dealings, tax crimes or embezzlement.

For many risks on which this report will shed light and to which a lending institution is exposed when entering into business relationships with prominent persons, it is even characteristically the case that these persons already legally own assets that are found either in the banking system or in the international securities trade and are embezzled or misappropriated at a later date, without ever leaving the banking system.

As will come to be shown, modern anti-money laundering measures, both on the part of the state and of the private sector, essentially start in the first phase (placement), to a far smaller extent even in the second phase (layering) and only to a small degree in the third phase (integration).

As mentioned at the beginning, given the multitude of possibilities it is clearly pointless to provide a generally valid definition or explanation of individual money laundering procedures: naturally, money laundering techniques evolve along with the modernising prevention systems, meaning that nowadays, for certain areas of money laundering, particularly in the area of derivatives, generally valid regulations could probably only be drawn up with difficulty. The crux of effective money laundering prevention even lies, to be precise, in the fact that prevention systems are only able to adapt to new money laundering trends reactively, are consequently therefore always one step behind the criminal, who ultimately is the first to set the standards as complex transactions progress.

1.3. Dimensions of global money laundering and damage

Money laundering causes global damage on a considerably large scale. The exact economic scope of global black money movements, however, has not yet been researched; only estimates and conjectures are doing the rounds regarding the dimensions of criminal cash flows.

However, most estimates refer to – going along with the traditional definitions – drug money laundering only. Thus, for example, the International Monetary Fund (IMF), backed by the Max-Planck-Institution, estimates the total volume of (drug) money laundering to be approximately 500 billion euro annually[14]. At a somewhat broader level the IMF assumes that 2 to 5 % of the entire world economy can be attributed to the black economy; for Great Britain, there was recently talk of a figure of 13 %, for Germany 16 % of the gross domestic product. If the Russian central bank can be believed, then in the first few years after the collapse of the Soviet Union already, at least 250 billion US dollars poured out of Russia into the financial centres of the Western world in connection with organised Russian crime[15]. In 1996 the IMF had estimated the overall annual volume of money laundering in the northern hemi-

---

14 See "Transnational Organised Crime and Money Laundering", [German] comments by Jürgen Storbek, Director of Europol, p.20 with further documented evidence, Berlin, 15 March 2001
15 See "Globalisation of the World Economy" [German] by the German Bundestag dated 24th September 2000, p.4, comment by the Federal Supervisory Bureau for Banking to the inquiry committee

sphere to be at least 690 billion US dollars (this corresponds, for example, to the gross national product of Spain), at least 1.5 trillion at the most (which corresponds, for example, to the gross domestic product of France)[16]. Even though the figures differ from each other significantly, the dimensions should still probably become clear to the reader.

At any rate, the types of damage and the groups of damaged persons can be identified even more clearly than the dimensions:

Individual victims

First of all – something which is frequently forgotten – the many individual victims of simple felonies must be identified as persons directly damaged by money laundering. A victim of investment fraud who has invested his or her assets in a pyramid scheme continually tries to get the invested money back from the criminal. The assertion of such damage compensation claims against the criminal is hindered by the criminal's bringing the illegally gotten assets to safety via money laundering, thus protecting them from his victims' intervention. Traditional definitions of money laundering, which often tie in with the criminal's attempt to merely protect the assets from state intervention, are founded on the above mentioned evolutionary history of existing criminal offences, namely that money laundering is primarily associated with crimes such as arms and drug dealing. Individual fates are frequently forgotten in this context. As the term "money laundering" broadens, victims of preliminary crimes must also be taken into account in considerations of the scope of the damage (and not only here).

Failure to confiscate as a form of damage

As mentioned, states are among the primary victims of money laundering. In the case of crimes of this type, in which naturally no immediately economically damaged person can be encountered – for example, in the case of arms trading, with drug crimes or in cases of corruption – the state has a claim to the handing over not only of the illegally traded objects, but also the proceeds. The ac-

---

16 See "Transnational Organised Crime and Money Laundering", p.35 with further documented evidence, comment by Luciano Violante, president of the Italian chamber of deputies

tual damage to states is founded in the fact that confiscation of precisely these instruments and proceeds is complicated or even foiled by the camouflaging of illegally gotten assets.

Damage to reputation

The dimensions of impairments arising through loss of reputation at companies or in states which consciously, or at least negligently, encourage money launderers or are at least obliged to admit to having defective prevention systems, have never even been recorded.

Abstract incidents of damage can veer rapidly into material damage. A globally operating American bank, for example, noticed in 1999 that a multinational concern of Russian criminal origin had laundered the equivalent of approximately EUR 6.5 billion via its accounts. German banks were implicated in this connection as correspondent banks. On the day it became aware, the bank concerned lost 7 % of its market capitalisation on the New York Stock Exchange.

Even entire economies are finding themselves exposed to losses of reputation that probably achieve barely conceivable dimensions. The FATF (an institution of the OECD, which we will return to) has even made itself a principle of this with its "name and shame" policy and published, in some cases several times per year, the list of "non-cooperating countries and territories", which admittedly has become considerably shorter in recent years. However, this initiative will be discontinued following a redistribution of roles among the international organisations. With this list the OECD sub organisation called on all participating states and companies to apply increased diligence (up to and including breaking off business relationships) and exposed deficiencies in the states concerned in clear terms and publicly.

Risk of the rise of parallel societies

A further economic risk, not to be underestimated, is the risk of the rise of entire "parallel societies". Criminal organisations and companies that systematically evade taxes and are permitted to enjoy the fruits of these deeds compete with legally functioning companies and, to this extent, contaminate the legitimate economic system. The Basel Banking Committee already recognised this particular threat in 1988 and warned of considerable market distortions that may arise due to such a shadow economy.

Damage due to reinvestment

Last but not least, it must also be pointed out that laundered assets from organised crime are often reinvested for the carrying out of further criminal offences, thereby indirectly causing further asset damage. This does not necessarily need to involve capital offences or terrorism, which naturally also uses money laundering. However, in any case, the funds received can continue to be used to finance simple organised economic crime, which is equally regrettable and disadvantageous for the respective economic systems.

2. Money laundering in the awareness of state and financial system

The outlined risks of money laundering have occasioned many states not only to render these punishable, but also to ensure complex formalities for controlling the financial sector in order to prevent money laundering. In this respect, too, only the broad lines can naturally be traced.

2.1. State measures

The role of the state in modern anti-money laundering is admittedly varied, but notwithstanding this it is evident today that the efforts of state criminal prosecution and regulation systems in modern anti-money laundering in mass circulation play an ever-smaller role in comparison with the efforts of the private economic sector.

As already mentioned, the original means of anti-money laundering is initially the confiscation of the instruments and proceeds of criminal offences. Figuratively speaking, the threat of confiscation of illegally gotten assets is the "spur" that motivates the criminal to make it impossible for the state to prove a connection between an asset and an actual criminal offence by laundering money. An effective anti-money laundering system therefore presupposes a functioning system for siphoning off proceeds, which, for example, due to legal bases that remain far behind international standards, is the case only to an extremely restricted extent in the Federal Republic of Germany.

An (obvious) state role in anti-money laundering lies in the punishment of money laundering in itself, but it is now the internationally held consensus that the efforts of a criminal or his accomplice to obliterate the connection between an asset and a criminal offence are grounds for a penal requirement of their own. However, prosecution authorities have only partially caught on to this: investigations still only frequently concentrate on the original crime alone (therefore the drug dealer or the corrupt civil servant) and let both confiscation and the money laundering pass by completely. Yet it is important to recognise that money laundering is also founded on its own particular definition of tort in criminal law dogma, and protects a completely different legally protected right than the primary crime, namely the above mentioned claim to confiscation by the public authorities and the victims' claim to the proceeds of serious crime. However, low conviction rates lead to the assumption that this recognition is held in less esteem in prosecution authorities than appears to be appropriate.

The third significant role of the state consists of creating joint international framework conditions that ensure effective anti-money laundering measures. Regrettably, this is occurring only to a smaller proportion through multinational conventions; predominantly, unfortunately, through bilateral "memorandums of understanding" whose practical enforceability often depends on the goodwill of the persons acting. Beyond this, the state intelligence services of the world's bigger states cooperate in the so-called EGMONT Group for the field of controlling international cash flows from organised crime.

Finally, individual states also assume a controlling function in respect of the private financial sector, which obliged to render its own considerable contributions and services. In recent years the impression has even arisen that many states have outsourced their money laundering prevention fully (and without service in return) to banks and financial service providers and other privately obligated persons. We will focus on this at another point.

These four above mentioned contributions by state authorities to money laundering prevention (punishment, confiscation, international coordination and control of the financial economy) are the points of departure for the effective combating of money laundering by the private economic sector.

2.2. Supranational developments: major international regulations for combating money laundering

Money laundering is an international business. Effective combating of transnational organised crime can only take place if anti-money laundering also occurs on an internationally standardised basis; only when international cooperation is simplified or, in many cases, actually enabled in the first place.

2.2.1. Early pioneers of international anti-money laundering

If the history of anti-money laundering at the international level is referred to, then Recommendation no. R80/10 of the European Council dated 27th June 1980 should be mentioned. In this recommendation the Council of Ministers of the European states advised urging banks and financial service providers to take precautionary measures against the abuse of their services, for example obliging banks to identify their customers and install internal security precautions. At that point in time, behind these efforts was the notion of laying a retrospective "paper trail" between criminals and the associated assets in cases of serious criminal activity. To this end, of course, it was necessary to at least check the identity of the person dealing with the bank. Although the banks had already recognised the problem of the abuse of their services, the state's commitment was still hesitant, since in almost all states money laundering was erroneously understood not as its own grounds for punishment, but only as an "associated crime" to the actual criminal offence.

The first authoritative step at the broader international level was, however, the passing of the UN agreement against illicit trading with narcotic drugs and psychotropic substances ("Vienna Drugs Convention") of 20th December 1988. In addition to the obligation of individual UN member states to implement sensible measures for siphoning off proceeds, these states were also urged to form money laundering into its own grounds for punishment. This initial international agreement was borne by the effort to take away the economic bases from the international drug trade and was therefore only aimed at siphoning off drug money.

At the European level, this area of application was expanded in 1990 by the "Strasbourg Convention" ("Convention on Laundering, Search, Seizure and Confiscation of the Proceeds of Crime"). In the Strasbourg Convention the contract parties agreed to undertake to set up more effective confiscation systems, something which, however, soon fell at national constitutional hurdles in a number of member states. Further, it was agreed in 1990 to universally establish grounds for punishment for money laundering as a crime in itself with a broader catalogue of preliminary crimes. All forms of covering up assets from organised crime were to be made a criminal offence immediately.

In 2000, the UN member states extended this obligation to all UN member states under the "Palermo Convention" ("Convention against Transnational Organised Crime") and agreed the foundations for international cooperation; these foundations were, however – as mentioned - largely annulled again due to circuitous and bureaucratic agreements on mutuality.

Alongside the law institutions, the international banking sector had also become active. At approximately the same time as the Vienna Convention, namely in December 1988, the central bank governors of the G7 states had, at the initiative of the Bank of International Settlements (BIS), agreed the basic measures and procedures in the so-called "Basel Declaration of Principles" that they wanted to see implemented in the banking system's combat against money laundering in the future. On one hand, all banks were called upon under item 2 of the declaration of principles to introduce effective procedures in order to obtain proof of identity from new customers. This measure had also come to be seen as necessary by the governors of the central banks of the G7 states, in order to lay a paper trail and thus be able to provide proof of a preliminary crime connection for tainted assets in the event of unwitting money laundering transactions. Furthermore, the central bank governors called upon the banking economy to stop providing services or actively assisting transactions which they have grounds to associate with money laundering. This ethical principle applies to this day.

A further significant point was the call upon the financial economy – initially formulated as a guideline only and of course non-binding – to cooperate unrestrictedly with state execution bodies, if the financial economy was permitted to do so by the respective national legislation, particularly in respect of regulations on customer secrecy. All banks were to formally adopt a business policy that was in accordance with the principles of this declaration, therefore cooperation while guaranteeing customer secrecy. A conflict of goals between banking customer secrecy and anti-money laundering therefore became evident right from the early days of anti-money laundering, and exists to this day.

2.2.2. The founding of the FATF

The OECD stepped onto the scene alongside the activities of the Basel Banking Committee. At the world economic summit in Paris an action group was called into life in June 1989, designed to eliminate the serious deficiencies in securing financial markets against abuse by organised crime which had been noted by the G7 and a "money laundering" working group from the EC. From now on, the Financial Action Task Force (FATF), deployed by the OECD, was to evaluate the standards of international anti-money laundering, denounce deficiencies and, above all, coordinate international cooperation – the bureaucratic obstacles of which were acknowledged ever more clearly as a stumbling block to effective money laundering prevention.

In the course of the year the FATF became the effective engine of international anti-money laundering: only just under one year following its founding, on 19th April 1990 the FATF issued a research paper with 40 recommendations that were aimed at the entire global community. At the time of founding the Financial Action Task Force consisted of representatives from the G7 states, the European Commission and a further 8 strategic member states. With time, the number of members of the FATF grew to the present 33 countries and more than 30 international organisations (including the IMF, Europol, Interpol and the World Bank) enjoy observer status. Additionally, regional groups have formed to take account of the corresponding needs and the varying degree of development of individual regions of the world.

Textually speaking, the recommendations ruled a request to all states of the world to implement the Vienna Convention definitively and in full, to alter national stipulations on banking secrecy (because this still stood in opposition to anti-money laundering in some jurisdictions), and to bring about conditions favourable to multinational cooperation in anti-money laundering. With regard to the more detailed form of individual national legislation, the FATF requested a general extension of the preliminary crime catalogue for money laundering going beyond drug crime to all serious crimes. Since, to date, only deliberate money laundering is punishable in some states, but it was practically impossible for public prosecution services to provide proof of intent precisely because of mass-volume banking transactions, the FATF called upon the OECD states to also penalise "trifling" perpetration of money laundering. Since, to the FATF's knowledge, many criminals were hiding behind corporate facades in order to put more pressure on the credit institutions at the same time, the FATF also called for the introduction of general criminal law liability of companies in the field of money laundering; however, this request is, incomprehensibly, incompatible with some national criminal law systems due to differences in dogma.

However, the significant point of the FATF's 40 recommendations lay in the fact that, for the first time, states were required to create favourable conditions for successfully confiscating proceeds and assets from serious crimes and subjecting financial service providers and bank to a broad range of obligations allegedly intended to contribute preventively to anti-money laundering. However, in reality, these were quasi-penal investigatory interventions of a barely preventive nature.

In detail it concerned the following obligations which were to be served to banks and financial service providers by means of laws, ordinances or other probate acts:
- Obligation to identify customers on the basis of an identity document or, in the case of legal persons, of official registers;
- Retention of customer documentation for at least five years;

- Transferral of the corresponding customer identification documents to the examining authorities in the event of a penal investigation;
- Obligation to report suspicious financial transactions to the authorities without informing the customer of this;
- Breaking off the business relationship in the extreme case;
- Creating internal regulatory mechanisms and structures for the effective prevention of money laundering.

At the time the FATF was founded the global community was faced with the problem that international standards on combating money laundering were extremely varied and banking systems also had different characteristics. The FATF therefore directed the recommendation to banks, via the member states, to universally subject business relationships with those states lacking appropriate formalities to a wider-reaching examination of diligence and, in the event of doubt, to conduct no business relationships.

For the remainder the FATF's recommendations essentially concerned the creation of official administrative structures, in particular, for example, the creation of a respective national Financial Intelligence Unit (FIU) which evaluates the reported suspicions and, where necessary, is required to forward them to the prosecution authorities. The 40 recommendations also governed essential matters of the international collaboration and transnational cooperation of banks, facilitators and FIUs.

2.2.3. The first European money laundering directive

At the European level the European Commission developed, alongside the efforts of the Financial Task Force, its own proposal for a "Council directive on the prevention of the use of the financial system for the purpose of money laundering" (first EU money laundering directive).

While resolving the directive, the Council of EC finance ministers took the decision to prescribe regular threshold value announcements for financial transactions over ECU 15,000.00. After the European Parliament and the Commission had made multiple changes to the money laundering directive, basic rules were passed at the European level which essentially followed the recommendations of the FATF but made use of freedoms of interpretation in individual sections. Within the framework of the directive procedure, for example, the obligation of the bank to generally distance itself from suspicious transactions (Art. 4 of the Commission proposal) was restricted, directly running counter to the FATF recommendations. Further, in a protocol declaration appended to the directive, the EU Commission and the Council of Ministers agreed, for example, that the banking supervision authorities can also be responsible for the investigation and analysis of reported suspicions, by which means the latter initially became more closely involved in the work of the prosecution authorities. Due to this misinterpretation of the stipulations of the FATF the setting up of competence centres, the Financial Intelligence Units, was delayed and anti-money laundering was incorporated into the general administrative apparatus.

In the subsequent period the member states passed the required legal and administrative regulations for implementing the directives. References will be made to the respective country reports[17] for the states under consideration here. In parallel with this, many countries outside the European Union also developed their own measures for combating money laundering, which were partially based on the specifications of the EU or the FATF.

An essential drawback of the first money laundering directive was, however, that it only obliged the member states to combat the laundering of proceeds from drug crimes. This deficiency again clearly demonstrates one of the design weaknesses of money laundering prevention concepts briefly indicated at the beginning: by the time it also became clear to the institutions setting the standards that not only drug dealers, but also other criminals were using the banking system to launder illegally gotten funds, channels of a shadow economy had long since formed which were to be far more difficult to dry up in retrospect than had been expected at the time the directive was passed.

2.2.4. The revision of the 40 recommendations

In the subsequent years international evaluations and working groups soon led the FATF to recognise that the established minimum standards written into the 40 recommendations from 1990

---

17   See p.75 (FL), p.137 (AUT), p.183 (GER), p.223 (SUI)

had now become obsolete and, in particular, did not appropriately reflect progress in banking. In 1995 and 1996, therefore, the 40 recommendations were considerably revised. The states were immediately recommended to expand their money laundering legislation to all serious criminal offences, or those crimes, respectively, which typically yield considerable proceeds. The obligations to cooperate which had previously been primarily directed towards banks were also expanded to those service providers who conduct, for example, financial committee transactions, asset management, currency exchange or, for instance, life insurance transactions.

In parallel with this, the European Council had also become active, passing on 8th November 1999 the already titled "Convention on the laundering and detection, the seizure and confiscation of proceeds from serious criminal offences" (Strasbourg Convention). Herein the member states (once more) bindingly undertook to penalise deliberate money laundering at least.

2.2.5. The US Patriot Act

Only five weeks after the events of 11th September 2001 a law was passed in the US parliaments which became known as the US Patriot Act (Providing Appropriate Tools Required to Intercept and Obstruct Terrorism). In addition to the alarming mutilation of civil rights due to the expansion of the prosecution bodies' opportunities to intervene (extended telephone tapping, prolongation of preliminary arrest etc.) stricter measures were also decided in the field of anti-money laundering and the confiscation opportunities involved with it.

The restrictions were now effective against previous anti-money laundering measures not only within the sovereign territory of the respective state. This was particularly felt by credit institutions conducting business relationships with US banks.

Those foreign credit institutions conducting a so-called "correspondent bank relationship" with US banks were obliged with immediate effect to cooperate extensively with US authorities. They were also required to hand over evidence within a few days, provided that this can be requested of the bank in accordance with the expanded American intervention rights. Since then, in extreme cases, foreign banks are even threatened with the confiscation of all correspondent bank accounts by the US prosecution authorities: the only pre-requirement for this is that a sufficient suspicion of money laundering has been raised against the foreign institution in a totally general manner, without the funds in the correspondent bank account having to be directly tainted.

Due to this further tightening of anti-money laundering measures, a new quality of intervention was achieved which, in addition to expanded procedural intervention competencies, is primarily characterised by the spread of national money laundering measures to other states via existing economic structures. The global issues of effective anti-money laundering associated with this consequence for institutions will be returned to at another point.[18]

2.2.6. The second EU money laundering directive

However, with the coming into effect of the second EU money laundering directive in December 2001, completely new dimensions in anti-money laundering were opened and – evidently in view of the events of 11th September 2001 in New York – civil rights were also alarmingly restricted in Europe for the first time for the purpose of a more stringent control of financial markets and allegedly for more effective criminal prosecution. In addition to banks and financial service providers, security traders, fund corporations, insurance companies and exchange offices were now expressly included in the catalogue of obligations. Member states were likewise obliged according to the directive to obligate auditors, tax consultants, real estate agents, notaries and lawyers executing suspicious orders from their clients within the scope of their business transactions to report their clients. The last mentioned changes in respect of the special relationship of trust between clients and lawyers came under particular discussion in the subsequent period.

Such extensive involvement of the non-financial sector with anti-money laundering had been barely conceivable up to this point and still appears disconcerting to many representatives of the last mentioned professions. The experiences of the FATF had actually demonstrated that, due to professional legal privileges, the pro-

---

18   See, for example p.48 onwards

fessional groups of lawyers and tax consultants should be viewed as being particularly exposed to risk. Yet this recognition was viewed by the broad majority of professionals less as a measure for raising the ethical standard, but rather as a demotion to "deputy sheriff" to the overstrained investigators and in many cases is still not taken seriously today. It will surely take years and require a number of convictions until the last mentioned professional groups become fully aware of their ethical obligations.

2.2.7. The renewed revision of the 40 recommendations of the FATF in 2003

The ever-more rapid developments on the financial markets occasioned the FATF in 2003 to again conduct a full revision and adjustment of the recommendations. Essentially, the stipulations for dealing with politically exposed persons, so-called PEPs (on this subject, see directly below) were tightened, a responsibility by the banks for correspondent bank accounts was established, the application of the 40 recommendations to electronic banking was improved and regulations for the identification of bank customers by third parties were passed. Furthermore, the FATF also associated itself with the principles for lawyers and tax consultants which had already been established in the EU directive from 2001.

2.2.8. The Commission proposal on the 3rd money laundering directive (2004)

Finally, the European Commission submitted a further directive proposal for a third money laundering directive[19] on 30th June 2004. Essentially, the revised 40 recommendations of the FATF from 2003 are to be implemented in this directive. The focuses of this directive include the tightening of due diligence obligations, consideration of various heightened money laundering risks, the evaluation of new trends and typologies and the expansion of the circle of persons subject to the stipulations of the money laundering directive. The directive also includes the binding obligation to

---

19 Directive "2005/60/EC for the prevention of the use of the financial system for the purpose of money laundering and terrorist financing" was published on 25th November 2005 in the official journal (L 309, p.15) of the European Union. Member states are set a deadline for implementation by 15th December 2007.

create a national centre for reporting suspicions (FIU) and the inclusion of terrorist financing in anti-money laundering. The latter change above all is currently causing disquiet in the associations and national regional authorities called upon to make a comment. If, to date, the barely avoidable financing of terrorism was theoretically segregated from money laundering prevention, then the concepts are now being intermixed, as had already happened in a number of US acts following the events of 11th September 2001. Additionally, the directive requires the respective entities addressed by standards to also identify, in the case of legal persons, those partners who control at least 25 % of the share capital, which, in view of the non-existence of publicly accessible partner lists in many European countries, will possibly encounter unimagined difficulties.

Following violent controversies and numerous special reports, the European Parliament agreed, in its session of 25th May 2005, to most of the changes proposed by a commission of experts led by the German MEP Nassauer. Even though the expansion of essential obligations to cooperate upon legal and tax consulting professions, particularly criticised by the public, was toned down, and a distinction between money laundering prevention and terrorist financing was drawn, a number of practical problems remain unaffected, in particular the deeper obligation to identify placed upon proprietors in the case of legal persons.

2.2.9. Outlook: fourth money laundering directive?

The carousel of legal standards, spinning faster and faster and sometimes binding, sometimes non-binding, led in the subsequent period not only to the general confusion of all concerned in the combat against money laundering, but also to the development of entire service sectors attempting to implement the requirements on the banking economy that so far have only been outlined briefly in each case. So, service providers, often consisting of lawyers, IT specialists and banking experts, advertised tailored outsourcing services, particularly to banks and financial service providers who could no longer keep up with the rapid legal development due to their size. Owing not least to the considerably increased density of regulations, banks' money laundering departments bucked the general trend of staff redundancies among mid-European financial service providers; combating money laundering was certainly one of the few booming sectors in terms of staff in the banking industry.

Following the specifications of the 3rd EU money laundering directive, according to which further specifications on the part of the EU for the firm establishment of uncertain legal notions are to be issued in a further directive by June 2006, work on a further "design directive" already began at the end of 2005. The first working drafts have been available since January 2006 and will be dealt with more detail further on. The requirement to issue a directive for firmly establishing a directive alone demonstrates the paradoxical legislative developments in the field of anti-money laundering.

Whether the actual goal of international efforts, namely to seize international organised crime by its roots and bleed it dry financially, can be constructively pursued with a short-term, excessively detailed regulatory frenzy of this nature, definitely appears uncertain. On the other hand, the rapid technical developments of recent years demanded ever-faster adaptation of international stipulations to the increasing technical opportunities. The regulations referred to above, however, also clearly show that state authority alone cannot win the fight against money laundering. To this end the cooperation of other responsible entities, the financial economy to name names, is required.

2.3. Self-imposed obligations of the "Wolfsberg" banks

Globally active banks recognised the legislator's considerable risks and difficulties (in some cases inability, too) in passing effective anti-money laundering measures. Therefore, in 2000, leading international banks developed their own due diligence benchmarks in parallel with the state regulations which, in a number of details, go far beyond the obligations that had previously been valid in respect of banks based on international or national standardisation. The aim of these self-obligations was not only to implement the ethical stipulations of the Basel Banking Committee, but also to establish a risk management system in order to safeguard credit institutions against reputational risks and damage compensation claims.

While the changes in customer due diligence that are relevant to the treatment of publicly and politically exposed persons shall be dealt with later,[20] it should already be pointed out here that the declarations of self-obligation by the Wolfsberg banks primarily differ from state measures in that self-imposed obligations typically result from (industry-typical) risk monitoring of the business areas. Whereas the state interventions briefly outlined above "steamrollered" a broadly applied normative approach, the banks developed far more effective instruments with which individual transactions are assessed in closer detail and the money laundering risks of individual transactions can be limited much more effectively from a statistical point of view.

Thus, for example, when judging the degree of suspiciousness of individual financial transactions, the banks undertook to conduct an individual risk assessment of the individual transactions based on precisely defined objective parameters. As opposed to the previous approach followed by governments and supranational organisations, this represented a complete change of perspectives and, precisely because of this, very far-reaching progress in modern anti-money laundering. The Wolfsberg banks then set down, in the regulations revised in 2002/03, industry-internal minimum standards in respect of the nature of the customer information to be obtained in order to establish identity. In addition to the identification documents which had previously been customary, the bank customer is must now be asked, for example, for:

- Reason for and purpose of opening the account;
- Likely account activities;
- Origin of the assets;
- Foreseeable net deposit;
- Bases of funding;
- References or verification possibilities in respect of customer indications.

Additionally, the Wolfsberg banks set down that within the banks, three criteria occasion closer verification of an account activity, namely:

- The origin of the account holder or payer,
- Sector risks or

---

20   See p.51

- The classification of an individual as a politically or publicly relevant person ("PEP").

The Wolfsberg banks also agreed among themselves to introduce an ongoing monitoring system for the existing databases, the design of which went far beyond international stipulations in terms of detail. In particular, on these latter points the Wolfsberg group passed, in September 2003, a supplementary "Statement on Monitoring, Screening and Searching", in which the technical minimum requirements for EDP-supported monitoring are set down.

Public criticism, particularly on the part of lawyers, was incomprehensibly vigorous after the first Wolfsberg agreements were closed. According to the opinion of some, the agreements were of no value since in terms of detail they did not go beyond the legally existing duties to report as concerns threshold values and communication density.

This opinion – still commonly encountered today – is not correct. The Wolfsberg banks had recognised that a compilation of all customer and transaction data – which is also critical against the background of modern civic rights – appeared, on the one hand, extremely costly and on the other, of little effect due to aspects of risk. Due to the combination of requirements to report and the risk analysis extremely familiar to the banking sector, a change of dogma was initiated by the industry itself which – as the remarks by committee chairman Nassauer on the 3rd EU money laundering directive at least give grounds to hope – is now already reflected in national anti-money laundering.

In terms of subject matter, too, the banks sometimes went far beyond what the law required: particularly worth mentioning is the agreement to take on full responsibility for respective correspondence partners within the framework of global correspondent bank relationships. Such a form of banks' full downstream responsibility for cooperation partners – which had never previously been stipulated in legislation anywhere in the world – was associated with considerable financial expenditure and logistical efforts and, in most cases, led to a reduction in correspondent bank relationships deemed to be particularly risk-inducing without the legislator's necessarily having to stipulate this.

2.4. Outlook

Increasing regulation density and exterritorial effects of money laundering stipulations?

The numerous national and international regulations – which are hard to overlook – will probably not necessarily encourage effective anti-money laundering.

An initial major weakness of international money laundering prevention was certainly the fact that there were practically no globally uniform standards. Due to the commitment of the FATF regional standards were indeed brought into line theoretically but, of course, there are still considerable practical differences in the form and practical implementation of anti-money laundering measures today. An ever more complex codification of obligations and laws, of due diligence conditions and intervention principles is rendering international alignment difficult and completely hindering it in practice.

A further weakness of anti-money laundering was certainly also that many standards regulators suddenly (sometimes even without a mandate) felt themselves called upon to define standards and regulations for themselves which are, in some cases, inherently incongruent. For example, under the umbrella of the FATF a multitude of regional bodies have now formed which all operate their own standards regulation.[21] Further, many of the organisations with which the FATF cooperates[22] set their own standards,

---

21 For example the Asia Pacific Group on Money Laundering (APG), the Caribbean Financial Action Task Force (CFATF), the Council of Europe Select Committee of Experts on the Evaluation of Anti-Money Laundering Measures (MONEYVAL, formerly "PC-R-EV"), the Eurasian Group (EAG), the Eastern and Southern Africa Anti Money Laundering Group (ESAAMLG), the Financial Action Task Force on Money Laundering in South America (GAFISUD) or the Middle East and North Africa Financial Action Task Force (MENAFATF)

22 For example the African Development Bank, the Asia Development Bank, The Commonwealth Secretariat, the Association of Intelligence Services ("Egmont Group"), the European Bank for Reconstruction and Development (EBRD), the European Central Bank (ECB), Europol, the Inter-American Development Bank (IDB), Intergovernmental Action Group against Money-Laundering in Africa (GIABA), the International Association of Insurance Supervisors (IAIS), the International Monetary Fund (IMF), the International Organisation of Securities Commissions (IOSCO), Interpol,

maintain their own groups of experts or pursue their own strategies for combating money laundering.

Additionally, the FATF has no democratic mandate, but operates merely under the umbrella of the OECD. The actual legislative and regulatory competencies naturally remain with the individual states, which in turn pursue their own strategies and interests and of course draw up their own regulations. International associations such as the EU and AU, too, provide impetus, not to mention the innumerable NGOs, interest groups and the sometimes globally active financial service providers and their associations. According to the latest plans, an indirect mandate in matters of anti-money laundering is to be transferred to the World Bank in particular.

Just this brief outline shows that money laundering prevention to date has particularly suffered from the fact that too many unions and bodies are developing their own models. Although the FATF has established itself as the driving force, this organisation's hands are often tied – as will come to be particularly demonstrated using the example of PEPs – by the fact that compromises are made among members and, therefore, only "lowest common denominators" are passed and raised to the rank of a recommendation which is still informal and not obligatory for any member state.

The exterritorial effect of the US Patriot Act on international correspondent bank relationships has already been addressed above. This legislation does ultimately take the needs of modern anti-money laundering into account in that it not only applies within territorial borders, but is also imposed on any form of international economic structure, namely bank details, which produces a domestic reference. Although this is thoroughly welcome from the point of view of particularly effective anti-money laundering, this opens the door for exterritorial applicability of legal standards in

---

the Organization of American States / Inter-American Committee Against Terrorism (OAS/CICTE), the Organization of American States/ Inter-American Drug Abuse Control Commission (OAS/CICAD), the Organisation for Economic Co-operation and Development (OECD), the Offshore Group of Banking Supervisors (OGBS), United Nations Office on Drugs and Crime (UNODC), the World Bank, the World Customs Organisation (WCO), to name but a few

the guise of anti-terrorism which cannot necessarily be described as "common sense".

From this standpoint, it appears timely to create clear, binding regulations under international law via the bodies provided for the purpose in order to reduce the application uncertainties that have arisen from the ensuing tangle of regulations, in some cases now also with anti-money laundering regulations having exterritorial effects, to a bearable extent.

In any case, the banking economy renders the major service provisions listed in the following for individual states free of charge and now bears the main burden of international anti-money laundering.

3. The currently internationally customary bank measures in the combat against money laundering

On the playing field of the diverse international, national and group-internal regulatory mechanisms, banks are attempting to find a balance between the expectations of prosecution authorities, effective protection of their institutions and their employees against money laundering, and the company's business interests. Depending on the size of the institution, risk deflection occupies up to several hundreds of employees who, in their daily work, are repeatedly presented with the almost impossible task of probing transactions – mostly of a completely neutral appearance – for suspected cases of money laundering.

3.1. Obligations of the banks

National legislation particularly obligates banks and financial service providers, based on the international framework conditions outlined above, to undertake due diligence in the name of the general public. Sometimes the banks allege that states have "outsourced" their criminal prosecution in the field of financial crime and perceive themselves as "worthless deputy sheriffs". On closer inspection, however, banks act only partially as the "long arm of the law". Overwhelmingly, banks attempt to distance criminal prosecution and reputational risks from themselves for their own industrial law-based interest. In addition to precise customer identification based on public documents and verification of customer identity based on public certificates or independent sources, banks' obligation to report to national FIUs is at the heart of the financial sector's efforts against money laundering. Owing to international standards, banks are additionally obliged to retain the documents for at least five years and repeat all customer verification measures at regular intervals.

The national laws passed because of the first EU money laundering directive initially obligate domestic banks to submit regular threshold amount reports to the FIUs. The threshold amount here in the European region is generally EUR 15,000.00. Additionally, banks must send so-called "suspicious transaction reports" (STRs) to the FIUs when undertaking a financial transaction below this threshold if there is a founded suspicion that a financial transaction is made for the purposes of money laundering. However, due to the complex form of most money laundering activity, instances of suspicion may not be evidenced in one single transaction, meaning that banks are also obliged in some cases to report suspicious activities that may consist of a number of transactions and/or do not directly bring about any form of asset movements.

At the organisational level, banks must nominate a commissioner for money laundering together with a deputy, who is personally responsible for compliance with obligations and who manages the money laundering avoidance apparatus. Expenditure for a money laundering prevention organisation varies from institution to institution. While the big Wolfsberg banks, which together transact approximately 80 % of payments worldwide, not uncommonly deploy more than 100 employees in money laundering prevention, money laundering departments in smaller banks not uncommonly comprise only the commissioner for money laundering himself and his/her deputy, who both carry out other tasks in addition. However, all institutions are obliged to evolve and modernise their respective prevention systems.

3.2. Banks as "police deputies"?

There is often the popular opinion while these activities are being carried out that banks are obligated, possibly against their will, to act as "police deputies". This wholesale label is, on closer inspection, not only incomplete, but also incorrect in its basic approach.

Describing the banks as "police deputies" is not appropriate as interests stand. It is true that the investigatory authorities increasingly rely on the data material provided by the banks, inasmuch as the bank actually plays a role in effective prosecution. Primarily, however, the bank attempts to avoid the perversion of its own business activity above all by strictly complying with due diligence obligations concerning the prevention of money laundering. The risks associated with business activity of this kind will be returned to later.[23] However, it remains to be emphasised here that banks have an original interest in not cooperating in any criminal acts of their customers and comply with precautionary measures on their own initiative. This is documented to a particular extent by the activities of the Wolfsberg banks, whose further-reaching self-imposed obligation (for example in the field of correspondent banking or in the field of electronic monitoring) has precisely this as its objective.

Another question which still needs to be clarified in respect of the respective individual regulation is whether banks behave with near sovereignty; further, whether, and in the improbable event that a bank customer incurs asset damages because of the money laundering prevention measures, liability of the bank or also of the state comes under consideration. This aspect was overlooked by the standards regulators to a large extent.

3.3 The search for the needle in the haystack – which possibly is not even there

With the revision of the 40 recommendations in 2002, the FATF made it clear that when assessing the matter of whether a transaction is a suspicious one, the individual key figures of an asset transaction should be of less importance to banks than evaluating the transaction against the background of typical customer activity

---

23   See also the case study section from p.273 of the present publication

on the customer accounts being observed. Behind this strategic adjustment was the recognition that, in by far the most cases, individual financial transactions appear fully neutral from the outside, but may only emerge as part of a money laundering activity in retrospect when further interconnections are being considered. This naturally places considerable requirements upon the evaluators of potentially many thousands of transactions and makes it clear that considering the overall activities of one or a number of bank customers involved an extremely highly placed aim: the impossibility of sufficiently anticipating connections in meaning between individual transactions, in particular, regularly leads to considerable headaches among investigators and banks to an equal extent to this day.

It has therefore always been a practical necessity to find constant, objective criteria that allow the existence of suspicious customer behaviour to become manifest. This type of filtering of financial transactions according to particularly risk-laden elements (country of origin or destination, suspicious senders or recipients, circular payments etc.) corresponds not only to banking-typical risk evaluation models, as they are known from the field of lending for example, but also represents the only favourable way of filtering out risk-laden transactions from an infinite number of orders and subjecting them to closer scrutiny where necessary.

Banks have therefore predominantly developed a control matrix, on the basis of which electronic scoring systems examine individual transactions for specific suspicion criteria. The system triggers the alarm in the event of an accumulated high risk, but releases apparently unsuspicious transactions for implementation without further delay. The detailed form of these scoring systems will be dealt with later.

4. International standards on customer due diligence: from KYC to "politically exposed persons"

It was therefore necessary to develop sufficient criteria and allocate these to a risk estimate. It is clear to everyone that some fields of business at banks are by nature already more vulnerable to abuse by money launderers than others. Therefore, only correspondent bank connections, cash transactions or business connections with "non-cooperating states and territories" were mentioned. Further instances which the banking industry is urged to view with greater scepticism are, for example, over-the-counter transactions or dealings with bearer documents, business relationships with (rarely regulated) aid organisations or e-money, to name but a few examples of more greatly risk-laden transactions.

Coming to light through a number of particularly spectacular incidents in which state assets were embezzled in grand style by emerging or developing country rulers and allowed to circulate through the West's banking system, a number of persons in the public eye were also universally classified as risk-laden in earlier scoring systems. This caused a loud call for "special treatment" of this entire group of persons. Completing bank transactions with prominent or very wealthy persons was subjected to restrictions as a result, the detailed form of which should at least occasion questions to be raised concerning compatibility of interests. In order to actually identify a prominent person or his or her representative as a risk person, it is naturally necessary for the bank to know its customers in the first place – a question which is just as simple as it is complex.

4.1. History of the KYC approach / History of PEP regulations

Effective observation of business relationships with prominent and politically exposed persons, who already represent a higher money laundering risk due to their influence in politics and the economy, presupposes the implementation of a secure "know your customer" system. This again requires those financial service providers carrying out financial transactions or other forms of asset movements to make their contribution to verifying and documenting the identity of the economic beneficiaries.

Until the end of the 1980's, the predominant attitude in the US was to precisely analyse as many financial transactions as possible in order to be able to subsequently lay the "paper trail" with as much precision as possible in the event of a state attorney investigation. As early as 1970 the Bank Secrecy Act required banks to compile threshold value reports (so-called currency transaction reports). Out of this developed a comprehensive network of suspicious transaction reporting systems, which led to a considerable volume of data without shedding light on the individual transaction report any further in terms of risk aspects. Large quantities of data like this accumulated over the years, but were barely able to express anything about actual individual money laundering risks.

Although the "know your customer" approaches were not unknown to US securities traders, these were initially categorised as being a personal encroachment and too costly for application in the wider banking system. In this regard, it was conjectured by scholars that the hesitancy of American securities service providers to introduce a "know your customer" policy could also be due to the fact that these principles reflected European notions of risk control, which were not necessarily suited to American banking traditions.

Accordingly, the original US delegation at the first major session of the Financial Action Task Force in autumn 1989 had opposed recommending KYC policies or even a system of risk-evaluated suspicious transaction reports to the member states.

This attitude of US banks need not necessarily be seen as a low opinion or rejection of risk-oriented customer inspection and transaction checks. Much more than the European notion of anti-money laundering, the US view was based on the assumption that organised crime could best be dried up by strict handling and control of the placement phase of a money laundering operation, and this, according to the American view, should optimally take place through the blanket recording of higher-volume cash transactions and dealings.

However, an encouraging compromise was arrived at during the FATF discussions: whereas the United States made a significant contribution to ensuring that FATF member states were able to agree on a common definition and sanctioning of money laundering on the criminal law side, the Swiss, French and English financial supervisory bodies in particular contributed to ensuring that banking and financial service providers, who found themselves globally obligated within the framework of the OECD, place much higher value on customer due diligence than previously. The KYC principle had found its way into international standards.

In the original 40 recommendations the banks were therefore instructed not to conduct any anonymous accounts or numbered accounts, to check the customer on the basis of reliable documents, to verify the customer's identity and to establish the entitled economic beneficiary (recommendations no. 12 to 14). Additionally, the banks were obligated to terminate the business relationship with the customer in the event of nonsensical or questionable transactions, or, as was the case, not to execute the transaction.

At the proposal of the Council of EU finance ministers, not only were these general KYC regulations introduced in the 1st EU directive on combating money laundering, but a duty to identify when undertaking financial transactions from an upper limit of currently EUR 15,000.00 was also adopted. At the second reading on the modified proposal of the Commission on 17th April 1991 the European Parliament added, among other things, a duty to identify when closing certain insurance contracts.

However, unlike the FATF recommendations, the first EU money laundering directive did not initially require banks to distance themselves from a suspicious transaction; in Art. 7 of the directive it was established that the transaction need only be held up for as long as no report has been made to the responsible authorities.

In the subsequent period, in particular around the middle of the 1990's, things were very quiet in the field of customer identification. Both the FATF and the EU occupied themselves with other problems in the anti-money laundering field (P.O. box banks, non-cooperating territories and states etc.), pushing effective improvement of KYC standards somewhat into the background.

Alongside the developments in anti-money laundering, however, the OECD, together with the Basel Banking Committee, established that, in respect of the abuse of a number of financial centres in the field of corruption money laundering, considerable deficiencies were apparently arising. After a number of particularly drastic and publicly influential examples shook the public in the nineties, in which banks – predominantly unwittingly – had assisted in the money laundering of embezzled potentates' funds and corruption funds, the international banking community, together with the OECD working group for anti-corruption and the non-governmental organisation Transparency International, felt itself required to take up the topic of "customer due diligence" once again.

Shortly after the internationally significant major banks, which together – as mentioned – transacted approximately 80 % of the payments globally, had universally agreed to establish an industry standard and began to exchange details about their money laundering prevention systems, the first more solid Wolfsberg principles were published on 30th October 2000. In these principles, the leading retail banks acknowledged the "know your customer" approach and recognised for the first time the particular status of interests in respect of the association of corruption, misappropriation and embezzlement on the one hand, and money laundering on the other.

On this subject in the Wolfsberg Principles, under Art. 2.5:

> *"2.5 Public Officials*
> *Individuals who have or have had positions of public trust such as government officials, senior executives of government corporations, politicians, important political party officials, etc., and their families and close associates require heightened scrutiny."*

Meanwhile the Financial Action Task Force – rudely awakened by a number of publicly influential scandals of European and US banks in which potentates' funds were laundered and/or came to light – had also recognised the explosiveness of the topic. The topic of corruption and private banking was granted significant priority during the 13th round of discussions of the FATF on 1st February 2000 on the topic of corruption and private banking. The formulation "politically exposed person", abbreviated to "PEP", which had initially been coined by the Basel Banking Committee, was now in use OECD-wide. According to the view of the FATF in 2000, the role of those individuals who assumed prominent public functions – such as, for example, heads of governments, high-ranking politician, high-ranking civil servants, members of the judiciary or military, party chairmen and boards of management of publicly operated companies – should be under particular scrutiny. According to the view of the FATF, these individuals were, especially when they came from countries where corruption predominated, a particularly high risk for the integrity of international financial markets.

Private banks, especially, recognised the particular explosiveness of this topic. After it became evident in 1999 and 2000 that, in one case, up to 70 million USD had been laundered via five financial institutions, of which two had implemented no form of warning systems with reference to PEPs, the Basel Committee and Banking Supervision stepped in again and in October 2001 passed regulations for "Customer Due Diligence for Banks", according to which banks called for particular value to be placed in the context of customer due diligence on particularly risk-rich customer groups, in particular trusts, fiduciary customers, customers not pronouncing in person, and, precisely, PEPs.

Since then, recommendation 2.2.5 rules that:

"Business relationships with individuals holding important public positions and with persons or companies clearly related to them may expose a bank to significant reputations and/or legal risks. Such politically exposed persons ("PEPs") are individuals who are or have been entrusted with prominent public functions, including heads of state or of government, senior politicians, senior government, judicial or military officials, senior executives of publicly owned corporations and important political party officials. There is always a possibility, especially in countries where corruption is widespread, that such persons abuse their public powers for their own illicit enrichment through the receipt of bribes, embezzlement, etc."

The motivating force behind the Basel Committee was clear: the acceptance and management of funds belonging to corrupt politically exposed persons damages the reputation of the bank and can undermine the public's trust in the ethical standards of the entire financial centre. The past had already shown that such cases generally trigger great media interest as well as strong political reactions, which can lead to considerable damage to reputation both for the bank concerned and for the relevant host country.

Even if the illicit origin of the assets is often difficult to prove, further damage is possible at a credit institution: the bank may find itself confronted with costly reports and arrest orders from execution and judiciary authorities (including international citizens' advice requested in criminal cases), and it may be sued for damages by the affected state or the victims of a regime. Under certain circumstances the bank and/or its employees themselves may be accused of money laundering if they knew or must have known that the funds originated from corruption or another serious crime.

After a number of countries had modified their laws and regulations with regard to the OECD convention on anti-corruption to the effect that the active bribery of foreign officials was punishable and had been raised to the status of a crime preliminary to money laundering, according to the Basel Committee it was

"incompatible with the professional ethical principles of the banking business to enter into or maintain a business relationship if the bank knows or has grounds to assume that the funds originate from corruption or embezzlement of public assets. It is urgently necessary for a bank, before entering into a business relationship with a person whom it suspects to be politically exposed, to scrutinise the identity of this person and of persons and companies which are obviously associated with him."

In order to establish whether a new customer is a PEP, the bank should therefore obtain sufficient information from him and examine publicly available information. Before entering into a business relationship with a politically exposed person the bank should investigate the origin of the funds more rigorously. The decision as to whether to open an account was to be taken at management level.

When revising the 40 recommendations the FATF took up these notions and, in Recommendation No. 5, underlined the importance of properly conducted customer due diligence.

Recommendation No. 6 of the FATF reads:

"Financial institutions should, in relation to politically exposed persons, in addition to performing normal due diligence measures:

a) Have appropriate risk management systems to determine whether the customer is a politically exposed person.
b) Obtain senior management approval for establishing business relationships with such customers.
c) Take reasonable measures to establish the source of wealth and source of funds.
d) Conduct enhanced ongoing monitoring of the business relationship."

These recommendations were still encouragingly solid. However, during the overall process of renewing the 40 recommendations a diplomatic conflict of interests had revealed itself within the FATF which was to have significant effects on the treatment of PEPs within the scope of anti-money laundering: in a number of emerging and developing countries in particular, banking and state affairs are to this day so barely separably mixed that there were fears that the recommendations would completely run into a void in practice.

On the other hand, the viewpoint existed in the FATF that an important goal of PEP scrutiny was to prevent potentates from being able to get their illicit assets out of the country. Therefore, according to one view, it was major progress at any rate if transnational financial transactions were to be better documented and observed.

Following tough negotiations the FATF recommended classifying as "politically exposed persons":

"... individuals, who are or have been entrusted with prominent public functions in a foreign country, for example Heads of State or of government, senior politicians, senior government, judicial or military officials, senior executives of state owned corporations, important political party officials. Business relationships with family members or close associates of PEPs involve reputational risks similar to those with PEPs themselves. The definition is not intended to cover middle ranking or more junior individuals in the foregoing categories."

Handling the recommendations of the FATF proved to be difficult in the subsequent period probably because the chosen delimitation criteria appeared inconclusive for many money laundering consultants.

Considered in the light of day, the differentiation is actually thoroughly questionable: whereas banks were to be obligated to wage increased customer diligence in the case of foreign persons in the public eye, this was, incomprehensibly, not to apply for prominent persons at home. A complete extension of obligations to foreign and domestic prominent persons was not, as mentioned, politically implementable even after bitter negotiations, since it is known that there is no sufficient segregation to this day between banking systems and legislature in some countries. In the face of the ever louder discussion, however, the FATF saw itself obliged to add an "Interpretative Note" to Recommendation No. 6, which reads:

"Countries are encouraged to extend the requirements of Recommendation 6 to individuals who hold prominent public functions in their own country."

Although this recommendation cushioned public opposition, on the other hand it cemented different approaches to the question of who is actually a PEP into the 40 + 9 recommendations.

Since the aforementioned mechanism – according to which the FATF standards were adopted through EU directives in Europe, then implemented by the member states and finally transcribed in administrative instructions – had meanwhile developed, the EU also saw itself obligated to adapt the regulations concerning PEPs: the proposal for a third EU money laundering directive was published on 30th June 2004. In its Art. 11 it reads:

"In respect of the relationship with politically exposed persons the member states rule that these institutions and persons shall
- *have appropriate risk management systems, on the basis of which it can be determined whether the customer is a politically exposed person or not;*

- *have obtained the approval of their management before they take up business relationships with these customers;*
- *have taken sensible measures, on the basis of which the source of the assets and funds is determined or, respectively, to guarantee continuous monitoring of the business relationship."*

The proposals essentially resume the recommendations of the FATF, without, however, adopting the apparently questionable differentiation according to foreign and domestic officials. Pursuant to grounds for consideration no. 10 of the directive, politically exposed persons are namely, quite sweepingly, all natural persons who exercise or have exercised important public functions and whose significant complex financial or business transactions are sometimes liable to an increased risk of money laundering, as well as their family members or persons close to these persons.

Following the previously mentioned controversial discussions and at the proposal of EU parliamentary Nassauer, the European Parliament altered the passages again when it convened. They now read:

"With regard to <u>transactions or business relationships</u> with politically exposed persons <u>who are resident in another member state or in a third country</u>, the member states rule that the institutions and persons <u>falling under this directive</u> shall,
- a) *have appropriate <u>risk-based procedures</u>, on the basis of which it can be determined whether the customer is a politically exposed person or not;*
- b) *have obtained the approval of their management before they take up business relationships with these customers;*
- c) *take <u>appropriate</u> measures, with which the source of the assets and the source of funds <u>which are deployed</u> during the business relationship <u>or transaction can be determined</u>;*
- d) <u>*subject the business relationship to enhanced continuous monitoring.*</u>*"*

Through these modifications the EU directive was adapted, on the one hand, to the stipulations of the FATF, on the other – in a manner to be welcomed – the risk-orientation of the procedure for establishing PEP suitability was underlined. Additionally, with the "appropriateness" criterion, a regulating agent found its way into the directive which should to protect the standards' addressees from fully disproportionate stipulations by the national legislators or financial supervisory bodies.

4.2. The scope of application of regulations concerning PEPs

As already demonstrated using the example of the foreign reference criterion, international standards differ fairly considerably when it comes to the question of who actually is to be deemed a "PEP". There is disunity in respect of further criteria, too:

According to the directives of the Swiss Banking Committee, falling under the category of PEP risk group are persons "who hold a major public function". According to the US Interagency Guidance the PEP, on the other hand, is defined as a Senior Foreign Political Figure, while the Basel Banking Committee in its "Customer Due Diligence for Banks" from 2001 merely mentions "potentates".

These uncertainties were not acceptable for the financial service providers. In the event of criminal proceedings a credit institution would have to prove, in order to avoid an accusation of gross negligence or carelessness, that the international industry standards on money laundering prevention were complied with. How, though, is that supposed to be possible if not even the international standards were uniform, but diverged as concerns all measures?

An initially somewhat clumsy attempt to narrow down the term "PEP" came from the OECD: the once again revised forty recommendations of the FATF, though, merely made it clear that the middle or lower levels of government, politics, the military or administration should not fall under the term "PEP"; positive examples were nowhere to be found.

Much more helpful, on the other hand, were the criteria that were compiled by the Wolfsberg Group as a follow-up to the revised

Wolfsberg Principles, which, although they still did not represent a globally applicable description of a PEP, did establish an international industry standard.

According to the view of the Wolfsberg members the term "Politically Exposed Person" referred to persons who exercise *"major public functions within a state"*. It was clearly explained that this included both persons who *"currently"* exercise such an office and those persons who have done this *"recently"* and *"whose financial circumstances could possibly be an object of public interest"*. In individual cases – according to the Wolfsberg Group – it should be determined on the basis of the *"political and social environment"* in the *"individual case"*, whether a person fell under this group of persons or not. In any event, according to the view of the Wolfsberg banks, the following persons are named as prime examples in order to facilitate such a classification in individual cases:

- Heads of government and state as well as cabinet ministers;
- Influential functionaries in state-owned industrial operations or administration;
- Senior judges;
- Senior party functionaries;
- Leading or influential officials, functionaries, military leaders and persons with similar functions in international or supranational organisations;
- Associated royal families;
- The senior or most influential representatives of religious organisations, if these functions are associated with political, legal or military responsibility or responsibility under administrative law or competency.

Further, the Wolfsberg banks made it clear that the family members of relevant PEPs were also to be subjected to increased due diligence scrutiny. According to the view of the Wolfsberg bank they include (marriage) partners, children, parents and siblings. Depending on the circumstances, other blood relations and those who married into the family may also be included under this term.

Far more vague, on the other hand, is the description of *"close associates"*, also covered by the Wolfsberg definition. According to the view of the Wolfsberg banks, to avoid self-responsibility of the banks, *"Business partners, personal advisors/consultants"* of the PEP and those who may obviously profit from such a person or his activities should be included in the industry standard.

In clear terms – and in one aspect certainly deviating from the rules of the FATF – the Wolfsberg banks pointed out that political parties were not PEPs, but banks should comply with the highest standard of diligence when entering into business relationships with political parties. Whether this qualification may be helpful in relation to most emerging or developing countries, in which not appointed governments, but individual members of party cadres frequently control the fate of a country, may possibly be doubted.

In practice, money laundering experts find themselves repeatedly confronted with the almost impossible task of, based on only a few details from the new customer interview, precisely judging whether the bank is dealing with a PEP. The situation with individual transactions presents itself as not being much easier.

For one thing, there is the above-mentioned dogma dispute concerning domestic or foreign references. Following the opinion of the FATF in its revised recommendations, a domestic head of government would potentially not be qualified as a PEP, but a successful foreign business would be. For another thing, according to the initial proposal by the EU Commission, no distinction between a German head of government and his counterpart from a foreign despot state would need to be drawn – which sounded at least just as inappropriate.

Through the resolution of 25th May 2005, this matter – at the EU level initially – was provisionally decided to the effect that only PEPs residing abroad (referring to another member state and third countries) should be included in the EU regulations. However, whereas according to the Commission's proposal, PEPs were

> *"those natural persons who exercise or have exercised important public functions and whose significant or complex financial or business transactions are in some cases burdened with an increased money laundering risk, as well as their family members or persons closely associated with these persons"*

The Parliament changed this wording as follows:

"those natural persons who exercise or have exercised important public functions, and their immediate family members or persons known by them to be closely associated."

Whether the restriction of "closely associated persons" to persons "known by them to be closely associated" will be of any help, may certainly already be regarded with appropriate scepticism.

As a "final blow" by the European legislator for the time being, an initial draft of the already mentioned "money laundering definition directive" was compiled at the beginning of 2006, in Art. 3 of which the term PEP is defined in closer detail. According to the draft the following persons should be treated as PEPs in the application area of the 3rd money laundering directive:

- Members of the executive body down to regional level
- Members of parliaments, including regional parliaments
- Judges of the respective supreme courts, including at regional level
- Management boards of (independently administrated) corporations exercising sovereign rights
- High-ranking diplomats, militia or other state civil servants
- Persons exercising management functions in state-owned operations which either deal with mineral resources, exercise a monopoly or make a considerable contribution to the state budget
- Leading party functionaries in those countries where there is a high degree of identification between party and government.

As a "drip tray" the draft also provides for equalising all other persons holding "similar influence" with all those who are affected.

In respect of "close associates", the draft brings further confusion: namely, "close associates" should not only include natural, but also legal persons who are connected with the PEP either at the functional or economic level, even if a connection only exists through a not more closely described "legal arrangement".

In a similar way to the FATF recommendations the draft does, on the one hand, make it clear that middle ranks should not fall under the PEP definitions. On the other hand, the Commission draft emphasises throughout that regional levels must also be included.

Such a distinction can barely be comprehended and in practice will probably lead to confusion when assessing a customer who, for example, is a provincial high court judge or the president of a local bar association. However, the judgement whether there is a high level of identification between party and government in a country, possibly in a federal state, will probably be just as difficult for a bank employee.

4.3. Individual risk benchmarks as a solution?

The previously mentioned discussion about the abstract concepts of "PEP" clearly shows the effects that a too exacting codification frenzy among a variety of standards regulators can have. Neither the lengthy discussion about the identity of the PEP nor the results found so far are of help in the matter. It is of no importance what the member states of the European Union will decide and rule for the respective states of Europe – in the consideration of domestic or foreign nationals it is already clear that every wholesale pre-definition of a politically exposed person is doomed to failure and an individual risk benchmark will need to be established.

On the other hand, the EU's draft on the third money laundering directive, clarifications in a further directive and the FATF recommendations alike took no account of the risks of an actual individual case. In any case, from the point of view of risk it appears tenable to subject the wife of a manager of a local construction authority to precise PEP risk scrutiny far preferably to, for example, a cabinet minister who reckons with standing in the spotlight anyway and who must disclose all income. The limitation of PEPs articulated by the FATF in particular, according to which no middle and lower functionaries, politicians and similar bearers of responsibility should be included, is diametrically opposed to the risk intensity of many economic sectors or administrative fields in which larger budgets are entirely managed by middle or lower employees – who could definitely be potentially susceptible to accepting gifts or misappropriating funds.

The discussion about the abstract concepts of the PEP can clearly be attributed to the fact that the regulations concerning PEPs – as with a number of special recommendations compiled by the FATF and meantime raised to legal status by other institutions – are basically retroactive regulations for individual cases. When at around the end of the 1990s a number of individual cases of undisclosed despots shook the banking industry, all alarmed standards regulators – and of those there are, as mentioned at the beginning, a number – found themselves immediately put in a tight spot by the public. The result was laws for the special treatment of PEPs which, for one thing, infringe on civic rights and for another, though, were probably already obsolete at the time they were passed.

Additionally, the discussion concerning the special treatment of PEPs is definitely being used as a market-political instrument. Major banks, in particular, are self-evidently making things easier for themselves by setting up, in the face of existing ingenious screening systems, ever stricter identification directives which smaller banking establishments can only copy with difficulty.

For this reason, a way out from the futile discussion about who is who is not to be included in the stricter money laundering regulations and can only be seen in the individual recording of personal profiles, fully independently of a classification as a PEP. Instead of trying to define the abstract concepts ever more closely, it would be done with one single brief sentence: banks must include the professional, economic, familial and personal background of a bank customer when assessing risk. Most establishments already do this in reality.

5. Practical organisation and form of PEP inspection by institutions

Motivated by the Wolfsberg agreements and the recommendations of the FATF, which had granted a considerably higher status to the treatment of prominent persons, heads of state or other exposed persons following the basic revision in 2003, the majority of German lending institutions have already installed security systems which minimise the reputational risks mentioned at the beginning and/or are designed to prevent abuse of banking services by prominent persons. It can be expected that the recommendations of the FATF reflected in the third EU money laundering directive will be implemented by member states in coming years. It can likewise be expected that a number of national financial supervisory bodies will at least adopt the stipulations of the FATF and the EU directive, or possibly even tighten them.

At the current point in time lending institutions have already taken measures arising from risk considerations in order to protect the respective institutions from reputational damage, prosecution or civil law disputes.

5.1. Scoring systems for establishing the degree of risk of a transaction or business relationship

In principle, lending institutions which, for example, have implemented automated transaction scanning procedures, examine payments and extended business connections via an electronic matrix. Individual precisely defined risk factors are amalgamated in this matrix and a certain value is assigned to them. Customary risk criteria include, for example, a customer's country of origin or the origin of a payment. If an EU, OECD or FATF country is involved in this connection, then fewer risk points are allocated to this transaction, for example, than would be the case for a payment originating from a state located outside these territories. Naturally, the highest geographical risk attribution takes place in respect of states which are placed by the FATF on the list of so-called "non-cooperating states and territories" or were only recently deleted from this list but are still subject to a "close monitoring" procedure. Further criteria are, for example, amount transacted, economic owner etc. Individual banks kept their respective scoring systems secret until a few years ago. This was due to the consideration that better management of reputational risks self-evidently promised long-term commercial success in respect of a competitor who has potentially implemented a poorer scoring system. Only the Wolfsberg discussions in recent years have reversed this dogma. As mentioned at the beginning, the world's leading payment banks now exchange their inspection matrices within the Wolfsberg group, in order together to achieve higher statistical precision through which money launderers can be identified with more precision.

If one takes up the notion cited above, according to which individual risk features can be apportioned to every person, then it becomes apparent that basically no more precise a description of PEPs is required, but simply a reliable empirical evaluation of other parameters such as previous convictions, profession, public functions etc.

5.2. PEP identification via "blacklists"

In parallel with the transaction-related scoring systems, banks use (electronic) suspect lists of customers which are compared with both the transaction data bases and with the customer master data. Names of war criminals, terrorists, criminals at large etc. are recorded on these checklists. It goes without saying that implementing financial transactions for or in the economic interest of such persons is high-risk.

So-called PEP lists, however, also exist several levels below this degree of risk. Naturally, it is hardly possible for money laundering experts to know foreign ministers from every state by name, or to react to potential changes quickly enough. In addition to criminal and terrorism databases, therefore, systems have been established that can quickly compile lists of leading personalities from the military, politics, judiciary or similar. Numerous service providers offer banks either online scanning of their customer or transaction data bases or allow the money laundering specialist to call up individual names in a library. Money laundering prevention has now given rise to an entire economic sector in which master data for improving risk management is updated and centrally controlled.

Additionally there are, of course, in many cases, black lists conducted by the institutions themselves from which political leaders or economic captains can be deduced who, in the institution's view, imply a high money laundering risk. These institution-owned lists are, for reasons of data protection, possibly dubious in some countries.

5.3. Consequences of PEP identification

If a lending institution establishes that a PEP wishes to enter into a business relationship, then the internal organisation structures of lending institutions must rule that the decision to establish a business relationship can only be taken at senior management level. Behind this aspect it can clearly be seen that, in the case of PEPs generally classified as high-risk, positions of risk are involved whose reputational risk may jeopardise the continued existence of the bank as well. In this respect it is only appropriate, from the point of view of risk, to require so-called senior management approval.

During the discussions about the third EU money laundering directive, it was repeatedly discussed in this connection whether an opinion of a managing board or chief executive needs to be obtained in every single case precisely in bulk business. In this respect, however, the general agreement on the part of the EU was that, owing to translation errors, the term "senior management" should be understood to the effect that a bank employee must obtain instructions from the next higher employee, which was probably more in correspondence with necessities in practice.

If senior management grants its consent to establishing a customer relationship, a PEP's account and custodian account movements must also be observed with particular care, analysed periodically and specifically investigated for aspects of risk. Enhanced customer due diligence also presupposes that potentially deposited assets such as high amounts of money or extensive bond assets are carefully examined as to their origin by the money laundering consultant. In this point, in particular, the bank is frequently reliant upon the cooperation of the PEPs.

6. Deficiencies and implementation problems when applying inspection programmes

Naturally, implementing the abstract regulations described above concerning the particular risk instances of a business relationship with PEPs is not particularly easy. To this day, for example, in Germany considerable uncertainty predominates as to which definition of "PEP" should actually be decisive for German industrial law. It has already been described in detail that even at the international level, no unity can be achieved as to whether, for example, only potentates and criminals known to the public, or European heads of state, too, should trigger the measures described above.

The money laundering consultant of a banking establishment very frequently finds himself facing the practical problem that, although he clarifies the formal identity of the customer, he has to rely on the customer's information alone when making statements about economic justifiability. PEPs that are trying, in particular, with criminal intent to feed assets into the legal circular flow, not uncommonly use family members, business partners or lawyers and tax consultants to appear to a certain degree as "front men" on their own behalf. Establishing the "economically entitled person" becomes even more important in this connection.

Additionally, database solutions on offer on the open market predominantly only contain publicly obtainable data material. Owing to the need to name high-risk persons but without exposing oneself to the accusation of slander or a breach of general personal rights, market providers ultimately have no other possibility than to cite public sources without making their own appraisals. This does preserve service providers from a dilemma, but it does not help banks and financial service providers any further in the event of doubt than their own Internet research would accomplish. Although more practical in application than individual research, industry solutions therefore provide hardly any added value during the decision whether a business relationship should be entered into or not.

In addition, industry-provided system solutions are also susceptible to errors, because links are often only made to natural persons but not to family trustees or addresses. For this reason both spelling errors, which are only actually caught by one part of the software, and duplications and broken links are possible.

Particular problems arise in small credit institutions or in establishments which only conduct a small number of payments or deposits. Probably due to the fact that commercial providers for PEP databases have only emerged in recent years and considerable start-up costs first need to be recouped, such programs are often simply too expensive for small credit institutions. Small banks, in particular, are repeatedly heard to claim that when new customer numbers are low or there are only a few payment transactions, acquiring corresponding scoring systems is likewise not worthwhile. The consequence of which is that, to this day, manual checks on the customer and transaction inventory have gained acceptance in many small banks, with many financial service providers and, most often, in companies not directly regulated by the money laundering legislation. Basically there are no objections to this type of check if it is proportionate with the individual risk situation of the respective company. Frequently, carefully conducted internet research will probably lead to qualitatively identical aims to a data base comparison from a commercial provider.

As a result, the question therefore arises how a lending institution can take control of the fact that more or less anybody could be a "PEP".

A look back at the backgrounds described above reveals that the "special treatments" required in respect of politically exposed persons can be attributed to dramatic individual cases in the 1990s, in which despotic heads of state, ruthless and corrupt economic captains or military leaders seriously jeopardised the reputation of major banking establishments. Even though it must be the presumed aim of every credit institution to prevent business contacts with South American drug barons, African despots or Asian triads, the escalating suspicion of broad swathes of the public clearly demonstrates the limits of an effective anti-money laundering opportunity. The "tightrope" between the well-understood interests of a credit institution and the interests of the general public from the point of view of the banking sector shall be dealt with later.[24]

However, it remains to be stressed even at this point that, although the wholesale implementation of lists or data bases will probably ensure that banks comply with the usual due diligence benchmarks, combating government criminal activity, the misappropriation of public funds or the corruption behind the PEP risk cannot be enabled through PEP special treatment measures. Realistically speaking, only further customisation of risk scoring systems can help to uncover money launderers in this context.

---

24   See for example section on jeopardising reputation, p.273

7. Outlook

It is a fact that criminals will always need to launder illegally obtained assets in order to make it difficult for the state to gain direct access to the acquired assets, which is why criminals will continue to develop ever more complex money laundering methods in the future. Criminal PEPs also attempt to make it difficult to trace accounts to their person.

An inevitable consequence of this is that even prosecution authorities – and with them obligated groups such as banks and lawyers – need to continue to develop their methods for avoiding self-responsibility. However, it appears questionable how far financial service providers can actually effectively trace connections back across five dummy firms or front men.

In the area of PEPs it will continue to be the case that a small group of persons with access to state assets will attempt to use these for their own ends. There is definitely a consensus between the legislator, banks, financial supervision bodies and the prosecution authorities that the financial sector also needs to become aware of its responsibility and work to counter this.

From the point of view of the banks, however, another question arises in this area that they have to weigh up ex-ante reputational risks and punishable offence risks against their own commercial interests.
Essentially, therefore, two questions will be posed in the future:

Firstly: Which group of persons should actually be monitored within the framework of "enhanced due diligence"? Are not even broad sections of the population potential PEPs or could they not at least become so in the future?

Secondly: To what extent does a financial service provider actually need to pursue investigations – is it enough to exclude (gross or simple) negligence by observing industry standards, or should future solution approaches even be associated with absolute, (therefore independent of blame), liability of the bank?

The solution approaches on this subject are equally as manifold as the conflict situations that arise. The answers – and this is clear – will range within the area of conflict between active risk management for avoiding each money laundering case or the avoidance of civic law or criminal law responsibility of the company or its employees.

In the process, an indispensable benchmark will be a customised risk evaluation, based on the actual institution, which is based on the fundamental concepts of the Wolfsberg group. At any rate it is welcome that the European standards regulator, too, has decided to unrestrictedly recognise the concept of the "risk-based approach" in this area. In the long view it will remain the only opportunity to sufficiently narrow down the almost inconceivably broad term of PEP and obtain uniform parameters based on empirical experience.

B.
Combating Money Laundering in Liechtenstein[25]

---

[25] The present essay was compiled by the author with the considerable collaboration of Dr. Christa Burschowsky

Dr. Erek NUENER

Dr. Erek Nuener, born 1968, is a national of Liechtenstein. After finishing his studies in legal sciences and his doctorate at the University of Innsbruck he served for one year in the administrative district of the Innsbruck local court. From autumn 1993 until the spring of 1995, he completed postgraduate university studies at Schloss Hofen (Austria) in the field of European law. From 1994 until 1997 Dr. Erek Nuener acted as articled clerk to a Liechtenstein legal firm. He successfully completed the Liechtenstein government's lawyer examination in 1997. From August 1997 until May 1998 he completed postgraduate studies at Boston University (USA) in the field of international banking and financial law. Dr. Erek Nuener has been an independent lawyer and partner of the trustee office IMT Internationale Management- und Treuhand-Anstalt, Vaduz. Dr. Erek Nuener holds various administrative board positions in financial service companies.

1. Liechtenstein in general

1.1. History of the Principality of Liechtenstein

Prince Johann Adam Andreas von Liechtenstein successively acquired the estate of Schellenberg and the earldom of Vaduz at the beginning of the eighteenth century. When Emperor Charles VI raised both regions to the status of principality in 1719, the country's prince as owner of an area immediately adjacent to the empire received a seat and a vote at the German Council of Electors. In addition the country received the right to bear the name of "Principality of Liechtenstein".

Through its acceptance as a member of Napoleon's Confederation of the Rhine, Liechtenstein achieved recognition of its sovereignty in 1806. Liechtenstein's sovereignty was confirmed at the Vienna Conference in 1815, at which the 39 German states formed the German Confederation. Liechtenstein belonged to the German Confederation until 1866 and is today the only state from this alliance to remain independent.

However, Liechtenstein's situation was very difficult. Commerce and industry had difficulties developing due to the economic isolation, peasant farming was burdened by feudal taxes and the level of education, despite universal compulsory schooling, was low.

Due to the absolutist manner of proceeding the population mistrusted necessary legal reforms (such as, for example, the introduction of the General Civil Code). The ideology behind the revolution of 1848 therefore also found resonance in Liechtenstein and subjects demanded from the Prince the abolition of feudal taxes, but also a new constitution which was to include free election of public representatives. However, the absolutist system remained prevalent for the time being, because Prince Alois II initially wanted to await developments in Germany and Austria.

Liechtenstein's economy was first able to slowly develop when the customs treaty with Austria-Hungary was signed in 1852.

Liechtenstein did not turn to the neighbouring state of Switzerland until after the collapse of the Danube monarchy. The first political parties in Liechtenstein came into being at the end of the First World War (Christian Social People's Party and the Progressive Citizens' Party). Account was taken of the demand for a more democratic constitution in 1921, when the constitution recently negotiated between Prince and Parliament, which prescribed essential directly democratic institutions and prevented foreign dominance, came into force.

Liechtenstein eventually announced the customs treaty with Austria. Relations with Switzerland were increasingly deepened. Among other treaties Liechtenstein and Switzerland eventually signed the customs treaty of 1923, on the basis of which Liechtenstein forms a common economic area with Switzerland.

Liechtenstein suffered a serious economic crisis during the interwar period, which on the one hand can be traced back to the penetration of the Rhine in 1927, which inundated more than half of the valleys, but also to the so-called savings bank scandal in particular. The young democracy was additionally strongly burdened by the domestic political tensions between the two parties, which only gradually subsided under the effect of the German invasion of Austria in March 1938. The parties eventually formed a government coalition and introduced proportional representation, which stabilised the country's domestic politics.

Thanks to Liechtenstein's neutral position and its partnership with Switzerland, Liechtenstein was not only protected from acts of war during the Second World War, but also survived its economic problems.

In the post-war period Liechtenstein experienced a lasting economic upturn, principally due to the customs treaty with Switzerland, but also due to the Swiss franc, its stable political and social conditions and its liberal economic regulations, combined with moderate taxation. Liechtenstein transformed itself from an agricultural state to a modern society with competitive industrial operations. Internationally, however, financial services, trustees and banks, in particular, received the most attention.

1.2. Liechtenstein's foreign policy

Liechtenstein's foreign policy position was significantly characterised as history progressed by its geographical location at an important European north-south connecting route. Liechtenstein's foreign policy, like that of its neighbouring states, is therefore in harmony with the concept of neutrality. Not only does it not belong to any political or military alliance, but it also has no military forces.

Liechtenstein has close bilateral relations with Switzerland. The most important treaty between the two states is the customs treaty of 1923. Due to this customs agreement the entire Swiss customs legislation as well as the remaining federal legislation, as far as the customs integration necessitates its application, applies to Liechtenstein.[26] Additionally, all trade and customs treaties signed by Switzerland with third countries find application in Liechtenstein. The customs treaty enables Switzerland to represent Liechtenstein in negotiations of this kind and sign such treaties with effect for Liechtenstein.

However, since the customs treaty was adapted to contemporary requirements in 1990 and 1995, Liechtenstein can itself become a treaty state in international agreements and a member of international organisation in the area covered by the customs treaty if Switzerland also belongs to these agreements and organisations. Liechtenstein and Switzerland now sign separate agreements in case Switzerland does not join an organisation or agreement, as was the case for example in 1994 for the preparation of Liechtenstein's accession to the European Economic Area.

In 1981 a currency treaty entered into force between the two states, on the basis of which Liechtenstein, which has been using the Swiss franc as legal tender since 1921, was integrated into the currency region of Switzerland. Due to general liberalisation, a postal agreement signed as early as 1921 and revised in 1978 was dissolved in the mutual agreement of 1999. Liechtenstein has also signed bilateral agreements with other states. Treaties in the

---

26 With the exception of all regulations of the Swiss federal legislature which establish the federation's liability to pay contributions

fields of double taxation, legal assistance and education and social services have been signed with Austria in particular.

In recent decades Liechtenstein has been able to expand its interstate relationships considerably. Although Liechtenstein did not belong to any international organisations a few years ago, it is now a member of a multitude of international bodies and organisations, of which only the most important can be listed here:

- International Court in The Hague (ICC)
  Joined: 29th March 1950
- International Police Association (INTERPOL)
  Joined: 1960
- Organisation for Security and Cooperation in Europe (OSCE)
  Participating state in the former CSCE from 1st August 1975
- European Council
  Joined: 23rd November 1978
- United Nations Organisation (UNO)
  Joined: 18th September 1990
- European Free Trade Association (EFTA)
  Joined 1st September 1991, previously special status from 3rd May 1960
- Treaty on the European Economic Area (EEA)
  Joined 1st Mai 1995
- World Trade Organisation (WTO)
  Joined: 1st September 1995

The multilateral agreements which Liechtenstein has joined, deal in particular with matters of the economy, law, health, education, culture, environmental conservation, transport, telecommunications, the combat against criminal organisations and terrorism, etc.

Through Liechtenstein's participation in such organisation the Principality, even as a small state has the opportunity to act out its interests in specific areas of international life and prove its willingness for cooperation and solidarity.[27]

---

27 *Vaduz Press and Information Bureau*, Principality of Liechtenstein/A Documentary [German], 2. revised edition 2003, page 56ff.

2 The decisive legal stipulations for combating money laundering in the Principality of Liechtenstein

2.1. Introduction

The Liechtenstein banking centre covers 15 licensed credit institutions. As at 31st December 2004 the balance of all banks amounted to CHF 34.21 billion. The generated annual profit was CHF 424 million, which corresponds to an achieved net profit per employee (part-time not included) of CHF 278,000.00.

At the same key date 1,526 full and part-time employees were active in the Liechtenstein banking sector. Off-balance-sheet customer assets amounted to CHF 29 billion and on-balance business covered CHF 78 billion of customer funds.

These figures show the status held by the banking sector in the small Liechtenstein economy.[28] Due to this special status of the banking sector in the Liechtenstein economy, effective legislation is required in order to protect the sector against abuse, money laundering and organised crime.

Although Liechtenstein had a basically European law-compliant anti-money laundering regime from 1996 (implementation of EU money laundering directive 91/308), weaknesses could be observed in the area of enforcement in particular. Various measures to improve the situation at the time have been launched in the meantime.

The legal assistance act (RHG),[29] for example, entered into force on 6th November 2000. Competencies of the institutions were legally established with the law dated 14th March 2002 concerning the administrative department Financial Intelligence Unit (FIU) LGBl. 2002 No. 57.

The FIU is primarily designed to be the contact partner for financial intermediaries in the event of suspicions concerning money

---

28 See 2004 annual report of the Liechtenstein Bankers' Association
29 Law dated 15th September 2000 concerning international legal assistance in criminal matters (Rechtshilfegesetz, legal assistance act (RHG)), LGBl. 2000 No. 215

laundering, organised crime or terrorism. It analyses and assesses the reports made to it in accordance with due diligence legislation, occasions the required sanctions according to due diligence legislation and, should the need arise, reports to the public prosecutor's office if the suspicion of money laundering, crimes preliminary to money laundering or organised crime hardens. It also obtains information from publicly accessible and non-publicly accessible sources which are necessary for recognising money laundering, crimes preliminary to money laundering and organised crime.[30]

In addition, on 1st January 1997 a due diligence act[31] entered into force which initially proved itself to be a solid basis for securing the financial service centre Liechtenstein.

However, Liechtenstein wanted to blaze further trails in respect of its responsibility in the financial field and behave even more decisively against money laundering and organised crime. The deficiencies observed during the application of due diligence act 1997 were seized upon and revised. A tightened due diligence act was the result, entering into force on 1st January 2001.[32] The due diligence act was accompanied by a likewise completely revised new due diligence ordinance. Additionally, the legal assistance act (RHG) was adapted to international requirements and the facts of money laundering (§ 165 criminal code (StGB)) were tightened.

Due diligence act was finally totally revised when the recently reworked due diligence act[33] (SPG) complete with implementation regulations[34] (due diligence regulations (SPV)) entered into force on 1st February 2005. The Principality of Liechtenstein, as a contract party to the treaty on the European Economic Area (EEA), herewith fulfilled its obligation in respect of due diligence to implement the 1st EU money laundering directive (directive

---

30 On the further tasks of the FIU see Art. 5 of the law of 14th March 2002 concerning the Financial Intelligence Unit (FIU) LGBl 2002 No. 57
31 Due diligence act (SPG) 1997, LGBl 1996/116
32 Due diligence act (SPG) 2001, LGBl 2000/213
33 Law of 26th November 2004 concerning professional duties of diligence during business transactions (Sorgfaltspflichtgesetz, due diligence act (SPG)), LGBl 2005 No. 5
34 Regulations concerning the due diligence act (Sorgfaltspflichtverordnung, due diligence regulations (SPV)) year 2004 No. 6

91/308/EEA) as well as the 2nd EU money laundering directive (directive 2001/97/EC).

In addition, the law[35] aimed at the setting up of a financial market supervisory body and its organisation, tasks and competencies was passed by the FMA on 18th June 2004.

Among other tasks the FMA is responsible for supervising and executing the due diligence act and its implementation regulations. In this vein, the FMA checks compliance with due diligence stipulations within the context of an annual formal and material inspection pursuant to Art. 24ff. due diligence act (SPG). Breaches of the obligations resulting from the due diligence act may be punished with on-the-spot fines, court fines or imprisonment.

In its report published in August 2003 concerning the OFC[36] assessment carried out in Liechtenstein in October/November 2002, the International Monetary Fund established that Liechtenstein legal stipulations in the field of anti-money laundering, as well as terrorist financing, were to a large extent in harmony with international standards requirements and that Liechtenstein generally has modern legislature of a qualitatively high standard which represents an excellent basis for effective supervision.[37]

Additionally, Liechtenstein is a member of the United Nations and is a contract party to numerous international agreements on protection against money laundering, anti-terror financing and international legal assistance.[38]

---

35 Financial market supervision law; FMAG LGBl. No. 175
36 Offshore Financial Center
37 On this subject see *FMA*, Liechtenstein Financial Market Association, 1st. Feb. 2005, due diligence regulations for banks in the Principality of Liechtenstein [German]
38 See government sanctions paper concerning the Liechtenstein financial centre "Combating money laundering and organised crime" [German] of December 2002

2.2. Criminal law coverage of money laundering in the Principality of Liechtenstein

2.2.1. General

In the course of the criminal code revisions[39] criminal stipulations concerning money laundering and criminal organisations were tightened and the facts of "terrorist association" were re-established. Additionally, bribery crimes (§§ 304ff. criminal code (StGB)) in the field of corruption were revised and active bribery was extended to foreign civil servants and/or officials.

In order to be able to meet the pressure of international obligations,[40] Liechtenstein integrated into its criminal code and criminal trial regulations[41] the sanctions according to asset law which were fully revised in Austria with the criminal law modification law of 1996. The sanctions concerned siphoning off financial gains, expiry and confiscation.

Extending the regulation concerning the siphoning off of financial gains (§§ 20 and 20a criminal code (StGB)) led to an independent sanction (not in the form of a punishment) in the event all criminal offences which have led to an illegal asset-related advantage, in which connection this sanction also affects members of criminal organisations or terrorist associations.[42]

Additionally, in accordance with § 20b criminal code (StGB), which governs the confiscation of assets arising from criminal offences, expiry was extended to foreign crimes and assets of criminal organisations or terrorist associations which were provided for terrorist financing.

---

39 LGBl. 2000 No. 256 and LGBl. 2003 No. 236
40 In particular European Council Convention No. 141 concerning money laundering
41 Striking in this respect is the change to the burden of certification with reference to the legality of the origin or assets in continued or recurrent criminal activity or membership in a criminal association. See government sanctions paper on the Liechtenstein financial centre "Combating money laundering and organised crime" [German] dated December 2002, p.7
42 See government sanctions paper on the Liechtenstein financial centre "Combating money laundering and organised crime" [German] dated December 2002, p.7

Due to the revisions of the criminal code, corresponding modifications to formal law eventually needed to be undertaken in the context of criminal trial regulations, narcotics law and other criminal by-laws.

2.2.2. The facts of money laundering (§ 165 criminal code (StGB))

2.2.2.1. The legal text

"1) Someone who conceals or obscures the origin of asset components arising from a crime, an offence according to § 278d or according to §§ 304 to 308 or an offence according to the narcotics law, particularly by providing false information in legal circulation concerning the origin or the true nature of these asset components, their ownership or other rights on them, the authorisations to possess them, their transfer or as to where they are located, shall be punished with imprisonment of up to three years or with a fine of up to 360 daily earnings.

2) Someone who takes possession of, receives for safekeeping, asset components arising from a crime, an offence according to § 287d or according to §§ 304 to 308 or an offence according to the narcotics law, be it merely for the purpose of keeping safe, investing or managing these asset components, transforms, exploits or transfers such assets to a third party, shall be punished with imprisonment of up to two years or with a fine of up to 360 daily earnings.

3) Someone who commits the crime in reference to a value surpassing 75 000 francs or as a member of a gang that has associated itself with repeated money laundering, shall be punished with imprisonment of six months to five years.

4) An asset component arises from a criminal act if the perpetrator acquires it through the crime or in return for committing the crime, or if the value of the originally obtained or received asset is embodied in the asset component.

5) Not punishable for money laundering is someone who has been punished for taking part in the preliminary crime.

6) Someone who takes possession of, receives for safekeeping, components of the assets of a criminal organisation (§ 278a) or of a terrorist association (§ 278b) by its orders or in its interests, be it merely for the purpose of keeping safe, investing or managing these assets, transforms, exploits or transfers such components to a third party, shall be punished with imprisonment of up to three years, someone who commits the crime in reference to a value surpassing 75 000 francs, with imprisonment of six months to five years."

Before going into the criminal inventory of money laundering in closer detail, it should be pointed out that the Liechtenstein regulation concerning money laundering is based on § 165 of the Austrian criminal code[43].

Since the Austrian criminal code largely formed the basis of the Liechtenstein criminal code, the attempt was made to avoid having the two criminal legislations "drift apart" in areas on which great importance is placed internationally. The fear was that in the event that money laundering crimes diverged, Austrian theory and jurisdiction in this area could now be brought in for interpretation to an only very limited extent.[44] The assumption should therefore be made that in the event of inadequate public Liechtenstein judiciary and theory, Liechtenstein courts will lean on Austrian judiciary and theory.

2.2.2.2. The objective facts

a. The perpetrator

The facts of money laundering can essentially be committed by anyone, since the terms of § 165 criminal code (StGB) do not restrict the circle of potential perpetrators to members of organised crime or persons acting in the financial sector.

---

43 BGBl 193/527
44 On this subject see report and application of the government to the parliament of the Principality of Liechtenstein concerning alteration of the criminal code in respect of the introduction of siphoning off financial gains, money laundering and the facts of insider crime, No. 18/1995, p.10

The preliminary perpetrator and the participant in the preliminary crime as subsequent money launderer:

Originally, neither the immediate preliminary perpetrator not participants in the preliminary crime could be prosecuted for money laundering according to § 165 criminal code (StGB). This was because, on the one hand, Liechtenstein recognises self-preferential treatment exempt from punishment, and on the other hand, because the original legal text of § 165 para. 1 criminal code (StGB) expressly made reference to asset components that originate *"from the crime of another"*.

In the meantime the legislator deleted the characteristic of "another" in § 165 para. 1 criminal code (StGB) and therefore created the possibility of punishing laundering of one's own funds.[45] At the same time, however, it was established in § 165 para. 5 criminal code (StGB) that someone who has been punished for participating in the preliminary crime is not punishable for money laundering. This ruled out a double penalty.[46]

b. The object of the crime

ba. Preliminary acts relevant to the crime

Money laundering can only be committed on asset components which arise from preliminary crimes listed in § 165 criminal code (StGB).

On the one hand, these are crimes and, on the other, the following stipulated offences:

- Terrorist financing offences (§ 278d criminal code (StGB))
- Gift acceptance offences
  - by civil servants (§ 304 criminal code (StGB))
  - by senior managers of a public company (§ 305 criminal code (StGB))
- By experts (§ 306 criminal code (StGB))
- By employees and expert consultants (§ 306a criminal code (StGB))

---

45 This although European Council convention No. 141 had expressly provided for the self-protection privilege in Art. 6 item 2 component b
46 On this subject see comments by *Mag. iur. Johannes Grabher*, Regulations on combating money laundering, page 11ff.

- Corruption offences (§ 107 criminal code (StGB))
- Forbidden intervention offences (§ 308 criminal code (StGB))
- Offences according to the narcotics law

bb. Origin of the assets

§ 165 para. 4 criminal code (StGB) says that an asset component arises from a crime if the perpetrator of the punishable crime has acquired it through the crime or received it for committing the crime or if it embodies the value of the originally acquired or received asset.

The asset immediately acquired from punishable action:

Primarily, the object of the crime of money laundering is considered as the asset acquired directly through or, respectively, for the preliminary crime. Whether money laundering is also to be assumed possible if the object originally acquired through the preliminary crime is transferred to a third party, or, respectively, how long the object is to be deemed tainted, is disputable.

Correspondingly, according to the wording of § 165 para. 4 criminal code (StGB), assets originally acquired through the preliminary crime would probably still be suitable for money laundering even after any number of transactions. However, this would result in avalanche-like contamination of all potential assets in the circular flow.

Up to this point there are no relevant opinions in Liechtenstein on the topic of surrogate money laundering or, respectively, the problem of the contamination of "clean" assets. It remains to be supposed that Liechtenstein courts will make use of the general similarity of Liechtenstein and Austrian criminal law and will base themselves on the relevant Austrian jurisdiction and literature when solving this problem.

The theories essentially agree that excluding objects from the circle of assets suitable for money laundering must be made possible. However, the solution approaches for this differ.[47]

---

47 On this subject see *Klippl Irene*, Money Laundering [German], Vienna 1995, 149; Klippel refers to the fact that § 165 criminal code (StGB) deals with a perpetual offence. There is therefore the possibility, she says, and that the facts of money laundering may become reality even after the mo-

One of the most frequently represented solution approaches is that of Bertel/Schwaighofer, according to which an asset component arises from a crime if and as long as it embodies the economic value that the preliminary perpetrator has acquired through a crime or has received for a crime. According to the approach, when determining the object of the crime only the identity of the economic value that the preliminary perpetrator has acquired is relevant. This is embodied sometimes in the fortune of the preliminary perpetrator or sometimes in that of the front man.[48]

§ 165 para. 4 criminal code (StGB) expressly declares that even those assets assuming a place in the fortune of the preliminary perpetrator originally assumed by the assets directly acquired through the preliminary crime are objects of money laundering. In such a case this is defined as surrogate money laundering.

The surrogate embodies the originally acquired object as long as it is economically identical with it in the broadest sense. However, this means that a closed chain of exchange dealings ranging between originally acquired assets and surrogate needs to be proven, which is probably not easy to do in general.

If this legal view is favoured, the conclusion is an antithesis to Swiss law. For in Switzerland, according to today's theory the originally criminally acquired asset remains an object of money

---

ment of acquisition in good faith of the contaminated asset. In order to effect that a contaminated asset which, without committing a criminal offence, was acquired in good faith and is not possessed in the interest of the previous owner and can be excluded as an object of money laundering, Klippl additionally takes account of suitable compensation in the event of subsequent bad faith. Klippl's intention by this is to see an object which was not possessed in good faith up until the end of the period of ownership prevented from being an object of crime because, in this case, the owner who acquired the object against suitable compensation would no longer be able to transfer this object without making himself liable to punishment and subjecting his successors to the same risk. According to Klippl, therefore, in the event of acquisition against suitable payment only non-culpable good-faith acquisition is relevant, not, however, good faith throughout the whole period of ownership

48 *Bertel /Schwaighofer*, Austrian Criminal Law, Special Section I [German], 6th edition, 2000, § 165, 165a, marginal notes 3,4

laundering if it was acquired in malicious faith via a service in return.[49]

Contamination of "clean" assets:

However, schools of thought also diverge on the question of proceeding in the event of the mixing of clean and tainted assets. There is an absence of emphatically clear regulations so far. Current theory, however, at least predominantly concurs that such assets must be at least partially suitable for money laundering. However, this legal view has very different foundations.[50]

bc. Manner of committing

The crime preliminary to money laundering must at least be in accordance with the facts and contrary to the law. Incapability of guilt and the presence or absence of other elements of guilt in the preliminary perpetrator have no influence on the money launderer's liability to punishment. Therefore, even the person who manages funds originating from a crime, an offence according to § 278d criminal code (StGB) or according to §§ 304 to 308 criminal code (StGB) or an offence according to the narcotics law, or from an inculpably acting preliminary perpetrator, commits money laundering.[51]

bd. Preliminary crime committed abroad

As far as can be seen, there is no Liechtenstein jurisdiction available providing information as to whether an asset component arising from a preliminary crime committed abroad may be laundered in Liechtenstein.

---

49   *Arzt Gunther*, Mutual dependency of the legal regulation of money laundering and confiscation [German], in: Trechsel (ed.) Money Laundering, Prevention and Combative Measures [German], Zurich, 1997, 30, Example 1

50   *Ackermann Jürg Beat*, Money laundering [German] (criminal code (StGB) Art. 305bis), in Niklaus Schmid (ed.) Commentary on Confiscation, Organised Crime and Money Laundering [German], Vol. I, Zurich 1998, § 5 criminal code (StGB) 305bis marginal note 232 refers to opinion and resolutions of 4th March 1997 by the Zurich District Court, trial no. U/DG960499, 8, 16f

51   *Kienapfel Diethelm*, Outline of Austrian Criminal Law, Special Section II, Crimes against assets [German], Vienna 1993, § 165 marginal note 24 in connection with § 164 marginal note 47-54; *Klippl*, 133, *Mag. iur. Christa Rothenbücher*, 30

The EC money laundering directive[52] also having legal effect for Liechtenstein as an EEA member state is designed to prevent transnationally active money launderers from using free capital flow and freedom of movement in financial services for their criminal transaction. Accordingly, the facts of money laundering are also deemed to be fulfilled if the preliminary crime was committed abroad – within or outside the Community.[53]

In principle, however, crimes committed abroad are only money laundering-suitable preliminary crimes in Liechtenstein if they are punishable both in Liechtenstein and at the location of the offence.[54]

Irrespective of the criminal laws of the location of the offence, in Liechtenstein preliminary crimes which were committed abroad are punishable if one of the crimes contained in § 64 criminal code (StGB) is involved. For many of these crimes there is the additional condition that Liechtenstein's interests have to be damaged or the perpetrator is not extradited.

Money laundering committed abroad is punishable in Liechtenstein according to § 64 para. 1 item 4 criminal code (StGB) if the perpetrator is not extradited or if Liechtenstein's interests have been damaged; this is the case if the preliminary crime was committed in Liechtenstein.[55]

c. Behaviour in accordance with the facts

ca. General

The variants of the facts of § 165 criminal code (StGB) refer to an active and a circumstantial crime. The acts contained in § 165 para. 2 criminal code (StGB) can, however, represent no perpetual crime, since the maintenance or continuation, respectively, of

---

52 See on this subject *Baudenbacher*, Financial Centre Liechtenstein in the EEA: Directive and Legal Political Aspects [German], LJZ, 13th year., 2/92, 51
53 However, preliminary crimes are necessarily also merely drug crimes. The directive refers to this extent to the Vienna Convention, Art. 3 para. 1 letter A of the United Nations Convention Against Illicit Traffic In Narcotic Drugs and Psychotropic Substances, Doc. E/CONF 82/15
54 See on this subject § 65 criminal code (StGB)
55 § 64 para. 1 item 4 modified by LGBl. 1996/64

the disreputable status of a subsequent actor in malicious faith, without active behaviour, is not punishable in Liechtenstein in accordance with § 165 criminal code (StGB).

cb. Variants of the facts of § 165 para. 1 criminal code (StGB)

§ 165 para. 1 criminal code (StGB) includes the "concealment" as well as the "obscuring of the origin" of contaminated asset components. These variants of the facts are put in concrete terms by means of a demonstrative list of procedures.

Concealment:
Concealment covers all actions in aid of thwarting or hampering the discovery of a material object suitable for crime by the victim or prosecution bodies by keeping the contaminated assets at an unusual location or in a hiding place.[56]

Obscuring of the origin:
Obscuring includes every form of behaviour with the aim of hampering or thwarting anticipated or commenced investigations into the criminal origin of the asset component by means of deception. This should particularly be interpreted as the camouflaging of criminally acquired gains, lending an appearance of legality to criminal assets through transactions that are as opaque as possible which make the illicit origin of the asset appear no longer traceable and provable, but also as the obliteration of the criminal cash flow.[57]

cc. Variants of the fact of § 165 para. 2 criminal code (StGB)

§ 165 para. 2 criminal code (StGB) punishes whoever takes possession of the contaminated assets, be it merely in order to keep the asset components safe, to invest them or to manage them, or transforms, exploits or transfers such assets.

---

[56] ÖJZ 1996/32/EvBl; 14 Os 181/95-6 5.12.1995 [Austrian legal newspaper]
[57] *Fehérvàry*, in: Kilchling/Kaiser (eds.), Opportunities to Siphon Off Gains in order to Combat Organised Crime. Review of the Situation and Perspectives in International Comparison [German], Freiburg i. Br. 1997, 174, footnote 3; *Mag. iur. Rothenbücher*, 55

These behaviours are typical safekeeping and management activities which are not condemnable per se. On the contrary, they represent actions in every day business transactions which are continuously enacted, which is why liability to punishment due to money laundering originally required an enhanced degree of deliberate intent, namely knowingness.

In the course of the revisions of the money laundering facts the subjective factual feature of "knowingness", which can only be proven with difficulty in criminal trials and represented a significant obstacle to convicting an accused person, was eliminated from the money laundering facts according to § 165 para. 2 criminal code (StGB) (receipt, transportation, exploitation and transferral of contaminated assets) as well as from § 278a para. 2 criminal code (StGB) (money laundering for criminal organisations). For the fulfilment of the money laundering facts according to § 165 para. 1 criminal code (StGB) (acts of obscuring) simple intent was sufficient from the start.

The formulation of § 165 para. 2 criminal code (StGB) differs from the Austrian criminal code particularly in that according to Liechtenstein law, the "knowing taking possession of" alone does not constitute a fact, but the "taking possession of with simple intent, in order to keep safe, invest or manage contaminated asset components" does.

This difference, which appears insignificant in the first instance, has a certain effect. According to Austrian law, liable to punishment is someone who has taken over contaminated asset components for safekeeping, investment and management without knowing at the moment "of taking possession of" that a disreputable asset is involved. As soon as he becomes aware of the disreputable origin of the asset, he renders himself liable to punishment if he continues to keep this asset safe, invests it or manages it or transfers to third parties.

Due to the formulation chosen in Liechtenstein criminal law, however, precisely this is prevented. Only the person who takes possession of contaminated assets with simple intent to manage them, etc., is liable to punishment, but not the person who continues to manage, keep safe or invest contaminated assets even though he subsequently learns of their disreputable origin or, respectively, satisfies the subjective fact of simple intent.

The Liechtenstein legislator therefore cleverly removes himself from the problem of how a bank employee or trustee, example, should behave in such a case.

Whereas according to Austrian law, traceable back-transferral to the previous owner, in addition to reporting to the responsible authorities, represents the only opportunity for a bank employee not to subsequently become liable to punishment despite knowingness, according to Liechtenstein law everything can be left at the present status without a second thought.

However, in Liechtenstein, too, active conduct applied with simple intent in respect of the origin of the asset components would be punishable. Merely leaving the present circumstance as it is, such as, for example, the continued safekeeping of the asset in a safe, or keeping an investment from the contaminated assets, is exempted from punishment according to § 165 criminal code (StGB).[58]

d. The qualified facts of money laundering

While the variants of the facts of money laundering according to § 165 para. 1 criminal code (StGB) (acts of obscuring) are punishable with imprisonment of up to three years or with a fine of up to 360 daily earnings and the variants of the facts of money laundering according to § 165 para. 2 criminal code (StGB) (receipt, transformation, exploitation and transferral of contaminated assets) with imprisonment of up to two years or with a fine of up to 360 daily earnings, according to § 165 para. 3 criminal code (StGB) acts of money laundering which take place in reference to a value surpassing CHF 75,000.00 or are committed as a member of a gang which has associated itself with repeated money laundering are punishable with imprisonment of six months to five years.

Additionally § 165 Abs. 6 criminal code (StGB) was introduced through LGBl. No. 236. According to this the variants of the facts of § 165 para. 2 criminal code (StGB) (receipt, transformation, exploitation and transferral of contaminated assets) are threat-

---

58   *Mag. iur. Christa Rothenbücher*, 63f

ened with stricter punishment if these are committed on components of the assets of a criminal organisation (§ 278a criminal code (StGB)) or a terrorist organisation (§ 278b criminal code (StGB)), by its orders or in its interest.

2.2.2.3. The subjective facts

As according to Swiss and Austrian law, money laundering also represents a crime of intent in Liechtenstein. Unlike § 165 para. 2 Austrian criminal code, according to which knowingness is required with regard to the receipt, transformation, exploitation or transferral of contaminated assets, according to Swiss law (Art. 305bis Swiss criminal code) and Liechtenstein law for the punishment of all variants of money laundering facts only potential intent is generally required.[59]

The required intent must have reference to all objective factual features. In concrete terms this means that every person who commits, through his behaviour, a criminal act in the sense of § 165 Liechtenstein criminal code (StGB) and *"seriously believes this to be possible and accepts that the assets are contaminated"* renders himself punishable for money laundering.[60]

In principle, according to Liechtenstein law the subjective preconditions must be present at the time the facts become reality.[61]

2.2.3. Active remorse (§ 165a criminal code (StGB))

According to § 165a para. 1 criminal code (StGB) every money launderer who voluntarily contributes to securing a significant proportion of the assets before the authority has become aware of his guilt, enjoys impunity. If the money launderer behaves in this sense and other circumstances, however, ultimately lead to secur-

---

59 *Bertel/Schwaighofer*, BT I, § 165, 165a, marginal note 10, 12; *Kienapfel*, BT II, § 165 marginal note 42ff.; *Triffterer Otto*, Criminal Code (StGB)-Commentary on System and Practice [German], Orac Verlag, concerning § 165 Margin no. 36, *Burgstaller Manfred*, The New Money Laundering Crimes [German] ÖBA 3/94, 175f; *Mag. iur. Christa Rothenbücher*, 78
60 § 5 para. 1 criminal code (StGB)
61 A referral is made to p.92 with regard to subsequent awareness of contaminated assets

ing of the assets, the money launderer also becomes not subject to punishment according to § 165a para. 2 criminal code (StGB).

2.3. The due diligence act

2.3.1. General

The due diligence act (SPG) governs the assurance of diligence during the professional exercising of financial transactions and serves to combat money laundering, organised crime and terrorist financing in the sense of the criminal code (§§ 165, 278 to 278d criminal code (StGB)).

Central aspects of combating money laundering by means of the due diligence act are the duties to inform and report, by which, on the one hand, due diligence providers are obligated to clarify the identity of contract partners and the origin of assets and, on the other hand, are obligated under certain circumstances to submit a written report immediately to the Financial Intelligence Unit (FIU). For reasons of space, only these central aspects can be dealt with in closer detail in this present study.

2.3.1.1. Personal area of application (Art. 3 due diligence act due diligence act (SPG))

Generally speaking, all companies and persons exercising financial transactions as part of their profession are due diligence providers; institutions for company staff benefits are excluded from the scope of the law.[62]

---

62   Art. 3 para. 3 due diligence act (SPG)

"The modern way of balancing bank interests according to the due diligence act"

However, pursuant to Art. 3 due diligence act (SPG) the personal area of application does not only cover traditional financial intermediaries, but likewise auditors, revision companies and revision companies and dedicated revision departments, real estate agents, traders in valuable commodities, auctioneers and casinos.[63]

In order to guarantee inspection of compliance with due diligence, exchange offices, real estate agents, traders in valuable commodities and auctioneers, together with all companies and persons exercising financial transactions as part of their profession

---

63 Art. 3 due diligence act (SPG)

which are not explicitly listed in Art. 3 Abs. 1 due diligence act (SPG), must report commencement of their activity to the FMA.

2.3.1.2. Material area of application (Art. 4 due diligence act due diligence act (SPG))

The due diligence act (SPG) also applies to the exercising of financial transactions as part of a profession. Basically deemed a financial transaction in the sense of the due diligence act (SPG) is every instance of acceptance or safekeeping of external assets, together with assistance in the acceptance, investment or transferral of such assets or the establishment of a legal entity not commercially active in the country of domicile for the account of a third party or activity as the instrument of such a representative.

On an equal footing with financial transactions are:
- Transactions by traders in valuable commodities and auctioneers, if a payment takes place in cash and the sum amounts to more than CHF 25,000.00, irrespective of whether the transaction is enacted in one single proceeding or in several proceedings between which a connection apparently exists: or
- The granting of entry into a casino to visitors, irrespective of whether the visitor actually takes part in the gambling or buys or sells chips.

The activity of "non-traditional" financial intermediaries only represents a financial transaction if they come into contact professionally, in the scope of conducting their business, with external assets to the effect that they actually accept or keep them, or they undertake a significant active supporting role in relation to an actual asset transfer. Art. 4 para. 3 due diligence act (SPG) finally lists those activities[64] which, although they would in principle be

---

64 - Contractual relationships of an investment company which neither conducts share accounts nor offers or operates shares itself
- Contractual relationships in the form of an exclusive asset management contract with limited power of attorney for a customer-personal bank account or custodian account
- The establishment of a holding company for the account of a third party or activity as agent of such a party represents no financial transaction insofar as the holding company serves as an agent for forming an operative group

subject to the due diligence act (SPG) in accordance with the elements listed above, represent no financial transactions in the sense of the due diligence act (SPG).

2.3.2. Identification of the contract partner and establishment of the economically entitled person

2.3.2.1. Identification of the contract partners

Due diligence providers are obligated, in accordance with Art. 5 due diligence act (SPG), to identify their contract partners on the basis of documented evidence when taking up a business relationship. Viewing a certified copy[65] of the documentary evidence is sufficient here.[66]

For the identification of natural persons, valid official identification with a photograph is enough; this does not need to be a passport or ID card.[67] Legal persons etc. must be identified at least on the basis of a written extract from corresponding data bases.[68]

When taking up a business relationship by way of a personal visit it is sufficient if the due diligence providers

- create a copy of the original or of the certified copy,
- confirm upon it that the original or the certified copy has been viewed, and
- integrate the signed and dated copy with the due diligence documents.

The documents required for identification must reflect current circumstances. Confirmations of authenticity, register extracts and

---

- The activity of lawyers and legal agents, unless they render services which are not exclusively reserved for their professional group
[65] Confirmation concerning the authenticity of the copy of documentary evidence can take place through a branch or subsidiary of institutional due diligence providers, through another institution subject to due diligence, a lawyer, a trustee, an auditor or an asset manager who is subject to directive 91/308 EEC in the version of 2001/97/EC or an equivalent regulation and an appropriate supervisory body, or through a notary public or another public position ordinarily issuing such confirmations of authenticity
[66] See on this subject Art. 3 para. 1 due diligence regulations (SPV)
[67] See on this subject Art. 4 due diligence regulations (SPV)
[68] See on this subject Art. 5 due diligence regulations (SPV)

confirmations by the chosen annual report auditor must not be older than twelve months.[69]

For natural persons must be documented: last name, first name, date of birth, residential address, country of residence and nationality. For legal persons, name or company name, location, country of location, date of founding and, where necessary, place and date of entry into the pubic register must be recorded.

When taking up a business relationship by way of correspondence, due diligence providers must integrate the original or the certified copy of the documentary evidence with the due diligence documents. The creation and keeping of copies is allowed if the original is provided for the identification by a person who is able to issue confirmations of authenticity.[70]

Provided that there are no instances of suspicion that assets are associated with money laundering, a crime preliminary to money laundering, organised crime or terrorist financing, the duty to identify placed on due diligence providers does not apply:

- if the maximum value of CHF 25,000.00 is not exceeded during banking transactions;
- if the maximum value of CHF 5,000.00 is not exceeded during cash or data transfers;
- if the amount of a periodical insurance premium does not exceed the amount of CHF 1,500.00 annually;
- if the one-time insurance premium amounts to less than CHF 4,000.00 or less than CHF 4,000.00 is paid to a premium custodian account;
- if a tenant custodian account for a property rented in an EEA member state or in Switzerland is concerned;
- in the case of paid-up capital accounts;
- in the case of legal persons quoted on the stock exchange;
- in the case of group or company-internal pre-identification;
- in the case of pre-identification by a due diligence provider in the context of insurance applications;
- In the case of the transfer of insurance premiums from an EEA bank account.

---

[69] See on this subject Art. 7 para. 2 and 3 due diligence regulations (SPV)
[70] See on this subject Art. 7 para. 1 due diligence regulations (SPV)

If the due diligence provider refuses to enter into a business relationship, there is no duty to identify irrespective of potential instances of suspicion.[71]

2.3.2.2. Establishment of the economic contract partner

Due diligence providers must establish the economically entitled person with the diligence appropriate to the circumstances when taking up a business relationship. In this process, persons who are ultimately economically entitled to the assets in question are deemed to be the economically entitled.[72]

In this respect, a legal entity not commercially active in a country of domicile can be an economically entitled person if a holding company is concerned,

- which serves as an instrument to forming an operative group;
- the purpose of which is to preserve the interests of its members in joint self-assistance or which pursues statutory and actual political, religious, scientific, artistic, and charitable, entertainment or similar purposes.

The ultimately economically entitled person must be established in the case of other holding companies. In the event of revocable constructions, such as, for example, a revocable trust, the effective founder is deemed to be the person economically entitled. In the case of insurance contracts, the person paying the insurance premium is economically entitled.[73]

In principle, it may be assumed that the contract partner is identical to the economically entitled person. The due diligence provider must, however, have the economically entitled person confirmed to him in writing by the contract partner if:[74]

- doubts exist as to whether the contract partner is the economically entitled person;[75]

---

71 See on this subject Art 6 due diligence act (SPG)
72 See on this subject Art. 11. due diligence regulations (SPV)
73 See on this subject Art. 11. para. 3 and 4 due diligence regulations (SPV)
74 See on this subject Art. 10 due diligence regulations (SPV)
75 See on this subject Art. 7 due diligence act (SPG)

- a bank or insurance transaction of more than CHF 25,000.00 or a transfer of cash or data transferral of more than CHF 5,000.00 is enacted;
- the business relationship with a natural person is taken up by way of correspondence;
- The contract partner is a legal entity not commercially active in the country of domicile.[76]

Art. 8 due diligence act (SPG) lists the circumstances in which the duty to establish the economically entitled person does not apply. These are essentially in line with those according to which the duty to identify with reference to the contract partner does not apply.[77]

With regard to economically entitled persons who are not commercially active legal entities in the country of domicile[78], the duty to establish the economically entitled person does not apply if they are quoted on the stock exchange.[79] Additionally, the duty to establish economically entitled persons does not apply for:

- banks and post offices in the case of accounts or custodian accounts which are conducted on behalf of lawyers authorised in an EEA member state or in Switzerland for the account of their clients within the framework of a forensic activity or in the capacity of executioner of wills, escrow agent or a similar capacity;[80]

---

[76] See on this subject Art. 4 para. 2 letter b due diligence act (SPG)
[77] See on this subject Item 3.2.1
[78] Pursuant to Art. 4 para. 2 letter b due diligence act (SPG) a legal entity not commercially active in the country of domicile is namely a legal person, a company, a trust or other community or asset unit, irrespective of its legal form, which conducts no operations in the field of trade, manufacturing or other trade conducted commercially
[79] See on this subject Art. 8 due diligence act (SPG) in connection with Art. 12 due diligence regulations (SPV)
[80] See on this subject Art. 8 para. 1 letter c. due diligence act (SPG) in connection with Art. 12 due diligence regulations (SPV): If a bank or post office waives the establishment of the economically entitled person in the case of lawyers' dedicated accounts, the lawyer must provide a written declaration that the accounts or custodian accounts exclusively serve one of the purposes enumerated in Art. 12 due diligence regulations (SPV), and the bank or post office must identify the accounts or custodian accounts accordingly. If a bank or post office notes that such a declaration has been falsely emitted, then it must demand a written declaration concerning the economically

- institutional due diligence providers, namely a bank, a post office, an investment company or an insurance company, if their contract partner is another corresponding company located domestically or abroad or is á stocks and bonds trader, which is subject to 91/308/EEA in the version of directive 2001/97/EC or an equivalent regulation and an appropriate supervisory body;
- Or, respectively, if the contract partner is a tax-exempted institution for company staff benefits.[81]

Art. 8 para. 2 due diligence act (SPG) additionally restricts the duty to establish the economically entitled person if the contract partner is a representative of a collective form of investment or a holding company with more than twenty economically entitled persons as investors. The duty to establish the economically entitled person falls away entirely in respect of collective forms of investment with are quoted on the stock exchange.

2.3.2.3. Time of the availability of information and documentation concerning the identification of the contract partner and the establishment of the economically entitled person

In principle, all required information and documents in connection with the identification of the contract partner or the establishment of the economically entitled person have to be available on "*commencement of the business relationship in full and in an appropriate form*".

Under the condition that the due diligence provider ensures that no flow of assets is taking place, as an exception it is sufficient if the required information and documents are available after 30 days at the latest.

If the required information and documents are still not available 30 days following commencement of the business relationship, the

---

entitled person from the contract partner. If the declaration is not provided, the business relationship must be broken off under provision of sufficient documentation of the flow of the assets, unless the pre-requirements of the duty to inform according to Art. 16 para. 1 due diligence act (SPG) had been met

81   Art. 8 due diligence act (SPG)

due diligence providers must break off the business relationship under provision of sufficient documentation of the flow of the assets, unless the pre-requirements of the duty to inform according to Art. 16 para. 1 due diligence act (SPG) had been fulfilled.[82]

2.3.2.4. Repetition of the identification and establishment

Due diligence providers must repeat the identification of the contract partner or the establishment of the economically entitled persons if, in the course of the business relationship, doubts arise concerning the identity of the contract partner or concerning the economically entitled person.

If, despite repeating the identification or establishment, doubts continue to exist concerning the contract partner's information, the due diligence providers may break off the business relationship, unless the pre-requirements for the duty to inform according to Art. 16 para. 1 due diligence act (SPG) had been fulfilled.[83] When breaking off the business relationship the due diligence providers must sufficiently document the flow of the assets in any case.

If, in the case of an existing insurance contract, the insured is replaced by another insured person, then the contract partner must be identified again and, where necessary, the economically entitled person must again be established.[84]

2.3.3. Monitoring

2.3.3.1. Criteria for limiting risks and their monitoring

Due diligence providers are obligated, with regard to their permanent business relationships, to ensure monitoring of their permanent business relationships in line with the risks. To do so they must establish criteria, and issue internal instructions, as to how these risks are to be limited and monitored.[85]

In its directive 2005/1, monitoring of business relationships, the FMA bindingly stipulated certain risk criteria for all due diligence

---

[82] Art. 16 due diligence regulations (SPV)
[83] Art. 9 due diligence act (SPG)
[84] Art. 13 due diligence regulations (SPV)
[85] Art. 13 due diligence act (SPG)

providers.[86] Due diligence providers must not abuse their foreign branches and their foreign subsidiaries in order to circumvent this directive. Rather, they must ensure that the subsidiaries and branches in countries which are not members of the FATF follow the FATF recommendations applicable to them, provided that local regulations do not oppose this.

Pursuant to the foregoing FMA directive the following three criteria in particular are deemed as being high-risk according to Art. 13 para. 2 due diligence act (SPG):

1. The physical bringing in of assets of a current value "*of more than 100,000.00 francs*" at one time or in phases at the beginning of the business relationship;
2. Business relationships with "*politically exposed persons*"; "politically exposed persons" designates persons with prominent public functions abroad: heads of state and government, senior politicians, senior functionaries in administration, the judiciary, the military and parties, the supreme decision makers in state-owned companies and persons closely associated with the above named persons for familial, personal or business reasons.[87]
3. "*Indications of money laundering*" according to the appendix to the FMA directive.
    According to the "FMA directive", particular risks with regard to money laundering are contained in transactions
    "*a) whose construction hints at an illegal purpose, whose economic purpose is not recognisable or which even appear to be economically nonsensical;*
    b) during which assets are withdrawn shortly after their arrival with the due diligence provider (transit accounts), if no plausible reason for this immediate withdrawal can be deduced from the customer's business activity;
    c) which lie outside the usual business activity or the usual customer circle of a certain due diligence provider or a certain place of business of a due diligence provider and for which it cannot be discovered why the customer

---

86   Passed on the basis of Art. 13 para. 2 due diligence act (SPG)
87   Art. 1 letter c. due diligence regulations (SPV), compare also Dr. Kaetzler's comments on PEPs from p.51

> *has selected precisely this due diligence provider or this place of business for his transactions;*
> *d) which lead to a previously largely inactive account becoming active again, without there being an apparent reason for this;*
> *e) which cannot be reconciled with the knowledge and experience of the due diligence provider concerning the customer and concerning the purpose of the business relationship;*
> *f) in principle, every customer is suspicious who provides the due diligence provider with false or misleading information or, without plausible grounds, refuses him information or documents necessary for the business relationship and customary for the activity concerned."*

In respect of banking transactions, the following transactions contain clues to money laundering according to the FMA directive:

> *"a) Changing a large amount in bank notes (foreign and domestic) of a small denomination into notes of a large denomination;*
> *b) Monetary exchange of a considerable scale without booking on a customer account;*
> *c) Cashing larger amounts by means of cheques, including traveller's cheques;*
> *d) Purchase or sale of larger amounts of precious metals by occasional customers (an occasional customer is a customer who conducts no permanent business relationship with the bank concerned – e.g. account or custodian account relationship, safe etc.);*
> *e) Purchase of bank cheques to a considerable extent by occasional customers;*
> *f) Transferral of orders to countries abroad by occasional customers, without apparent legitimate grounds;*
> *g) multiple closing of banking transactions just under the identification limit."*

With regard to bank account and custodian accounts, according to the FMA directive the following transactions contain clues to money laundering:

"a) Recourse to funds which are indeed customary in international trade, but whose use conflicts with the customer's known activity;
b) Economically nonsensical structure of a customer's business relationships with the bank (large number of accounts at the same institution, frequent movements between various accounts, exaggerated liquidities etc.);
c) Placing of securities (pledges, guarantees) by third persons unknown to the bank, which have no recognisable close relationship with the customer and for whose placement there are no apparent plausible grounds;
d) Transfers to another bank without indication of the recipient;
e) Acceptance of cash transfers from other banks without indication of the beneficiary's name or account number;
f) Repeated transfers to countries abroad with the instruction that the amount be paid to the recipient in cash;
g) Larger and/or frequent transfers from and to drug-producing countries and/or frequent transfers from and to drug production countries or from and to countries which are named on the FATF list of non-cooperating states and territories;
h) Placing of guarantees of bank guarantees in order to secure non market-compliant loans among third parties;
i) Unexpected repayment of an idle loan without a credible explanation;
j) Use of pseudonym or numbered accounts for the completion of commercial transactions from trading, commercial or industrial operations."

In respect of trust companies, according to the FMA directive the following transactions contain clues to money laundering:

"a) Back-to-back loans without recognisable, legally binding permissible purpose;
b) Fiduciary behaviour by participants in non stock-exchange listed companies into whose activity the due diligence provider can have no insight."

Additionally, according to the FMA directive the following transactions contain clues to money laundering:

"a) Attempt by the customer to avoid the contact aspired to by the due diligence provider;
b) Account closure and opening of new accounts in the name of the same customer or of his family members without a paper trail;
c) The customer's wish for receipts for cash withdrawal or delivery of securities, which in fact and in actuality were not enacted or for which the assets were immediately re-deposited at the same institution;
d) The customer's wish to execute payment orders under indication of a non-applicable client;
e) Customer's desire that certain payments not run via his accounts, but via nostro accounts of the due diligence provider or via conti pro-diverse;
f) Acceptance and documentation of loan coverages not conforming to reality or fiduciary granting of loans under provision of fictitious cover;
g) Criminal proceedings against contract partners or economically entitled persons due to money laundering, a crime preliminary to money laundering or organised crime domestically or abroad."

2.3.3.2. Global monitoring of money laundering risks

Banks which own branches abroad or manage a financial group with foreign companies must globally record, limit and monitor their risks associated with money laundering, organised crime and terrorist financing.[88]

The banks must ensure on this subject that the group's internal revision and external revision department has access to information concerning individual business relationships in the event of need. Not required is a central data base of contract partners and economically entitled persons at the group level or central access by the group's internal monitoring departments to local data bases. They also have to ensure that the subsidiary provides the information fundamental to global monitoring of money laundering risks to the group's responsible departments.

---

88   Art. 13 para. 3 due diligence act (SPG)

In this respect, it must be considered in particular that banks which have branches abroad or manage a financial group with foreign companies must also grant the group's internal revision and external revision department access to information concerning individual business relationships.[89] Banks are obligated to inform the FMA accordingly in the event of general obstacles to the flow of information.[90]

2.3.3.3. Profile

Due diligence providers must create a profile with the following content for every business relationship entered into permanently and keep this up to date:

a) Contract partners;
b) Power of attorney;
c) Economic background and origin of the introduced assets;
d) Profession and business activity of the economically entitled person or, in the event of activity as an agent of a legal entity not commercially active in the country of domicile or if the contract partner is a legal representative not commercially active in the country of domicile, of the effective founder and
e) Purpose of the assets.

In the process the level of detail must take account of the risk of the business relationship.[91]

2.3.3.4. Clarifications

a. IT-supported systems

In principle, the use of IT-supported systems is obligatory wherever their deployment makes sense and there is an appropriate cost-benefit ratio. Banks and post offices may only disregard the use of IT-supported systems in exceptional cases.[92]

---

89   Art. 13 para. 3 due diligence act (SPG) in connection with Art. 20 due diligence regulations (SPV)
90   Art. 20 para. 3 due diligence regulations (SPV)
91   Art. 14 due diligence act (SPG) in connection with Art. 21 due diligence regulations (SPV)
92   In principle, in the process, the use of a suitable system in optimum correspondence with the state of technical possibilities is required, insofar as the

If the ascertainment of business relationships with politically exposed persons is carried out without IT support, then another appropriate risk management system must be installed[93] The senior management must decide, in each case, whether to accept business relationships and, on an annual basis, whether to continue business relationships.[94]

b. Nature of the clarifications and content of clarifications

If, within the framework of a permanent business relationship, facts or transactions arise which deviate from the profile or which meet the risk criteria ascertained by the due diligence provider, due diligence providers must make appropriate efforts to undertake simple clarifications aimed at rendering facts or transactions plausible. The information to be obtained, exploited and documented is that which is suitable for rendering the background of facts or transactions traceable and comprehensible.[95]

If, within the framework of permanent business relationships, facts or transactions arise which justify instances of suspicion that assets are in association with criminal offences, such as money laundering, a crime preliminary to money laundering, organised crime or terrorist financing, due diligence providers must undertake special clarifications. In this respect they must obtain, exploit and document information that is suitable for discounting or hardening any instances of suspicion.[96]

Due diligence providers are not permitted to break off the business relationship until the special clarifications have been completed or if the pre-requirements for the duty to inform are in place.[97]

Pursuant to item 4 of the FMA directive, depending on the circumstances of the individual case, details concerning the following

---

costs for this are sufficiently proportionate with the aspired benefit. See on this subject Art. 19 due diligence regulations (SPV)
93   Art. 19 para. 3 due diligence regulations (SPV)
94   Art. 33 para. 1 due diligence regulations (SPV)
95   Art. 15 para. 1 due diligence act (SPG) in connection with Art. 22 para. 1 due diligence regulations (SPV)
96   Art. 15 para. 2 due diligence act (SPG) in connection with Art. 22 para. 2 due diligence regulations (SPV)
97   Art. 16 para. 2 due diligence regulations (SPV)

aspects in particular must be obtained and documented (provided that this cannot already be deduced from the profile of the business relationship):

"a) Purpose and nature of a certain transaction;
b) Financial circumstances of the contract partner or, respectively, of the economically entitled person, as far as they are known to the due diligence provider;
c) Professional or commercial activity of the contract partner, or the economically entitled person or the effective founder of a legal entity not commercially active in the country of domicile;
d) Origin of the disreputable or invested assets."

In the process the obtaining of information from third persons, likewise the involvement of experts in clarifying antecedents is expressly permitted. Explanations by the customer in respect of such transactions must be checked for plausibility. In so doing it is fundamental that not every explanation by the customer can be accepted indiscriminately.[98]

c. Proceeding on the basis of the clarification results

Due diligence providers must record the results of their clarifications and keep this report in the due diligence files.[99] If the facts or transactions obligating clarification are explained in a plausible manner, the business relationship may continue as before.

If due diligence providers continue the business relationship despite doubts, but without a suspicion on the basis of which a duty to inform the FIU would arise, they must monitor continued progress more thoroughly.[100] However, if they break off the business relationship in this respect, they may only permit withdrawal of the assets in a form allowing the prosecution authorities to continue following the trail if need be. They are not permitted to pay out any funds in cash or physically issue securities or precious metals, unless the contract partner has fulfilled his obligations to the full extent.

---

98   FMA directive, item 4
99   Art. 20 due diligence act (SPG); FMA directive, p.2
100 FMA directive, item 5.2.

Due diligence providers are not to break off the business relationship or permit the withdrawal of larger amounts if solid indications exist that public authority sanctions are imminent.[101]

2.3.3.5. Duty to inform

Due diligence providers must inform the Financial Intelligence Unit (FIU) immediately in writing if the suspicion arises in connection with business relationships, irrespective of whether these are permanent, that a connection exists with money laundering, a crime preliminary to money laundering, organised crime or terrorist financing. All official departments of the public administration and the FMA are also subject to this duty to inform.

Someone who undertakes such a communication to the FIU is exempted from every form of responsibility under civil and criminal law, provided that he has not acted with intent. Likewise exempted is someone who, despite the wish of his contract partner to break off the business relationship, does not break off this relationship in correspondence with Art. 16 para. 2 due diligence act (SPG) until the special clarifications have been completed or, respectively, does not break off the relationship because the pre-requirements for the duty to inform the FIU are in place.[102]

Until an order has arrived at the responsible prosecution authority, at the longest, however, up to the expiry of five working days from arrival of the communication at the FIU, due diligence providers must cease all actions that may thwart or prejudice any orders according to § 97a code of criminal procedure (code of criminal procedure (StPO)), provided that these are not approved in writing by the FIU.

Due diligence providers are not permitted to inform the contract partner, the economically entitled person or third parties that they have made their communication to the FIU until an order from the responsible prosecution authority has come in, at the longest, however, up to the expiry of twenty working days from arrival of the communication at the FIU.[103]

---

101 FMA directive, item 5.3.
102 Art. 16 para. 3 due diligence regulations (SPV)
103 Art. 16 due diligence regulations (SPV); lawyers and legal agents, auditors, revision companies and dedicated legal revision departments are not obli-

2.3.3.6. Right to report

In addition to the duty to report to the FIU a right to report to the FIU is contained in Art. 17 due diligence act (SPG), according to which due diligence providers have the right to make a written communication to the FIU if, in connection with the initiation of a business relationship without, however, this relationship being entered into, the suspicion arises that there is a connection with money laundering, a crime preliminary, to money laundering, organised crime or terrorist financing. In respect of the responsibility of due diligence providers according to civil and criminal law when utilising the duty to inform, the elements listed in section 2.3.3.4. "Clarifications" (p.109) in connection with the duty to report, apply accordingly.

2.3.3.7. Delegation

Due diligence providers may delegate identification of the contract partner, establishment of the economically entitled person, creation of the profile and the ongoing monitoring of the business relationship – with the exception of the duty to report to the FIU – to the following persons:

- a commissioned third party;
- a non-third party, if he is a due diligence provider or is the equivalent, if objective performance of the duties is guaranteed.

If the due diligence provider makes use of the opportunity to delegate in respect of identifying the contract partner, establishing the economically entitled person or ascertaining data for the profile, he must ensure that the delegate obtains or, respectively, compiles the documents and information according to the stipulations of the due diligence act (SPG) and due diligence regulations (SPV) and sends these, complete with a communication on the identity of

---

gated to inform the FIU if they have received the information from or via a client within the context of judging the legal situation for this client or have obtained it within the context of their activity as defence lawyers or representatives of this client in a legal proceeding or concerning such a proceeding, including consultation on the operating or avoidance of a proceeding, before or after such a proceeding or, respectively, during such a proceeding

the person conducting the identification, to Liechtenstein to the due diligence provider.

Additionally, the delegate must confirm with his signature that the copies created in the context of the identification are in compliance with the originals and that any written declarations to be obtained within the context of establishing the economically entitled person originate from the contract partner or from a person authorised according to Art. 10 para. 2 due diligence regulations (SPV).

If he has the monitoring of the business relationship carried out by a delegate, he must ensure that the delegate undertakes the clarifications prescribed according to due diligence act (SPG) and due diligence regulations (SPV) and sends the documentation concerning special clarifications and all documents, papers and pieces of evidence provided in this connection at least once a year to Liechtenstein to the due diligence provider.[104] Additionally, he must ensure that the documentation regarding simple clarifications is transferred to him on request within a useful period. The due diligence provider must have the documents from which transactions and, where applicable, the asset status in the corresponding period, can be deduced, delivered to him at least once a year, provided that he himself is not managing the accounts or custodian accounts of the business relationship concerned. The delegation must be documented, and onward delegation by the delegates is excluded.[105]

Due diligence providers remain responsible for complying with due diligence obligations even in the event of delegation. However, punishment of the due diligence provider due to breach of the corresponding obligations is excluded if the obligations were delegated according to the regulations to another due diligence provider or to an equivalent person and the selection of the delegate, the corre-

---

104 The forwarding can be omitted if the delegated person has his place of residence or business in Liechtenstein and keeps the documents, paperwork and evidence there, thus guaranteeing access to these at any time. See Art. 24 due diligence regulations (SPV)
105 On this entire subject see Art. 24 due diligence regulations (SPV)

sponding instructions and monitoring of the delegate were undertaken diligently.[106]

2.3.3.8. Rendering of joint services

If a number of due diligence providers are acting as an instrument of a legal entity not commercially active in the country of domicile, or if a number of due diligence providers render services for the same contract partner for their common account and using the same company name, it is sufficient if the mandate manager performs the duties of due diligence with reference to identification of the contract partner, establishment of the economically entitled person, creation of the profile as well as ongoing monitoring.

Due diligence providers who do not meet these obligations must, however, ensure that they receive access to the due diligence files at any time on request.

If a number of due diligence providers who are not acting for their common account and not using the same company name act as instruments of the same legal entity not commercially active in the country of domicile, it is permissible to have fulfilment of these duties undertaken by one of these instruments; those persons, however, not fulfilling this duty personally, remain responsible for compliance with this duty. Exempted from this responsibility are those persons who have appointed, in writing, a due diligence provider to undertake these duties and have checked the proper fulfilment of the obligations in an appropriate manner.[107]

2.3.4. Documentation and internal organisation

Due diligence providers must document compliance with the due diligence obligations during their business relationships according to the stipulations of the due diligence act (SPG) and due diligence regulations (SPV) in corresponding due diligence files.

Customer-relevant paperwork and pieces of evidence must be retained for at least ten years following termination of the business

---

106 Art. 18 para. 3 due diligence act (SPG) in connection with Art 30 para. 2 due diligence act (SPG)
107 Art. 19 due diligence act (SPG) in connection with Art. 30 para. 3 due diligence act (SPG)

relationship, transaction-related paperwork and evidence at least ten years following completion of the transaction or following compilation, respectively.[108]

Due diligence providers do not only need to take care of the necessary organisational measures concerning suitable internal control and monitoring measures and advanced and initial training of their personnel, but must also issue internal instructions. Additionally, due diligence providers must record in an internal annual report the measures which have been enacted in the past calendar year towards implementing the due diligence act (SPG). In addition, due diligence providers must appoint a contact person for the FMA and the FIU, as well as persons or departments for the internal functions of "commissioner for due diligence" and "commissioner for investigations".[109]

2.3.5. Inspections

The FMA monitors enforcement of the due diligence act (SPG), regularly carrying out spot-checks for this purpose. If the due diligence providers have a dedicated legal revision department at their disposal, in principle they are examined for compliance with the stipulations of the due diligence act (SPG) by order of the FMA by the revision department or by the FMA itself. All other due diligence providers are examined by the FMA or by order of the FMA by auditors or revision companies in reference to compliance with this law. The appointed due diligence providers may submit two proposals for auditors or revision companies with the FMA, communicating their preference. The FMA generally commissions the preferred proposed auditor or the preferred proposed revision company, respectively.

A report must be compiled concerning the results of the inspection. The paperwork and data from the inspection may be processed and stored exclusively in Liechtenstein. Knowledge

---

108 See on this subject in detail Art. 20 due diligence act (SPG) in connection with Art. 25 due diligence regulations (SPV)

109 *Dr. iur. Michael Breuer*, Combating Money Laundering in International Law, in the European Union and in the Principality of Liechtenstein [German], 2003, 277ff. or see on this subject in detail Art. 21 due diligence act (SPG) in connection with Art. 26-32 due diligence regulations (SPV)

acquired during the inspection may be used exclusively for combating money laundering, crimes preliminary to money laundering, organised crime and terrorist financing in the sense of the criminal code.[110]

2.3.6. Measures and legal methods

The FMA takes the measures required within the context of its supervision of due diligence providers.[111] Complaints can be made against decisions and orders of the FMA to the FMA complaints commission within 14 days of notification. Complaints can be made against decisions and orders of the FMA complaints commission to the administrative court within 14 days of notification.[112]

2.3.7. Criminal stipulations

The due diligence act (SPG) draws a distinction between delinquency and breaches. Pursuant to Art. 30 para. 1 due diligence act (SPG), subject to punishment by the District Court for delinquency with imprisonment of up to six months or with a fine of up to 360 daily earnings is someone who:

> "a) does not identify the contract partner in accordance with Art. 5 due diligence act (SPG);

---

110 See on this subject in detail Art. 24-28 due diligence act (SPG) in connection with Art. 34-38 due diligence regulations (SPV)
111 In detail these are:
- issuing orders, directives, recommendations
- carrying out or commissioning ordinary inspections
- carrying out or commissioning extraordinary inspections if there are indications for doubts about the undertaking of due diligence obligations or circumstances which make the reputation of the financial centre appear jeopardised
- in the event of repeated or serious breaches of individual regulations of the due diligence act (SPG), short-term prohibition of the commencement of new business relationships in order to avoid further breaches
- requesting the appropriate disciplinary measures from the responsible position
- The FMA can demand from the due diligence providers and from the persons commissioned for the inspection all information and documents that it requires for fulfilment of the supervisory activity within the framework of the due diligence act (SPG)
112 Art. 29 due diligence act (SPG)

b) does not establish the economically entitled person according to Art. 7 due diligence act (SPG);
c) does not repeat identification of the contract partner and establishment of the economically entitled person according to Art. 9 para. 1 due diligence act (SPG);
d) conducts a business relationship in opposition to Art. 12 para. 1 or 2 due diligence act (SPG);
e) opens, as bank or post office, bearer savings books, accounts or custodian accounts in opposition to Art. 12 para. 3 or, respectively, at the time of coming into force of this law does not dissolve existing contractual relationships in the sense of Art. 12 para. 3 due diligence act (SPG) according to the regulations of Art. 40 para. 4 due diligence act (SPG);
f) does not conduct special clarifications, in opposition to Art. 15 para. 2 due diligence act (SPG);
g) omits to inform the FIU according to Art. 16 para. 1 due diligence act (SPG);
h) breaks off the business relationship in opposition to Art. 16 para. 2 due diligence act (SPG);
i) does not desist in actions according to Art. 16 para. 4 due diligence act (SPG) which could thwart or may prejudice possible arrangements according § 97a code of criminal procedure (StPO), without these having been approved by the FIU;
j) breaches the obligation to block information according to Art. 16 para. 5 due diligence act (SPG);
k) does not open or retain the due diligence files according to Art. 20 para. 1 due diligence act (SPG);
l) as auditor, revision company or dedicated legal revision department grossly breaches his obligations according to Art. 27 letter b due diligence act (SPG), in particular, provides untrue details in the inspection report or conceals essential facts;
m) as auditor, revision company or dedicated legal revision department breaches the obligation to secrecy according to Art. 27 letter c due diligence act (SPG);
n) as auditor, revision company or dedicated legal revision department, processes or stores documents and data concerning inspections outside the region of the Principal-

ity of Liechtenstein in opposition to Art. 27 letter d due diligence act (SPG);

o) does not have the inspection carried out in full or in relation to individual areas of the due diligence obligations according to Art. 28 para. 1 letter b or c due diligence act (SPG)."

According to para. a) b) c) and f) not subject to punishment is someone who has transferred the relevant obligations by means of written agreement to a delegate according to Art. 18 para. 1 letter a due diligence act (SPG), if he has selected the delegate with the diligence appropriate to the circumstances, has instructed the delegate concerning his tasks and has examined the proper fulfilment of the tasks by the delegate.

Additionally, according to para. a) b) c) and f) not subject to punishment is someone who does not personally fulfil the relevant obligations under the presupposition of Art. 19 para. 1 or 2 due diligence act (SPG), if he has appointed a due diligence provider to undertake the duties by means of written agreement and checks proper fulfilment of the obligations in an appropriate manner.

Subject to punishment by the FMA according to Art. 31 due diligence act (SPG) for breach with a fine of up to CHF 100,000.00 is someone who:

"a) refuses to provide information to the FMA, an auditor, a revision company or a dedicated legal revision department, provides untrue details or conceals essential facts;

b) does not comply with a request to produce a situation in line with the law or with another order by the FMA issued within the framework of executing this law;

c) permits asset flows in opposition to Art. 35 due diligence act (SPG)."

Subject to a fine for breach by the FMA of up to CHF 10,000.00 is someone who omits to submit a report according to Art. 3 para. 4 or Art. 40 para. 2 due diligence act (SPG).

2.3.8. Measures in business dealings

In respect of accounts or custodian accounts within the context of business relationships which were opened before 1st January 2001 and which, according to the law applying then, required no profile of the business relationship with the inclusion of the economically entitled person, due diligence providers must not permit asset flows for as long as the required details and documents are not available.

As an exception, asset flows are allowed according to Art. 35 due diligence act (SPG) if:

"a) the balance of the assets of the business relationship does not exceed CHF 25,000.00;
b) there is no suspicion of a connection with money laundering, crimes preliminary to money laundering, organised crime or terrorist financing;
c) the name of the person to whom the assets are transferred can be deduced from the due diligence files;
d) the assets are transformed in a form allowing the authorities to following their trail; and
e) the business relationship is dissolved immediately after the assets are transferred."

2.3.9. Administrative assistance

The domestic authorities responsible in the area of combating money laundering, organised crime and terrorist financing are strictly obligated to cooperate and, in this vein, exchange the required information and documents.[113] Additionally, the due diligence act (SPG) in Art. 37 due diligence act (SPG) regulates cooperation with foreign authorities in case that it is not ruled otherwise in specific laws.

In accordance with this regulation the FMA was expressly granted the opportunity to get into contact with foreign financial supervisory authorities when fulfilling their tasks in order to request information or documents. At the same time the issuing of official, non-publicly accessible information by the FMA to foreign financial

---

113 See on this subject in detail Art. 36 due diligence act (SPG)

supervisory authorities is forbidden and only permitted for the following circumstances:

"a) if the public order, other major national interests, the area of secrecy and fiscal interests are not breached by this;
b) if the information corresponds to the purpose of the due diligence act (SPG);
c) if it is guaranteed that the requesting state would comply with a similar Liechtenstein request;
d) if it is guaranteed that the issued information is only used for checking compliance with due diligence obligations;
e) if it is guaranteed that the employees of the responsible authority as well as persons commissioned by the responsible authorities are subject to official or professional secrecy, respectively;
f) if the law concerning international legal assistance is not applicable in criminal cases; and
g) it is guaranteed that the issued information is not forwarded to other authorities or bodies without the prior consent of the FMA. If the information originates from a foreign authority, then the information may only be forwarded with its express consent and, where applicable, only for the purpose to which this authority has consented."

Unless otherwise defined in inter-state agreements, such received information from the responsible authorities may be used only for checking compliance with due diligence obligations, for imposing sanctions, within the scope of administrative procedures concerning the contestation of decisions by a responsible authority or within the scope of legal proceedings.[114]

3. Legal assistance

3.1. General

Owing to its state political interest in granting legal assistance in the international context, Liechtenstein closed bilateral and multilateral agreements in this area at a very early stage. For example, the first bilateral agreement concerning criminal intelligence ex-

---

114 See on this entire subject Art. 37 due diligence act (SPG)

change through exchange of notes with the German Empire as early as 1920, which was followed in 1931 by an agreement concerning legal assistance through questioning witnesses. Additionally, Liechtenstein closed an extradition treaty listing 27 elements of crime subject to extradition with the United States of America in 1936. An agreement concerning bilateral legal assistance exchange with the Republic of Austria also came about in 1955. In the multilateral context, Liechtenstein signed the European agreement concerning legal assistance in criminal cases as well as the European extradition agreement. Finally, a legal assistance act (RHG) came into force in 1992, undergoing total revision in 2000 whereby the legal as stance procedure was tightened and accelerated.[115]

3.2. Law concerning international legal assistance in criminal cases (legal assistance act (RHG))

3.2.1. General

The legal assistance act was absorbed "system-compliantly" from Austrian extradition and legal assistance act (RHG) and thus aligned with material criminal law and criminal procedure law. The result is clear delimitation of competencies between administration and jurisdiction in the legal aid procedure.

With the legal assistance act (RHG) the legislator at the Liechtenstein parliament extensively regulated the areas of extradition from Liechtenstein, transit through Liechtenstein, legal assistance for countries abroad, taking over of criminal prosecution and monitoring, enforcement of foreign penal decisions and effecting of extradition, transit, handing over, legal assistance as well as the taking over of criminal prosecution, monitoring and enforcement. It is fundamental to apply the criminal process regulations logically if

---

[115] Law of 11th November 1992 concerning international legal assistance in criminal cases (*Rechtshilfegesetz*), LGBl. 1993 No. 68 abolished and revised in 1993 by law of 15th September 2000 concerning international legal assistance in criminal cases (*Rechtshilfegesetz*, legal assistance act (RHG)) LGBl. 2000 No. 215

nothing can be deduced from the regulations of the legal assistance act (RHG).[116]

3.2.2. Extradition

3.2.2.1. Permissibility of extradition

Liechtenstein has to conduct legal assistance dealings with a not inconsiderable proportion of countries which are not members of the European legal assistance agreement, without there being contractual grounds.

For this reason, Liechtenstein strictly insists on granting legal assistance whilst requiring mutuality. This means that Liechtenstein strictly only complies with a legal assistance request from another country if the requesting state would comply with a similar Liechtenstein request. Additionally, legal assistance may strictly only be approved if nothing stands in the way of public order or other essential interests of the Principality of Liechtenstein.[117] Consequently, Liechtenstein authorities may likewise only place requests according to the legal assistance act (RHG) if a similar request from another state could be complied with, unless it would appear urgently necessary for special reasons.[118]

3.2.2.2. Extradition of persons to another state

In Liechtenstein, requests to extradite persons to another state are strictly only permissible for prosecution due to an act threatened domestically or abroad with imprisonment of more than one

---

116 Exceptions on this subject are recorded in the area of the procedure to extradite persons in Art. 9 para. 2 legal assistance act (RHG). See also on this subject Art. 58 legal assistance act (RHG)
117 Art. 2 and 3 legal assistance act (RHG)
118 Art. 1, 2,3 legal assistance act (RHG); *Liechtenstein Bankers' Association,* Financial centre Liechtenstein – Liechtenstein renders legal assistance internationally [German] Status May 03; in connection with a request according to legal assistance act (RHG), mutuality can also be assured to another state if, although there is no inter-state agreement, it would be permissible according to the regulations of the legal assistance act (RHG) to comply with a similar request by this state

year or for the enforcement of an imprisonment imposed due to such an act or a preventive sanction of this duration.[119]

However, extradition for enforcement is only permissible if at least four months of imprisonment are still to be enforced. Multiple imprisonments or their remaining durations still to be enforced must be added together.[120]

However, in any event, the requesting state must guarantee that the extradited person will not be prosecuted, punished, restricted in his personal freedom or delivered onwards to a third country on the basis of an act which he committed before his handover and to which the extradition consent does not extend. Additionally, the requesting state must guarantee that the extradited person will not be prosecuted, punished, restricted in his personal freedom or delivered onwards to a third country exclusively on the grounds of one or a number of acts not individually subject to extradition.[121]

However, following implementation of the extradition, Liechtenstein can agree to a fundamentally non-permissible prosecution or enforce an imprisonment or preventive sanction or forwarding to a third country if extradition for the act forming the basis of the request would be permissible in the relationship with the requesting state.[122]

---

119 Art. 10 legal assistance act (RHG); Art. 11 due diligence regulations (SPV); Art. 11 para. 1 legal assistance act (RHG); When judging whether a criminal act gives rise to an extradition, the impending criminalities modified by § 6 of the juvenile court law are not the point of departure. Whether a request to prosecute necessary according to Liechtenstein law or a similar authorisation is available, is insignificant

120 See on the entire subject Art. 11 legal assistance act (RHG); if an extradition is permissible in this sense, then extradition may take place also for prosecution due to other criminal acts or for enforcement of other imprisonments or preventive sanctions, regarding which, due to the extent of the impending criminality or the degree of the punishment or sanction still to be enforced, extradition would strictly not be permitted

121 Additionally, the requesting state must guarantee that, when modifying the legal appraisal of the act forming the basis of the extradition or during application of stipulations other than the originally accepted criminal law stipulations, the extradited person is only prosecuted and punished to the extent that the extradition would be permissible under the new standpoints

122 See Art. 23 legal assistance act (RHG)

Such consent on the part of Liechtenstein is, however, not required, if

- the extradited person remains in the territory of the requesting state for longer than forty five days after his release, even though he was able and permitted to leave it;
- the extradited person leaves the territory of the requesting state and returns to it voluntarily or is regularly brought back to it from a third country,
- the extradition took place according to Art. 32 legal assistance act (RHG) (with the acquiescence of the extradited person).

As soon as an extradition process against a foreigner is pending or sufficient grounds for initiating such a procedure exist, it is impermissible to bring him out of the country on the basis of other legal regulations.[123]

3.2.2.3. Extradition of nationals

However, the extradition of nationals is regulated considerably more restrictively in Art. 12 legal assistance act (RHG), according to which these nationals may only be extradited to another state or handed over for prosecution or penalty enforcement if they have expressly consented after being instructed on the consequences of their statement. The consent must be recorded by protocol and can be revoked up until the handover is ordered. The exceptions to this are the transiting and return of a national whom another state hands over to the Liechtenstein authorities temporarily.

In Art. 14ff. the legal assistance act (RHG) defines acts on the basis of which an extradition is strictly impermissible despite the implementations undertaken previously. This includes in particular criminal acts of a political nature[124], military and fiscal criminal acts[125] and criminal acts subject to Liechtenstein jurisdiction.[126]

---

123 See Art. 13 legal assistance act (RHG)
124 See Art. 14 legal assistance act (RHG)
125 SS Art. 15 legal assistance act (RHG)
126 See on this subject Art. 16 legal assistance act (RHG); Liechtenstein jurisdiction does not oppose an extradition if the jurisdiction is exercised only representatively for another state, or if preference should be given to im-

Pursuant to Art. 17 legal assistance act (RHG), an extradition is also impermissible if the person to be extradited for the criminal act has been legally released by a court in the state of perpetration or otherwise placed beyond prosecution, or has been legally convicted by a court in a third country and the punishment has been fully enforced or has been reprieved for the as yet unenforced part, or its enforcement has expired according to the law of the third country.

Additionally, a basically permissible extradition can be impermissible for reasons of expiry[127], the protection of constitutional principles, extradition asylum[128], criminal minority[129], impermissible punishments or preventive measures[130] or in cases of hardship.[131]

3.2.2.4. Responsibility

The Justice Department makes a finding concerning the extradition request according to inter-state agreements and the principles of inter-state legal relations. In the process it considers the interests of the Principality of Liechtenstein, international public law obligations, particularly in the area of asylum law, and the protection of human rights. It must reject the extradition if the Superior Court has declared it impermissible.[132]

3.2.3. Transit

The permissibility of transiting persons through Liechtenstein is regulated in the legal assistance act (RHG) in Art. 42ff. In the

---

plementing the criminal proceeding in the requesting state with consideration of the special circumstances, in particular for reasons of establishing the truth, assessing the punishment, enforcement or better social rehabilitation, unless the person to be extradited is already legally convicted domestically, legally released or placed beyond prosecution for other reasons listed in Art. 9 para. 3 legal assistance act (RHG). In the case of Art. 16 para. 2 item 2 legal assistance act (RHG), extradition is moreover impermissible if there are concerns that the person to be extradited would be placed in a considerably worse position overall due to a conviction in another state than according to Liechtenstein law

127 See Art. 18 legal assistance act (RHG)
128 See Art. 19 legal assistance act (RHG)
129 See Art. 21 legal assistance act (RHG)
130 See Art. 20 legal assistance act (RHG)
131 See Art. 22 legal assistance act (RHG)
132 On responsibility and procedures see Art. 26ff. legal assistance act (RHG)

process the permissibility criteria for transit are drawn on those which must be fulfilled in connection with an extradition of persons according to the legal assistance act (RHG), but do not concur with them in full.

The Justice Department must decide over the transit request. Execution of the transit is the responsibility of the country's police.[133]

3.2.4. Legal assistance for countries abroad

3.2.4.1. Permissibility of legal assistance in general

At the request of a foreign authority[134] legal assistance can be rendered in criminal cases, including procedures to order preventive sanctions and pronounce an order according to asset law as well as matters of removal and criminal record, procedures concerning damage compensation for criminal court arrests and conviction.[135]

Legal assistance is to be understood as every form of support which is granted for a foreign procedure in a matter of criminal law.

In principle, legal assistance may only be rendered when the facts of the case are apparent from the request and the legal judgement of the criminal act forming the basis of the request is apparent. A reference to the criminal law regulations to be applied, or applied, in the requesting state is sufficient in the case of delivery requests.

The copy, certified transcription or photocopy of the order from the responsible authority must be enclosed with a request to search persons or premises, confiscate objects or monitor telecommunications. If this does not involve an order by a court, then there must be a declaration from the authority requesting legal assistance that the pre-requirements required for this sanction according to the law applying in the requesting state are fulfilled.[136]

---

133 Art 47ff. legal assistance act (RHG)
134 A court, public prosecutor's office or an authority active in executing criminalities or sanctions should be regarded as an authority
135 Art. 50 legal assistance act (RHG)
136 See on this subject Art. 56 legal assistance act (RHG)

Art. 51 legal assistance act (RHG) restricts the permissibility of legal assistance and declares such assistance impermissible under the following circumstances:

> "1. *if the act forming the basis of the request is either not threatened with court punishment[137] or according to Art. 14 and 15 (impermissibility of extradition due to criminal acts of a political nature and military and fiscal criminal act) is not subject to extradition,*
> 2. *if the extradition would be impermissible for the procedure forming the basis of the request according to Art. 19 items 1 and 2 (impermissibility of the extradition due to protection of constitutional principles; extradition asylum)*
> 3. *if either the special pre-requirements for the conducting of certain investigations required according to the code of criminal procedure (StPO) are not in place or the rendering of legal assistance would result in the breach of a duty of secrecy to be protected according to Liechtenstein regulations and in respect of criminal courts.*"

In Articles 52 to 54 legal assistance act (RHG) it is explicitly ruled under which circumstances a transferral of objects and files, the delivery of a summons by a foreign authority to a person within Liechtenstein as well as the handing over of arrested persons for the purposes of evidence,[138] is possible.

According to the legal assistance act (RHG), foreign instruments are in principle not permitted to conduct inquiries and proceedings in the territory of the Principality of Liechtenstein. The collaboration of responsible foreign judges, public prosecutors or other persons participating in the proceeding is, however, permitted if this appears necessary for proper execution of the legal assistance request. The required service tasks of foreign instruments need, except in the case of transnational observations, the consent of the Justice Department.

---

[137] The absence of culpability according to Liechtensteinian law does not oppose the delivery of written items if the recipient is prepared to accept them; Art. 51 para. 2 legal assistance act (RHG)
[138] See also on this subject Art. 73 para. 2 legal assistance act (RHG)

3.2.4.2. Responsibility

In principle, the District Court is responsible for executing the legal assistance request. If a person to be handed over is in custody or undergoing enforcement of sanctions, the District Court decides on the request for handover. The decision must be communicated to the Justice Department, which must reject the handover under certain circumstances. The handover is effected by the national police.[139]

3.2.5. Taking over the prosecution and monitoring; enforcement of foreign criminal law decisions

3.2.5.1. Taking over of prosecution

Requests to take over prosecution made to Liechtenstein are first checked by the Justice Department as to whether there is occasion for this. If this is not the case, the Justice Department rejects further treatment of the request; otherwise it is forwarded to the public prosecutor's office. The requesting state must be informed of the orders made and of the result of a criminal proceeding.[140]

3.2.5.2. Taking over of monitoring

The pre-requirement of permissibility of the monitoring of a person legally convicted by a foreign court and for whom imposition of a penalty has been conditionally adjourned, a penalty or preventive sanction has been conditionally pardoned, or who has been released from imprisonment or from a preventive sanction associated with a prison term at the request of another state, is regulated in Art. 61 legal assistance act (RHG).

The District Court is responsible for the decision concerning the request to monitor as well as for ordering the monitoring measures. The public prosecutor's office and the convicted person have the opportunity to bring a complaint before the Superior Court within fourteen days.

The Justice Department is responsible for communicating the decision concerning the request for taking over of monitoring and of

---

139   See on this subject Art. 55 legal assistance act (RHG)
140   Art. 60 legal assistance act (RHG)

the sanctions ordered on the basis of this request and their result to the requesting state.[141]

3.2.5.3. Enforcement of foreign criminal court decisions

At the request of another state, the enforcement or further enforcement of the decision of a foreign court legally pronounced in the form of a fine or prison term, a preventive sanction or an order concerning asset law is permissible in Liechtenstein if:

> *"1. the decision of the foreign court has been issued during a procedure commensurate with the principles of Art. 6 of the convention on the protection of human rights and fundamental freedoms,*
> *2. the decision has been issued for an act which is threatened with court punishment according to Liechtenstein law,*
> *3. the decision has not been issued due to one of the criminal acts listed in Art. 14 (criminal acts of a political nature) and 15 (military and fiscal criminal acts),*
> *4. no expiry of enforceability would yet have been reached according to Liechtenstein law,*
> *5. the person affected by the decision of the foreign court is not being prosecuted for the crime domestically has been legally convicted or released or otherwise placed beyond prosecution."*[142]

Enforcement of the decision of a foreign court which has been expressed in the form of imprisonment or preventive sanction, is, however, strictly only permissible is the convicted person is a national, has his residence or abode domestically and has consented to the domestic enforcement.[143] Additionally, the enforcement of preventive sanctions is only permissible if the Liechtenstein law stipulates a similar sanction.

If orders according to asset law are taken in a decision by a foreign court, enforcement is only permissible to the extent that according to Liechtenstein law the pre-requirements for a fine, the siphoning off of gains, an expiry or a confiscation are in place and

---

141 See Art. 63 legal assistance act (RHG)
142 Art. 64 para. 1 legal assistance act (RHG)
143 Art. 64 para. 2 legal assistance act (RHG)

a corresponding domestic order has not yet been issued. Decisions by a foreign court which are expressed in the form of a fine or the siphoning off of gains are, moreover, only permissible if insertion can be expected domestically and the person concerned, if he can be reached, has been heard.

If the expiry or confiscation is legally expressed in the form of a decision by a foreign court, its enforcement is only permissible if the seized objects or assets are located domestically and the person concerned, if he can be reached, has been heard. Fines, siphoned-off cash sums, expired assets and confiscated assets go to the district.[144]

The District Court decides with a ruling on the request for enforcement and the adjustment of the punishment, of the preventive sanction or siphoning off of gains, of the expiry or confiscation. The public prosecutor's office and the concerned person have the opportunity to bring a complaint before the Superior Court within 14 days. The Justice Department informs the requesting state of the decision concerning the request to take over the enforcement. Following the takeover of the enforcement of a punishment or preventive sanction, a criminal proceeding for the crime forming the basis of the judgement may no longer be introduced and should in any case be terminated if its enforceability according to the law of the requesting state expires.[145]

3.2.6. Effecting extradition, transit, handing over, legal assistance and effecting the taking over of prosecution, legal assistance and monitoring and enforcement

3.2.6.1. Effecting extradition, transit and handing over

If there is occasion to effect the extradition of a person located abroad for prosecution or enforcement of a prison term or preventive sanction or to effect a transit or handover, the District Court must, at the request of the public prosecutor's office, transfer the required documents to the Justice Department.

---

144 Art. 64 legal assistance act (RHG)
145 Art. 67 legal assistance act (RHG)

The Justice Department may under certain circumstances dispense with effecting the extradition, transit or handover.[146]

If the pre-requirements for effecting the extradition are in place, the District Court may, at the request of the public prosecutor's office, request the imposition of the extradition arrest by the responsible foreign court via the prescribed route. This must be communicated to the Justice Department immediately.

However, a person who is extradited to Liechtenstein must strictly be prosecuted, punished, restricted in his personal freedom or forwarded onwards to the third country ("speciality of extradition") neither for an act committed before his handover nor exclusively for one or several acts which are not subject to extradition singly.

However, this is possible if

> "1. the extradited person remains on the territory of the Principality of Liechtenstein for longer than twenty five days following his release, even though he was able and permitted to leave it,
> 2. the extradited person leaves the territory of the Principality of Liechtenstein and returns voluntarily or is regularly brought back from a third country, or
> 3. the requested state dispenses with compliance with the speciality of extradition."[147]

In the event that the act forming the basis of the extradition is to be recognised in a manner legally different to that in the extradition request, or should other criminal law regulations be applied than those originally accepted, the extradited person may only be prosecuted and punished to the extent that the extradition would have been permitted under the new standpoints. If the extradition of a person convicted for several coinciding criminal acts is approved only for the enforcement of the part of the punishment falling to a single one of these criminal acts, only this part may be enforced. These stipulations must correspondingly also be applied to transit.[148]

---

146 See on this subject Art. 68 legal assistance act (RHG)
147 Art. 70 para. 1 legal assistance act (RHG)
148 See on this entire subject Art. 70 legal assistance act (RHG)

3.2.6.2. Effecting legal assistance

a. Effecting the summons of persons from abroad

If the personal appearance of a person to be heard before the court seems necessary, the foreign court must be requested to issue the summons. There may be no forced threats implied in the event of his non-compliance.

The summoned person may only be prosecuted, punished or restricted in his personal freedom for an act committed before his arrival,

> "*1. for a criminal act forming the subject of the summons of a person as the accused,*
> *2. if the summoned person remains on the territory of the Principality of Liechtenstein for longer than fifteen days following completion of the hearing, even though he was able and permitted to do so, or*
> *3. if he voluntarily returns to the territory of the Principality of Liechtenstein or is regularly brought back.*"[149]

b. Handing over of arrested persons for the purposes of evidence

A person under arrest abroad can only be handed over to Liechtenstein for the conducting of important investigations, in particular for the purpose of questioning or identification. Regarding this Art. 73 legal assistance act (RHG) refers to the stipulations of Art. 59 para. 2 and 3 legal assistance act (RHG).

---

149 Art. 72 para. 2 legal assistance act (RHG)

3.2.6.3. Effecting the taking over of prosecution, monitoring and enforcement of domestic criminal law convictions abroad

a. Effecting the taking over of prosecution

The Justice Department can request another state to introduce a criminal proceeding against for a criminal act subject to Liechtenstein jurisdiction if the jurisdiction of the state appears justified and the extradition of a person located abroad cannot be effected or the effecting of the extradition can be dispensed with for other reasons.

This likewise applies if the sentencing of a person located abroad in the other state is advisable in the interest of establishing the truth or for reasons of sentencing or enforcement and if this person is being extradited for another criminal act or it is otherwise to be assumed that the criminal proceeding will be undertaken in another state in the presence of this person.

However, such a request is impermissible if it is to be feared that the person would have been exposed to a disadvantage on one of the grounds listed in Art. 19 legal assistance act (RHG) (protection of constitutional principles; extradition asylum) or if the criminal act is threatened with the death penalty in the requested state. The suspect must be heard, if he is in Liechtenstein, before the request to take over prosecution.

b. Effecting monitoring and enforcement

Another state can, given an appropriate occasion, be requested by Liechtenstein to monitor a person for whom a probation period has been defined on the basis of the decision of a domestic court according to §§ 43, 45, 46 or 47 criminal code (StGB) or § 8 of the juvenile court law. A statement by the public prosecutor's office must be obtained before such a request and, if he is in Liechtenstein, the convicted person must be heard.[150]

A request for taking over the enforcement of an imprisonment or preventive sanction is essentially permissible if

---

[150] See on this subject Art 76 legal assistance act (RHG)

"1. the convicted person is in the requested state and his extradition cannot be effected or effecting the extradition can be dispensed with for another reason, or
2. the purposes of execution could be better achieved through enforcement or further enforcement in the requested state."[151]

However, this does not apply if

"1. the convicted person is a national, unless he has his residence or abode in the requested state and is located there,
2. it is to be feared that the punishment or preventive sanction would be executed in a manner contrary to the requirements of Art. 3 on the convention for the protection of human rights and fundamental freedoms,
3. it is to be feared that the convicted person would have to anticipate persecution or disadvantages of the nature described in Art. 19 item 3 legal assistance act (RHG) (extradition asylum) there in the event of his handing over to the requested state, or
4. it is to be feared that that the convicted person would be placed in a considerably worse position overall due to a conviction in another state than due to enforcement or further enforcement domestically."[152]

A request to take over the enforcement of a fine or the order to siphon off gains is permissible if insertion in the requested state can be expected.

Before a request to take over enforcement, a statement by the public prosecutor's office must be obtained and the person concerned heard, if he is located domestically.[153]

3.3. No legal assistance in fiscal matters

Liechtenstein strictly grants no legal assistance in fiscal matters. Accordingly, as explained before, it was expressly established in the legal assistance act (RHG) that legal assistance and extradi-

---

151   Art. 76 para. 2 legal assistance act (RHG)
152   Art. 76 para. 3 legal assistance act (RHG)
153   See on this subject Art. 76 legal assistance act (RHG)

tions cannot be granted if the criminal acts consist, according to Liechteinsteinian law, exclusively in the breach of payment regulations (fiscal proviso).

Additionally, in the event of legal assistance Liechtenstein demands assurance from the foreign authority that the material is not made available to another official entity, for example tax administration (speciality proviso).

In addition to the fiscal crimes, the impermissibility of legal assistance also covers the breach of payment, monopoly, customs or currency regulations as well as regulations concerning goods management and foreign trading. The reason for this is that, according to the Liechtenstein constitution, a breach of the financial or economic order of a state by another state does not necessary need to be interpreted as an impairment of interests protected by criminal law.[154]

---

[154] *Liechtenstein Bankers' Association*, Financial Centre Liechtenstein, Liechtenstein renders legal assistance internationally [German]

C.
Combating Money Laundering in Austria

Mag. Johannes TRENKWALDER, LL.M

Mag. Johannes Trenkwalder, LL.M was born in 1974 and is an Austrian citizen. Following his studies in legal sciences in Innsbruck he completed a post-graduate course in "International Business Law" at the University of Manchester. In 2000 he began as an associate at the legal partnership CMS Reich-Rohrwig Hainz Rechtsanwälte, where he became a partner in 2005. He is particularly active in the field of conducting national and international transactions and his specialist areas include company law, mergers & acquisitions and financing. In 2002/2003 he was a research assistant for comparative company law in the START project an der Vienna University of Economics and Business Administration. Johannes Trenkwalder is the author of publications particulary in the field of company law. He is also a guest lecturer at the College of Business Administration, Vienna.

1. Legal context

1.1. Legal sources

The central conditions of Austrian law concerning money laundering are found in the criminal code (Austrian criminal code (StGB)) and in the banking act (Austrian banking act (BWG)). More conditions can be found, among other locations, in the EU source tax act[155], the industry act 1994[156], the gambling act[157], lawyer regulations[158], in the insurance supervision act[159], in the customs rights implementation act[160], as well as in numerous international agreements in which the Republic of Austria is a contract partner.

At the European Union level, three money laundering directives have been drawn up so far, the third money laundering directive having recently been published in the Official Journal of the European Union.[161]
Alongside these are a series of national and international legal sources, which are of a "soft law" nature but assume an extremely central role in the consolidation and interpretation of legal regulations. International "soft law" legal sources having acquired significance for Austrian practice are, for example, the "Forty Recommendations"[162], which were formulated by the Financial

---

155 BGB (Austrian Civil Code)I I 33/2004
156 in the version BGB (Austrian Civil Code)I I 111/2002
157 BGB (Austrian Civil Code)I 620/1989 in the version BGB (Austrian Civil Code)I I 71/2003
158 RGBl 96/1868 in the version 93/2003
159 BGB (Austrian Civil Code)I 569/1978 in the version BGB (Austrian Civil Code)I I 46/2002
160 BGB (Austrian Civil Code)I 659/1994 in the version BGB (Austrian Civil Code)I I 26/2004
161 Directive 91/308/EEA of the Council of 10th June 1991 on the prevention of the use of the financial system for the purpose of money laundering; directive 2001/97/EC of the European Parliament and the European Council of 4th December 2001 on modification of the directive 91/308/EEA of the Council, respectively, directive 2005/60/EC of the European Parliament and Council of 26th October 2005 for the prevention of the use of the financial system for the purpose of money laundering and terrorist financing
162 The currently applicable version dates from 20th June 2003 and can be retrieved at http://www1.oecd.org/fatf/40Recs_en.htm (30th July 2005)

Action Task Force on Money Laundering (FATF)[163], and the "Wolfsberg Anti Money Laundering Principles"[164], which were issued by the Wolfsberg Group[165], together with the "Guidance Paper on Anti-Money Laundering and Combating the Financing of Terrorism"[166], which was published in October 2004 by the "International Association of Insurance Supervisors" and deals with measures for combating money laundering in the insurance sector.

The legal sources of national "soft law" particularly include the various circulars of the financial market authority (FMA) concerning money laundering and terrorist financing. Of note are:

- the FMA circular of 23rd April 2004 concerning credit institutions
- the FMA circular of 24th August 2004 concerning investment services companies
- the FMA circular of 16th December 2004 concerning insurance companies and
- the FMA circular of 9th October 2003 concerning money laundering regulations of the insurance supervision act.[167]

1.2. Statistics

2050 file entries were recorded at the money laundering reporting office in the calendar year 2004. Of these, 1579 reports were made by professional report providers, a majority, namely 1260, by banking and financial institutions. In total, 373 suspicious transaction reports were made, of which 349 originated from banking and financial institutions, eleven from insurance companies, five from the financial market authority, three from industrial-

---

163 The FATF is an inter-state organisation with currently 33 members (including Austria) and was founded by the governments of the G7 countries (as they still were at the time)
164 These consist of several different documents, retrievable at http://www.wolfsberg-principles.com/translations-german.html (30th July 2005)
165 The Wolfsberg Group consists of international financial institutions; on this subject see also Dr. Kaetzler's section from p.43
166 Retrievable at http://www.fma.gv.at/de/pdf/iais-gui.pdf (30th July 2005)
167 All circulars available at http://www.fma.gv.at/de/fma/geldwaes/grundleg/weiterei.htm. (30th July 2005)

ists, two from Casinos Austria, two from notaries public and one from a lawyer.[168]

Besides these, investigations arising from Interpol, Europol or Egmont inquiries or inquiries from liaison officers or the justice department were initiated in 349 cases. 100 charges due to the suspicion of money laundering were brought in the calendar year 2004. The most common preliminary crimes forming the basis of money laundering investigations were serious fraud (33 cases) and narcotics dealing (15 cases).

The observations of the money laundering reporting office revealed that many money laundering activities used the following systems: off-shore business, "money remittance" systems and "alternative remittance" systems. "Money remittance" is the (multiple) circulation and forwarding of money through which tracing is made difficult. According to the observations of the money laundering reporting office, drug dealers, pickpockets, housebreakers and internet tricksters in particular make use of this system – often using fake identities. "Alternative remittance" systems designate a transferral of money or goods without traceable movements and are founded on the trust of a section of the persons involved.[169]

1.3. Term of money laundering

Two different terms can be found in Austrian law: "money laundry" (*Geldwäscherei*) and "money laundering" (*Geldwäsche*). § 165 Austrian criminal code (StGB) uses the term "money laundry"; the Austrian banking act (BWG) incorporates this term in §§ 39ff. However, the term "money laundering" is also used in the Austrian banking act (BWG) (cf. § 78 para. 9 no. 2) – an investigation and comparison of the two terms would be beyond our scope here. Both terms are also used in the Austrian trade regulations (GewO) 1994, while the difference is not apparent from the legal text to the person seeking legal information. There is an express indication in some parts of the material concerning the Austrian trade regula-

---

168 See also the statistics section of this publication from p.313
169 More detailed information at http://www.interpol.int/Public/FinancialCrime/MoneyLaundering/hawala/default.asp#2 (30. July 2005)

tions (GewO) amendment[170] that the terms are used synonymously.[171]

The following is a subdivided depiction of aspects to be considered with regard to money laundering according to § 165 Austrian criminal code (StGB):

a) Punishable for money laundering[172] according to *§ 165 Austrian criminal code (StGB)* is someone who (i) conceals or obscures the origin of (para. 1) or (ii) takes possession of, keeps, invests, manages, transforms, exploits or transfers to a third party (para. 2) asset components originating from certain preliminary crimes.

b) Qualification of an act as money laundering presupposes that the asset component concerned originates from a *preliminary crime*. Preliminary crimes are all crimes which are threatened with more than three years' or lifelong imprisonment, certain other crimes listed in the law (e.g. forgery of certificates, suppression of certificates, resistance against state authority, founding of a criminal association, terrorist financing, provision of false evidence, forgery and/or suppression of evidence, accepting gifts, bribery) as well as certain financial delinquencies (smuggling and evasion of entry or exit contributions). The preliminary crime must be neither punished nor punishable. It is sufficient that the preliminary crime was exercised according to the profile of the crime and unlawfully.[173] Regarding the preliminary perpetrator, existing grounds for exculpation do not therefore simultaneously justify the impunity of the subsequent perpetrator in respect of his completion of the crime of money laundering.

---

170 BGB (Austrian Civil Code)I I 111/2002
171 1117 dB GP XXI, remark on § 365 m trade regulations (trade regulations (GewO))
172 The term "money laundering" will be used in the present essay from now on
173 *Kirchbacher/Presslauer* in Vienna Commentary on the Austrian criminal code (Austrian criminal code (StGB)) Volume II [German] § 165 marginal note 13

c) *Asset components* relevant to money laundering can be physical objects, claims, and other rights equivalent to assets.[174] Pursuant to § 165, paragraph 3 of the Austrian criminal code (StGB), an asset component arises from a criminal act if it was obtained by the perpetrator of the criminal act through the crime or received in exchange for committing the crime, or if the value of the originally obtained or received asset is embodied in the asset component. This includes, on one hand, both the actual booty directly obtained from the underlying offence and the remuneration paid for committing the underlying offence, income from bribery and graft, and similar. On the other hand, it also applies to objects, claims and other rights into which such an asset component has been transformed (for example, through the purchase of an object with the cash obtained from the underlying offence, through barter, etc. – surrogate asset components). Whether the asset component originally obtained through the underlying offence remains "permanently contaminated" – that is, whether it retains the property of "object of a crime" even after being transferred to a third party – has not yet been fully clarified.[175] At times, it has been stated that the characteristic of "object of a crime" should expire when ownership of the asset component is acquired in good faith[176], or when a third party has obtained the asset component against adequate compensation, without thereby having committed a criminal act.[177] With regard to surrogate asset components, the rule is that they can no longer be considered as objects of a crime in the context of money laundering as soon as they no longer embody the value of the original asset component.[178]

For example: if someone has therefore obtained money through forged certification (§ 223 Austrian criminal code (StGB)), with which a third party then (in awareness of the

---

174 *Kirchbacher/Presslauer* in Vienna Commentary on Volume II of the Criminal Code [German], § 165, marginal note 5.
175 *Kirchbacher/Presslauer* in Vienna Commentary on Volume II of the Criminal Code [German], § 165, marginal note 7.
176 Rainer in Triffterer/Rosbaud/Hinterhofer, Commentary to the Criminal Code [German], § 165, marginal note 24.
177 *Klippl*, Money Laundering, p.150 [German].
178 *Kirchbacher/Presslauer* in Vienna Commentary on Volume II of the Criminal Code [German], § 165, marginal note 9.

forged certification and the act of money laundering) acquires a car, the acquired car loses its property as an object of a crime when the car is sold to a third party. The compensation received for the sale now embodies, instead of the car, the asset component originating from the forged certification as the preliminary crime.

d) *Perpetrator* of money laundering can in principle be everybody who is not the direct perpetrator, designated perpetrator or joint perpetrator of the preliminary crime.[179]

e) § 165 para. 1 Austrian criminal code (StGB) renders the *concealment and* the *obscuring* of the origin of asset components originating from certain preliminary crimes liable to punishment. Concealment of such an asset component is every activity that makes the asset component's discovery (by the victim of the preliminary crime, prosecution authorities or a third party commissioned with the discovery) difficult.[180] Concealing the origin of such asset components according to § 165 para. 1 Austrian criminal code (StGB) is someone who "provides false information in legal circulation concerning the origin or the true nature of these asset components, their ownership or other rights on them, the authorisations to possess them, their transfer or as to where they are located."

§ 165 para. 2 Austrian criminal code (StGB) renders the *taking possession of, keeping, investment, management, transformation and exploitation* of such asset components or *transferring to a third party* liable to punishment:

- Taking possession of means establishment of safekeeping.
- Keeping means factual possession.
- Investing means investment of the asset components.
- Managing means the exercising of legal authority to dispose.
- Transforming means substituting the asset component for another.
- Exploiting means selling the asset component.

---

179 *Bertel/ Schwaighofer* – Austrian Criminal Law, Special Section I Volume VIII [German]
180 *Kirchbacher/Presslauer* in Vienna Commentary on Volume II Austrian criminal code (StGB) [German] § 165 marginal note 16

- Transferring to a third party means the granting of authority to dispose.

f) The manners of committing of § 165 para. 1 presuppose conditional intent (*dolus eventualis*) on the *subjective side of the crime*. Acting with conditional intent is someone who seriously believes it possible and accepts that he is realising the legal facts of a crime. The intent must also extend to the origin of the asset. The perpetrator must therefore know the circumstances of the preliminary crime from which the subsumability as a preliminary crime suitable for money laundering results and include them in his perception of the circumstances of the criminal act.[181] Correct legal classification of the preliminary crime is not required.

The manners of committing of § 165 para. 2 Austrian criminal code (StGB) do not only presuppose conditional intent, but knowingness. Knowingness in this context means that the perpetrator intends to apply the conduct indicated in § 165 para. 2 consciously. The presupposition of knowingness pursuant to § 165 para. 2 Austrian criminal code (StGB) also refers to the asset's origin/preliminary crime.

g) An *enhanced penal context* (imprisonment from six months to five years) exists in the event of committing money laundering as a member of a criminal association which has associated itself with repeated money laundering, or if the asset component concerned exceeds EUR 40,000.00 (§ 165 para. 3 Austrian criminal code (StGB)). Someone who knowingly takes possession of, keeps, invests, transforms, exploits or transfers to a third party components of the assets of a criminal organisation or a terrorist association is punishable with imprisonment of up to three years (§ 165 para. 5 Austrian criminal code (StGB)).

§ 165a para. 1 Austrian criminal code (StGB) provides for the possibility of *active remorse* for the perpetrator when money laundering has been committed: if the perpetrator voluntarily, and before the prosecution authority has learned of his guilt, effects the securing of significant asset components to which the money laundering refers by providing indications to the prose-

---

181 *Kirchbacher/Presslauer* in Vienna Commentary on Austrian criminal code (StGB) Volume II [German] § 165 marginal note 21f.

cution authority, he is not punishable. The same applies if, without assistance by the perpetrator, significant asset components are secured if the perpetrator voluntarily and seriously makes efforts to secure the asset components without being aware of the securing (§ 165a para. 2 Austrian criminal code (StGB)).

h) In implementation of international and European legal stipulations[182] at the beginning of 2006, Austria standardised the criminal responsibility of associations for all legally punishable acts – therefore also for money laundering. Association denotes every legal person, partnership and registered acquisition company, meaning that credit institutions and financial institutions are included in the term of association. The criminal facts requirements for the responsibility regulated in the association responsibility act (VbVG) must be checked in two phases. Initially a causal crime by a natural person, who must either be the decision maker or an employee of the association, is required. Furthermore, attribution requirements on the part of the association must be fulfilled, whereby the causal crime also becomes imputable to the association.

Every instance of responsibility of a banking/financial institution therefore requires a natural person who must have fulfilled all objective and subjective elements of the crime of § 165 Austrian criminal code (StGB) in connection with money laundering. In particular it is therefore necessary that the money laundering be committed with intent. On a broad scale, grounds for exemption for punishment also benefit the association.[183] In any case, causal crimes of every form of participation (immediate perpetrator, contributory perpetrator, designated perpetrator) and in the experimental stage also fulfil the material requirements of the VbVG.

In the second step, all elements must be checked on the basis of which the causal crime is attributed to the association. The general requirement in this process is that the crime was

---

182 See among others Second protocol on the agreement to protect the financial interests of the European Communities, [German] Official Journal of the European Communities 1997 C 221, p.11
183 On this subject in more detail *Soyer*, New corporate criminal law and prevention consulting [German], AnwBl [Austrian lawyers' journal] 2005, p.11

either committed for the benefit of the association or an obligation of the association was breached due to the crime (§ 3 para. 1 VbVG), while there is no general duty to prevent criminal offences. The VbVG therefore records no causal crimes which are committed entirely outside the activity of the natural person for the banking/financial institution. However, if a bank employee launders money for the banking/financial institution within the scope of his activity, the banking/financial institution is routinely enriched by the profits made on transaction costs.

In the following, then, a distinction will be drawn between groups of causal perpetrators – (straightforward) employees and decision makers. An employee is every person acting in personal dependency upon, or also only in economic dependency and for the account and by order of the banking/financial institution. Decision makers are all persons with comprehensive power of representation, with authorisations to control at the highest level (e.g. including managers of a controlling or revision department) or with more or less considerable influence on the senior management. The banking/financial institution is only responsible for an employee's causal crimes (with intent) if the crime was enabled or facilitated by decision makers' having omitted to apply the diligence appropriate under the circumstances (§ 3 para. 3 VbVG). In particular, breaches of organisational and personal obligations therefore lead to a causal crime being attributed to the banking/financial institution. On the other hand, if the decision maker acts illegally while exercising his managing role at the banking/financial institution, no further elements of the matter are required to bring about the attribution to the banking/financial institution.

As a sanction the VbVG provides for a fine commensurate with the gains of the association. The fine is calculable in the form of a daily earnings model. 180 days are set down as the highest fine, while the limit for a daily earning is EUR 10,000.00 (§ 4 VbVG).

2. §§ 39ff. Austrian banking act (BWG)

In fulfilment of European and international legal obligations[184] the Austrian legislator standardised the obligations of banking and financing institutions in §§ 39 to 41 Austrian banking act (BWG) for the combating of money laundering and terrorist financing. In respect of the term "money laundering," the Austrian banking act (BWG) refers to § 165 Austrian criminal code (StGB). This definition fulfils the requirements set by directive 2001/97/EC of 4th December 2001 to the legislature of the member states, according to which money laundering exists if, in awareness of the fact that assets originate from a criminal activity or participation in such an activity, these assets are exchanged or transferred in order to conceal their origin or to protect participants in the criminal act in a manner potentially thwarting prosecution; or the true origin, nature, location, disposal or movement of such assets is concealed and if such assets are acquired, possessed or used, if their origin was known upon acceptance of the assets.

Terrorist financing denotes the intentional provisioning or gathering of assets for execution of the terrorist acts listed in § 278d Austrian criminal code (StGB). Common to the listed terrorist acts is that they have the appropriate qualities for bringing about a serious or long-term disruption of public life or serious damage to economic life, and are committed with the intent to gravely intimidate the population, compel public figures or an international organisation to act, tolerate or abstain, or to severely shake or destroy the basic political, constitutional, economic or social structures of a state or international organisation. With regard to terrorist financing the origin of the asset is no criterion, meaning that funds of legal origin may also fall under the scope of application of §§ 39ff. Austrian banking act (BWG).[185]

---

184 See directive 2001/97/EC of 4th December 2001; 40 Recommendations of the FATF; Resolution 1373 of the United Nations Security Council
185 *Fletzberger* in *Fletzberger/Schopper*, Distance Selling of Financial Services [German], p.166

2.1. The obligations standardised for banking and financial institutions in §§ 39ff. Austrian banking act (BWG)

A range of obligations for banking and financial institutions are standardised in §§ 39ff. Austrian banking act (BWG). The due diligence benchmark to be complied with while fulfilling all these obligations is defined in § 39 Austrian banking act (BWG). According to this an examination of the § 39 Austrian banking act (BWG) forms the point of departure for the following remarks. This incorporates explanations on the most comprehensive obligation of banking and financial institutions, which is that concerning the identification of customers in accordance with §§ 40 and 41 Austrian banking act (BWG). The other obligations for banking and financial institutions contained in §§ 40 and 41 Austrian banking act (BWG) – for example, the duty to report and the organisational obligation – interact in a different manner, sometimes even conditioning one another. The structure of the following remarks is designed to take this relationship into consideration.

The obligations are presented in subdivisions according to points in each case.

2.1.1. Due diligence obligation

a) The *general due diligence obligation* for credit institutions and financial institutions is standardised in § 39 Austrian banking act (BWG). According to this, senior managers of a banking/financial are obligated to exhibit, during the course of their management, the diligence of an orderly and conscientious businessman in the sense of § 84 para. 1 companies law (AktG). This general benchmark also applies in principle in connection with the combating of money laundering and terrorist financing.

b) On the other hand, § 39 para. 3 Austrian banking act (BWG) establishes *an enhanced due diligence benchmark* for checking certain transactions. The condition is not aimed at the senior management, but directly at every individual employee of the credit institution or financial institution.[186] According to the regulation, the enhanced due diligence obligation on employees ap-

---

186 See Laurer in Fermuth, Laurer/Linc/Pötzelberger/Strobl, Austrian banking act (BWG) brief commentary [German], p.482

plies during transactions whose nature particularly suggests, in the estimation of the employees, that a transaction could be associated with money laundering or terrorist financing. The decisive factor in the process is not the arbitrary appraisal of the transaction by the employee, but rather his dutiful assessment at his own estimation based on experience and available information. The typologies of types of transactions commonly associated with money laundering published by the FATF and FMA play a decisive role when putting the "dutiful estimation" in Austrian administrative practice in concrete terms.[187] It should be noted that the special due diligence obligation does not already exist before or during the arbitrary decision, but not until after the decision.

Overall it is the case that the due diligence obligation generally formulated in § 39 Austrian banking act (BWG) is defined in concrete terms in §§ 40f. Austrian banking act (BWG).[188] The special character of the due diligence obligation lies mainly in additional duties of identification, checking and investigating.

c) The extent of the measures to which a credit institution/financial institution is obligated with the scope of § 39 para. 3 Austrian banking act (BWG) (put in concrete terms by the following paragraphs of the Austrian banking act (BWG)) varies depending on the individual case. The conditions concerning the duty to identify have the most comprehensive scope of application. The duty to identify exists in the run-up to a multitude of transactions, in order to counter the potential risk of anonymous business relationships; in contrast, there are duties to investigate for a considerably limited number of transactions. In contrast to the duty to identify, which generally exists due to the interest to rule out a (sweepingly) anonymous financial sector, the duty to investigate is generally only triggered by the (actual) form of a transaction that suggest that the transaction is being conducted for the purposes of money laundering. The extent of the duty to investigate will therefore generally be based on the type of the transaction. Accordingly, the assumption must not be made that the same procedure is routinely appropriate for

---

187 See www.fatf-gafi.org
188 See Laurer in Fermuth, Laurer/Linc/Pötzelberger/Strobl, Austrian banking act (BWG) brief commentary [German], p.483

fulfilling the duty to investigate. Rather, the requirements and facts of the matter of the individual case are decisive for the scope and type of the appropriate measures.

The elements requiring credit institutions/financial institutions to report to the money laundering reporting office are regulated in § 41 Austrian banking act (BWG). The duty to report primarily arises as a result of an estimation rounding off the investigations as to how probable a transaction's connection with money laundering is. In principle, the precise extent of the due diligence obligation is determined according to the size, business structure and risk potential of the credit institution or financial institution.[189]

2.1.2. Duties to identify

a) The central task for credit institutions and financial institutions according to § 40 Austrian banking act (BWG) lies in the identification of customers.[190] The aim is to render the flow of criminal funds or, respectively, funds for terrorist financing, traceable. It is all the easier for credit institutions and financial institutions to establish the purpose of a transaction the more information is available about the customer ("know your customer" principle). There is therefore the obligation to record the identity of a customer: on the one hand when initiating a *permanent business relationship* between the banking/financial institution and the customer (§ 40 para. 1 no. 1 Austrian banking act (BWG)); on the other hand, for all *transactions* not enacted within the context of a permanent business relationship whose transaction value is at least EUR 15,000.00 (or EUR equivalent) (§ 40 para. 1 no. 2 Austrian banking act (BWG)). It should be noted that one single transaction may also be completed in several procedures. The transaction should then be assessed in its entirety if the link between the procedures – due to their

---

[189] See FMA circular of 23rd April 2004 on inspection procedures and suspicious transaction reports in connection with money laundering and terrorist financing, p.3

[190] See FMA circular of 23rd April 2004 on inspection procedures and suspicious transaction reports in connection with money laundering and terrorist financing, p.25

temporal proximity, for example[191] – is obvious. The identity of the customer must also be established if the (overall) transaction value is initially unknown, but it emerges during implementation of the transaction that the amount will exceed EUR 15,000.00.

An actual suspicion of money laundering or terrorist financing is not implied in this context. In the interest of improved traceability of transactions and the preventive deterrence of money launderers, anonymous permanent or capital-intensive business relationships should generally be precluded.[192]

b) Additionally, the identity of a customer must always be established if there is the founded suspicion that the customer belongs to a terrorist association or that the customer is objectively collaborating in transactions that are conducted for the purposes of money laundering or terrorist financing (§ 40 para. 1 no. 3 Austrian banking act (BWG)). The probability of the connection between transaction and money laundering required by § 40 para. 1 no. 3 Austrian banking act (BWG) is therefore a higher one than the probability indicated in § 39 para. 3 Austrian banking act (BWG). When the suspicion is founded or how it is to be justified is not legally determined. An assumed founded suspicion of money laundering / terrorist financing will probably only be the case if a probability going beyond the merely possible exists that a certain transaction is conducted for the purposes of money laundering/terrorist financing. This probability must be suggested by objective circumstances.[193] The precise knowledge or provability of the criminal background is not required.[194]

From a practical point of view a suspicion is founded if a global consideration of a transaction (also on completion of the investigations of the credit institution or financial institution) suggests

---

191 See Laurer in Fermuth/Laure/Linc/Pötzelberger/Strobl, Austrian banking act (BWG) Brief commentary [German], p.488
192 See RL 91/308/EEA of 10th June 1991
193 See Laurer in Fermuth/Laurer/Linc/Pötzelberger/Strobl, Austrian banking act (BWG) brief commentary [German], p.491
194 See FMA circular of 23rd April 2004 on inspection procedures and suspicious transaction reports in connection with money laundering and terrorist financing, p.24

the conclusion that the transaction is conducted for the purposes of money laundering or terrorist financing. In other words, it can be said that a suspicion is founded if one is obliged to entertain it in the light of an enhanced due diligence obligation in the face of the objective circumstance because the correctness of the suspicion is considerably more likely than any other explanation.[195]

c) Certain types of transactions are deemed particularly high-risk with regard to money laundering and terrorist financing.[196] Worth mentioning here, for example, is the changing of banknotes of low denomination for banknotes of high denomination to a large extent, prematurely high repayments of, or high cash coverage of, loans and cash deposit of banknotes of low nominal value to a large extent to accounts with subsequent cash withdrawal or remittance. Major trade transactions with commodities which are financially completed via an otherwise uninvolved jurisdiction are also deemed high-risk. If a transaction falls under the scope of these typologies, duties to investigate may be triggered – provided that other circumstances of the individual case do not mitigate the suspicious appearance.

Owing to the multitude of transactions which may in practice be conducted for the purposes of money laundering, it must not be assumed that only the indicated types of transaction are high-risk. An enhanced risk of money laundering may arise, for example, with so-called PEP's (on this subject see below) or transactions of a similar nature to the types depicted above. In practice, the non-clarity of the case variants admittedly raises problems.

d) The circumstances to be paid attention to by the bank when assessing a transaction, which may justify the suspicion of money laundering, are generally[197]:

---

195 See *Maurer/Manhart*, The Second EC Money laundering Directive and the Duty of Discretion of Liberal Professions [German], wbl 2004 [magazine for Austrian and European economic law], p.401, which narrows down the result still further

196 See www.fatf-gafi.org; see also the Liechtenstein section of the present publication from p.105

197 See FMA circular of 23rd April 2004 on inspection procedures and suspicious transaction reports in connection with money laundering and terrorist

- the person of the customer and his behaviour (principally PEP's, incorrect or implausible information, avoidance of the bank, seeking certain employees, the absence of any cost sensitivity or the circumvention of sanctions concerning anti-money laundering or terrorist financing);
- Legal construction and owner relationships of a company (e.g. complexity which can only be explained at great pains, international interconnections, non-transparency);
- Opportunities to look into economic relationships and backgrounds of a customer's transactions (e.g. unwillingness of customers to explain their economic relationships or backgrounds of their transactions);
- The proximity of the customer to the credit institution or financial institution (particularly no direct contact with the bank, no place of residence in the country of the business relationship);
- Relationship of the origin or a transaction with Austria (e.g. absent logical economic link with the transaction);
- Controllability of the customer's business activity from Austria (e.g. distance of the commodity flow from Austria);
- The amount of the transaction with reference to the relevancy threshold of EUR 15,000.00 and absolute (in particular, high sums and repeated transactions just under the identification threshold);
- The type of the customer's dealings in the context of which the transaction is to be conducted with reference to the relationship between customer and credit institution/financial institution (e.g. one-time dealing, trade dealings in commodities, major project transactions).

The criteria indicated should not be considered in an isolated manner, but in one overall view. In any event they do not justify a suspicion. However, the purpose of the transaction must be checked with particular diligence.

e) Since 1st July 2002 duties to identify also exist for every payment into and withdrawal from savings deposits if the amount to

---

financing, p.19 and p.27; see in turn the counterpart in Liechtenstein in this publication from p.105

be paid in or withdrawn is at least 15,000.00 (§ 40 para. 1 no. 4 Austrian banking act (BWG)).

f) Within the framework of the duties to identify sufficient *data* must be recorded by the credit institution or financial institution in order to be able to identify the customer unambiguously. In principle, name and date of birth should be recorded for natural persons. In the case of legal persons, company name and head office must be ascertained; in both cases the data from the documents drawn on for the identification must be recorded (§ 40 para. 1 Austrian banking act (BWG)). How the data are documented – for example, as a copy of the documents submitted by the customer or as a transcription of these documents – is the responsibility of the credit institution or financial institution.[198]

Generally it is the case that in the event of a permanent business relationship the credit institution or financial institution must establish identity upon first customer contact. Further on in the business relationship, checking of the identity can take place in the customary manner (appropriate to business), for example through verifiable provision of signature, if it is assured that the person acting is identical to the legitimate customer or his authorised, identified representative. In the remaining cases the customer's identity must be established prior to the implementation of every transaction.[199]

g) Depending on whether the customer himself is in *direct or indirect contact* with the credit institution or financial institution, or whether a third party provides the connection with the credit institution / financial institution, the Austrian banking act (BWG) formulates the duty to identify of credit institutions and financial institutions in a different manner. Therefore, every customer must announce whether he is active for his own account or for the account of a third party (§ 40 para. 2 Austrian banking act (BWG)). If the customer breaches this obligation, both the delaying of transactions associated with a report to the money

---

[198] See *Kreisl*, Identifying the Customer according to the Austrian banking act (BWG) amendment 2003/35 [German], ecolex 2003, p.950
[199] See 1130 document no. 18.GP, p.142

laundering reporting office and an administrative penalty according to § 99 no. 9 Austrian banking act (BWG) is impending.

If the customer is in *direct contact* with the credit institution or financial institution and is acting for his own account, the banking / financial institution must establish the customer's identity by viewing an official photo ID submitted by the customer. The ID must contain a non-substitutable facial portrait of the customer, as well as the identification of the issuing authority (§ 40 para. 1 Austrian banking act (BWG)). In particular, therefore, personal identity card, passport and driving licence are suitable for proving the identity of a customer. However, the use of other forms of ID is also conceivable if they satisfy the requirements mentioned above. If it is not in keeping with the law of a foreigner's country of origin – as is possible with Arab countries, for example[200] – for the date of birth to appear on travel documents, recording the customer's name may be sufficient for meeting the duty to identify if identification even without establishing the date of birth can be done unambiguously (§ 40 para. 1 Austrian banking act (BWG)).

If the customer is a *legal person* (this also covers partnerships and registered acquisition companies[201]), the natural person with authorisation to represent must, on the one hand, prove his own identity. On the other hand, the credit institution or financial institution must check the authorisation to represent by means of suitable certificates and establish the identity of the legal person (§ 40 para. 1 Austrian banking act (BWG)). With regard to formalities, no excessively strict benchmark need be applied to the suitability of a certificate. Primarily, the use of a commercial register extract or an extract from a comparable register comes under consideration. If such a register does not exist in the customer's country of origin, recourse can also be had to agent appointment certificates or powers of attorney as a substitute.[202] The identification of legal persons also takes

---

200 See *Brandl/Wolfbauer*, The Austrian banking act (BWG) amendment of June 2003 [German], ecolex 2003, p.624
201 See *Schopper*, New due diligence obligations according to § 40 Austrian banking act (BWG), Austrian law of economics (RdW) [German] 2003, p.349.
202 See 32 document no. 22.GP, p.4

place on the basis of suitable certifications. In the event of the absence of a commercial register or a comparable register, possible state licences, chamber of commerce statements or minutes of general meetings may be drawn on for the identification.[203] Not all persons authorised to represent the legal person need be identified. The number of persons with power to represent is sufficient.

For *persons without their own entitlement* the Austrian banking act (BWG) provides a ruling analogous to the regulations concerning the legal person. An official written document is sufficient for certifying the power of representation. The customer's identity must be certified in a manner appropriate to their seniority.[204] In principle it must be observed that the more comprehensive the business capacity of the customer is, the higher the requirements on certifying the identity of the customer must be.

If the customer is acting as a *trustee* of a third party, then the customer must demonstrate his own identity by submitting an official photo ID in the manner described above. Proof of the identity of the trustor must take place via the submission of a copy of an official photo ID or, in the case of legal persons, via evidentiary certificates. Further, the trustee must confirm in writing that he has convinced himself in person or via reliable guarantors of the identity of the trustor (§ 40 para. 2 Austrian banking act (BWG)). According to law, reliable guarantors are courts and other public authorities, notaries public, lawyers and credit institutions, provided that they do not have their official scope of influence, head office or place of residence in a non-cooperating state. Non-cooperating states are identified according to § 78 para. 8 Austrian banking act (BWG) via an ordinance by the Austrian federal government.

At the moment there are no non-cooperating states after Myanmar and Nauru were deleted from the list of non-cooperating states.[205] The customer in an ongoing business relationship with the credit institution or financial institution must

---

203 See 32 document no. 22.GP, p.4
204 See 32 document no. 22.GP, p.4
205 See BGB (Austrian Civil Code)I II Nr 495/2004

announce an approximate date of commencement of activity as a trustee without delay.[206]

There are no regulations on establishing the identity of other customers acting via *legal representatives*. There are no indications that the acting of legal representatives in communication with banks is to be excluded. There is therefore a legal loophole.[207] The appropriate manner of proceeding of the credit institution or financial institution will have to be similar to the procedure depicted above in connection with trustees/trustors. On the one hand, the representative must demonstrate the power of representation in an appropriate manner, on the other, the identity of the customer must be certified. For this purpose (at least) one copy of an official photo ID of the customer and a written confirmation concerning the knowledge of the customer's identity by the representative will need to be submitted.

h) The identification opportunities indicated so far exclude straightforward *long distance business*. In order to effect no disadvantage for foreign credit institutions or financial institutions, or banking or financial institutions with a small branch network,[208] two possibilities are set forth by law as to how a credit institution or financial institution can fulfil its duties to identify even without direct contact with a customer or a representative.

The first possibility consists in identifying the customer by means of *secure electronic signature* in accordance with § 2 no. 3 Austrian signature act (SigG) (§ 40 para. 8 Austrian banking act (BWG)). According to this a signature can be regarded as secure if
  (i) it is assigned exclusively to the signatory,
  (ii) it enables the identification of the signatory,
  (iii) it is created using means which the signatory can keep under his exclusive control,

---

206 See Laurer in Fermuth/Laurer/Linc/Pötzelberger/Strobl, Austrian banking act (BWG) brief commentary [German], p.492
207 See *Schopper*, New due diligence obligations according to § 40 Austrian banking act (BWG) [German], RdW [Austrian law of economics] 2003, p.349
208 ibid.

(iv) the connection with the (signed) data is effected in such a form that a subsequent alteration can be established, and
(v) the signature concerns a qualified certificate and is created under application of the technical requirements of the signature act.

Ascertainment of the customer's identity is ensured by guaranteeing the authenticity and integrity of the signature. The relevance of this regulation will increase as the use of electronic signatures becomes more widespread.

The second permissible determination of the customer's identity in long-distance dealings takes place via the postal *route* (§ 40 para. 8 Austrian banking act (BWG)). In this connection a copy of an official photo ID of the customer or agent with power of representation in the case of legal persons must be sent to the credit institutions or financial institution. The name, date of birth and the address or, respectively, company name and head office, which must be the location of the customer's central administrative office at the same time, must be known to the credit institution or financial institution before the contract is closed.[209] The customer must therefore – if he is a legal person – also submit a declaration concerning the location of the central administrative office. Only after these pre-requirements are in place can the credit institution or financial institution submit to the customer, in writing by recorded delivery, the legal declaration establishing the contractual business relationship with the customer.

It is questionable whether completing a transaction in long-distance dealings is possible if – as is conceivable, for example, during mediations by banking/financial institutions – submission of a legal declaration to the business partner by the banking/financial institution is not customary in connection with the commencement of the business relationship. Occasionally the view is put forward that, in such cases, the conducting of a transaction in long-distance dealings is entirely permitted without the postal dispatch of a declaration.[210] This would create

---

209 See *Brandl/Wolfbauer*, The Austrian banking act (BWG) amendment of June 2003 [German], ecolex 2003, p.626
210 so *Brandl/Wolfbauer*, The Austrian banking act (BWG) amendment of June 2003 [German], ecolex 2003, p.626

the opportunity to circumvent the identity regulations which would thwart certain identification of customers subject to the regulations of § 40 para. 1 Austrian banking act (BWG). In view of the wording of the act, therefore, a confirmatory letter will need to be sent to the customer by post.[211]

i) There are *exceptions* to the possibilities for customer identification in *long-distance dealings* described above. Both forms of identification in long-distance dealings are excluded in the event of founded suspicion of the customer's belonging to a terrorist organisation or cooperating in money laundering or terrorist financing. There is also an exception in the event that the customer has his location or place of residence in a non-cooperating state. As already mentioned, there are currently no non-cooperating states. If the customer's location or place of residence is outside the EEA, a written confirmation by a credit institution or financial institution in a permanent business relationship with the customer that the customer has been identified in compliance with European legal requirements is needed in addition for the fulfilment of the depicted pre-requirements. The credit institution or financial institution must at least be subject to requirements that are equivalent to European legal regulations. Confirmation of the customer's identification by Austrian representative authorities or recognised accreditation offices is also possible.

j) Owing to the (relative) *anonymity* in the area of long-distance dealings there is an *enhanced risk* of data forgery and abuse. As a result the risk of using the long-distance transaction for the purposes of money laundering and terrorist financing is also an enhanced one. The (particular) due diligence obligation of credit institutions and financial institutions therefore demands enhanced caution in this area. This must be of particular relevance here in the face of the existing criticism concerning identification by post[212]. Also owing to the increased risk in long-

---

211 See *Kreisl*, Customer identification according to the Austrian banking act (BWG) amendment 2003/35 [German], ecolex 2003, p.953
212 See *Brandl/Wolfbauer*, The Austrian banking act (BWG) amendment of June 2003, ecolex 2003, p.624; *Kreisl*, Identifying the customer according to the Austrian banking act (BWG) amendment 2003/35 [German], ecolex 2003, p.950; *Schopper*, New due diligence obligations according to § 40

distance dealings, representation of the customer is only permissible in the case of natural persons without personal entitlement and legal persons within the framework of § 40 para. 1 Austrian banking act (BWG).

k) In order not to render business communication unduly difficult, § 40 Austrian banking act (BWG) prescribes *general conditions of exception* from the strict duty to identify. The strict duty to identify of the credit institution or financial institution may not be applicable in the case of third-party accounts of authorised party representatives located in the European Community. The basic requirement for this is the infeasibility of individual proof in the context of representing larger joint ownership communities of alternating composition (§ 40 para. 2 Austrian banking act (BWG)). Infeasibility is highly probable in the case of larger joint ownership communities of alternating composition. This exception is geared to the area of internal management.[213] The bank's duties to identify are basically incumbent upon the authorised party representative. For his part, this representative is subject to profession-specific duties to identify, whereby identification of the customer seems assured. For trustors whose location or place of residence is not in a cooperating state or against whom there is the founded suspicion of belonging to a terrorist association or cooperating in money laundering or terrorist financing, reduction of the duty to identify is excluded.

There are reduced formal regulations in the context of school savings (§ 40 para. 2a Austrian banking act (BWG)) since the school is obligated to check the identity of pupils when they are accepted.

The duties to identify of credit institutions and financial institutions fall away entirely if the customer is a credit institution or financial institution that is subject to the European legal requirements concerning anti-money laundering or equivalent regulations (§ 40 para. 9 Austrian banking act (BWG)).

Austrian banking act (BWG) [German], RdW [Austrian law of economics] 2003, p.349; *Fletzberger* in *Fletzberger/Schopper*, Distance Selling of Financial Services [German], p.178

213 32 document no. 22.GP, p.4

2.1.3. Duties to check and investigate

a) Owing to the large number of transactions potentially suitable for money laundering and the opportunities to circumvent the anti-money laundering system of the Austrian banking act (BWG) the duties to check and investigate – in addition to the duty to identify – are the most complex requirements on credit institutions and financial institutions set down in §§ 39ff. Austrian banking act (BWG). Duties to check or investigate concern the banking/financial institution, or its employees, respectively, in three cases in particular.

"Austrian washing machines??
Thanks – but they don't work!!"

b) If in the context of the duty to identify the identity of the customer is demonstrated by a (legal or legally transacting) representative, or if a foreign official photo ID does not include the customer's date of birth, the credit institution or financial institution must check the *authenticity* of the submitted documents and their correspondence with legal regulations. The scope of this duty should, however, be reduced to an extent appropriate to the facts of the business transaction and the knowledge of the employees. Detective work by a banking/financial institution is not required.[214]

c) If employees of a credit institution or financial institution entertain doubts that a customer is actually acting for his own account, appropriate measures must be taken to obtain information concerning the identity of the possible *trustor*. As the law appears, this obligation only arises in the case of transactions with compulsory identification. In conformity with the directive (Art 3 (7)) this obligation is, however, to be assumed in the case of every transaction if there is the suspicion that a customer is not, contrary to his statements, acting in his own interest.[215]

d) In order to substantiate the suspicion in the sense of § 41 para. 1 Austrian banking act (BWG) qualified in comparison with § 39 para. 3 Austrian banking act (BWG) that a transaction is being conducted for the purposes of terrorist financing or money laundering, investigations by credit institutions and financial institutions are required in some circumstances. These duties to investigate are initially restricted by the requirement that a suspicion must be founded in order to trigger legal consequences going beyond the duty to investigate, but knowledge or punishability of the transaction are not required. From this and from the regulations concerning other duties to check it can also be concluded that the investigations must neither be of a detective nature nor suitable for substituting the work of the prosecution authorities.

Therefore, the priority will be on the gathering and exploitation of the information that the credit institution or financial institution is able to acquire from the business relationship with the customer and on the basis of this relationship. Therefore, in the

---

[214] See 32 document no. 22.GP, p.4
[215] See *Schopper*, New due diligence obligations according to § 40 Austrian banking act (BWG) [German], RdW [Austrian law of economics] 2003, p.349

area of gathering internal information the duty to investigate is closely associated with the organisational obligations and duties to identify of the credit institution or financial institution. Usually the credit institution or financial institution can only substantiate the entertained suspicion via the opportunity to get an overview of the entirety of a customer's transactions, his general behaviours and the usual business activity. The so-called "know your customer" principle is one of the fundamental principles of money laundering prevention.[216] Therefore, it will basically be easier for a credit institution/financial institution to estimate the purpose of a transaction if there is a permanent business relationship. On the other hand, in the event of a non-permanent business relationship less strong clues must be sufficient in order to substantiate a suspicion.

The exploitation of information which an employee acquires outside the business relationship with the customer concerning the circumstances of a transaction is likewise suitable for substantiating a suspicion. Such information should therefore be included in the overall consideration of a transaction's risk.

e) Irrespective of the fact that the circumstances of a transaction whose nature suggests that it may be in connection with money laundering must be checked with particular diligence, it is not necessary to apply the same degree of investigation in all cases of a potential connection between a transaction and money laundering. Rather, the extent of the necessary investigations is determined by the individual case.

2.1.4. Organisational obligations

a) In order for the obligations standardised in §§ 39ff. Austrian banking act (BWG) particularly the duties to identify and investigate, to be able to be undertaken by the credit institution or financial institution, employees need to be appropriately informed on the topic of money laundering and terrorist financing and appropriate organisation of credit institutions and financial institutions is required. § 40 para. 4 no. 1 Austrian banking act (BWG) generally establishes on this subject that credit insti-

---

[216] See *Fletzberger* in *Fletzberger/Schopper*, Distance Selling of Financial Services [German], p.163

tutions and financial institutions must introduce suitable *inspection and communication procedures* in order to prevent transactions that are conducted for the purposes of money laundering. Employees of credit institutions and financial institutions dealing with the conducting of transactions must be familiarised with the regulations serving the prevention and combating of money laundering (§ 40 para. 4 no. 2 Austrian banking act (BWG)). The participation of these employees in special training programmes is explicitly ordered. These programmes should contribute to the employees' being trained to recognise transactions potentially being associated with money laundering and to take the correct action in such cases. Supplementary to this, employees must be regularly informed about current developments in the area of money laundering. Since § 39 para. 3 Austrian banking act (BWG) is aimed directly at employees of credit institutions and financial institutions, the obtaining of information concerning money laundering and terrorist financing by employees at their own initiative may also be necessary.

b) The introduction of inspection and communication procedures must enable rapid information exchange between employees and comprehensive access to information for employees. The adaptation of EDP systems and the optimisation of communication opportunities may be required. The appointment of a *money laundering commissioner* in every credit institution as a central point of anti-money laundering, which credit institutions undertook to do in the "Extended Due Diligence Declaration" of 13th January 1992, appears useful in any event. The money laundering commissioner should serve as a contact person for employees and as an inspector and decision maker. The money laundering commissioner is a responsible commissioner in the sense of § 9 Austrian administrative penal code (VStG).

c) The size and nature of the credit institution or financial institution is of crucial importance for the extent of the measures to be carried out. Although not expressly mentioned in the act, it can be assumed that the depicted organisational obligations should also apply in respect of combating terrorist financing and not merely in respect of money laundering.

2.1.5. Duties to report

a) Duties to report are mostly the (money laundering-suggesting) result of fulfilling the indicated obligations (particularly the duty to identify and investigate). While duty to identify, investigate and organisational obligation refer to the institution-internal area, the reporting is aimed at an authority. It is therefore a part of the information exchange between credit institutions/financial institutions and authorities.

b) If the result is a founded suspicion that a transaction that has already taken place, is ongoing or planned is conducted for the purposes of money laundering or terrorist financing (§ 41 para. 1 no. 1 Austrian banking act (BWG)), that the customer belongs to a terrorist association (§ 41 para. 1 no. 3 Austrian banking act (BWG)) or that the customer has contravened his duties to disclose as trustee (§ 41 para. 1 no. 2), the credit institutions and financial institutions must immediately inform the money laundering reporting office of the Austrian Federal Ministry for Internal Affairs. Concerning the founded suspicion, strict reference should be made to the description above.

c) All further processing of the transaction must cease from the *report* up to clarification of the facts. There is an exception to this if delaying the transaction hampers or prevents ascertainment of the facts. The rule in the event of doubt is that cash deposits may be made while cash withdrawals must be refrained from. In order to gain clarity, credit institutions and financial institutions have the opportunity to request the decision from the authority as to whether there are misgivings against the immediate processing of the transaction. If the money laundering reporting office makes no pronouncement on the request by the end of the next banking day, the transaction may be conducted (§ 41 para. 1 Austrian banking act (BWG)).

The reporting office will not be *obligated to pronounce* if it can be seen that the reporting office received only incomplete information from the credit institution or financial institution. Incomplete sending of information to the reporting office represents a breach of the duty to report of the credit institutions or financial institutions.

d) Further duties to report exist in the event of requests for payments from savings deposits for which no identity establishment has yet taken place if the credit amounts to at least EUR 15,000.00. Payments from such savings deposits may only take place following the lapse of one week following placement of the request, unless the reporting office orders a longer time bar (§ 41 para. 1a Austrian banking act (BWG)).

2.1.6. Duties to inform

The duty to inform is the counterpart to the duty to report in the exchange of information between credit institutions/financial institutions and the authority. The duty to inform is therefore the guarantor for the information flow between credit institution/financial institution and authority required for combating money laundering. In respect of the money laundering reporting office, credit institutions and financial institutions must, on request, communicate all information appearing necessary to the reporting office for the prevention or prosecution of money laundering (§ 41 para. 2 Austrian banking act (BWG)). This therefore constitutes an exception from banking secrecy.

2.1.7. Duties of secrecy

Credit institutions and financial institutions must keep all procedures serving the fulfilment of the duties to report and inform secret in respect of customers and third parties (§ 41 para. 4 Austrian banking act (BWG)). Only following authorisation by the money laundering reporting office is a credit institution or financial institution entitled to inform the customer of the postponed or refrained from conducting of a transaction. However, the customer may be referred to the reporting office even without authorisation from the reporting office.

2.1.8. Duties to retain

a) The duty to retain guarantees a minimum degree of traceability of transactions independently of an actual suspicion of money laundering or a suspicion of terrorism on the part of the credit institution or financial institution. It enables credit institutions/financial institutions and authorities to gain a better insight into the business activity of customers. The "know your customer" principle plays an important role in this connection too.

b) Credit institutions and financial institutions must retain the documents in which the identification features of customers are recorded for a minimum of five years more after termination of the business relationship with the customers (§ 40 para. 3 no. 1 Austrian banking act (BWG)). This applies for all documents which have been gathered within the scope of the duty to identify, therefore, for example, also for the confirmation by the trustee as having assured himself of the identity of a trustor. Credit institutions and financial institutions must also keep records and pieces of evidence from all *transactions* for up to five years from implementation (§ 40 para. 3 no. 2 Austrian banking act (BWG)).

2.1.9. Consequences of a breach of §§ 40f. Austrian banking act (BWG)

Pursuant to § 98 para. 2 no. 6 Austrian banking act (BWG) (for credit institutions) or, respectively, § 99 no. 8 Austrian banking act (BWG) (for financial institutions) breaching of the obligations of §§ 40 and 41 para. 1 no. 4 Austrian banking act (BWG), provided that the crime does not fulfil the facts of money laundering or terrorist financing, represents an administrative infringement and is punishable by the FMA with a fine of up to EUR 20,000.00. Responsible in terms of criminal law according to §§ 98 and 99 Austrian banking act (BWG) in connection with § 9 Austrian administrative penal code (VStG) is strictly someone who is authorised to represent the credit institution/financial institution externally. This is primarily the senior management.

There is an exception to this fundamental rule if a responsible commissioner is appointed (§ 9 para. 2 Austrian administrative penal code (VStG)). The responsible commissioner may originate from the circle of appointees to represent the credit institution/financial institution externally, but does not need to belong to this group of persons. Pre-requirements for appointment to responsible commissioner are

(i) the commissioner's place of residence in Austria,
(ii) the possibility to criminally prosecute the commissioner,

(iii) the provable consent of the commissioner

(iv) the holding of an authority to issue orders in the clearly delimited field of anti-money laundering.[217] Owing to these pre-requirements the money laundering commissioner comes under consideration as responsible commissioner in particular.

It is questionable whether a breach of the obligations of §§ 39ff. Austrian banking act (BWG) also justifies responsibility of the bank for (deliberate) money laundering by employees. Inasmuch as the obligations of §§ 39ff. Austrian banking act (BWG) refer exclusively to the prevention and traceability of money laundering crimes of third parties, but do not lay down any organisational obligations and duties to inspect with regard to an institution's own workforce, a breach of obligations probably does not lead to any attribution of money laundering to the credit institution/financial institution in the sense of the association responsibility act (VbVG). An alternative may apply, for example if – in implementation of the 3rd money laundering directive – an obligation to establish senior management approval concerning the commencement of business relationships/conducting of transactions with PEP's were to be introduced into the Austrian banking act (BWG). In this case the non-observance of the organisational obligation by the bank's decision makers may lead to an attribution of the (deliberate) money laundering by a bank employee to the credit institution/financial institution.

2.2. Digression: damage compensation

a) *Claims for damage compensation* by the customer may arise from the circumstance that, in negligent ignorance that the suspicion of money laundering or the suspicion of a contravention of disclosure regulations by trustees was incorrect, a transaction is delayed or not conducted at all (§ 41 para. 7 Austrian banking act (BWG)). Such claims for damage compensation exist neither in respect of credit institutions and financial institutions nor in respect of an employee. Since § 41 para. 7 Austrian banking act (BWG) obviously takes account of the duties to report of para. 1 leg cit, it can be assumed that incorrect suspi-

---

217 See *Hauer/Leukauf*, Administrative procedures [German], p.821

cion that the customer belongs to a terrorist association or that the transaction is conducted for the purposes of terrorist financing, is likewise subject to this regulation.

b) It is unclear, however, to what extent the standardised liability exclusion reaches. A multitude of opinions unfolded on this subject. On one hand the view is put forward that, in principle, no damage compensation claims can be raised from a negligently incorrect application of § 41 para. 1 Austrian banking act (BWG).[218] This would mean an entire liability exclusion for credit institutions and financial institutions or their employees, respectively, in the event of negligence. On the other hand it is accepted that the negligent assumption of the existence of a suspicion (founded or otherwise), which does not objectively exist, effects no liability exclusion.[219] The view is also put forward that only the opinion held in a negligent manner that a suspicion was founded in the sense of § 41 para. 1 Austrian banking act (BWG) would exclude liability according to damage compensation law.[220]

c) In order to be able to define the scope of the liability exclusion according to § 41 para. 7 Austrian banking act (BWG), it is first necessary to explain the term of *"negligent ignorance"* in the sense of para. 7. The negligent ignorance that a suspicion is false may be due to a culpable absence of information or to sufficient information being incorrectly assessed in a culpable manner. The culpable absence of information may be due to a breach of organisational obligations (the employee cannot retrieve all available information, for example) or to a breach of duties to investigate (the employee omits, for example, to obtain available information). The misassessment of available information can in turn be based on an incorrect assumption of facts – therefore on a factual error – or on the incorrect assumption that the facts substantiated a suspicion – therefore on a legal error. The act does not distinguish between these cases, meaning that initially there are no grounds for distin-

---

218 See *Vertneg*, Money launder versus duty of discretion [German], RdW [Austrian law of economics] 1993, p.329
219 See Laurer in Fermuth/Laurer/Linc/Pötzelberger/Strobl, Austrian banking act (BWG) brief commentary [German], p.502
220 See *Borns*, Austrian banking law [German], p.263

guishing between these cases of ignorance. In principle, therefore, the liability of a financial institution/credit institution or of an employee can be excluded on the basis of a negligent lack of information as much as on the basis of a negligent misassessment of available information according to § 41 para. 7 Austrian banking act (BWG). Even a combination of erroneous actions, so, for example, the incorrect legal assessment of insufficient information, could also exclude liability.

d) The second term to be investigated from para. 7 is that of "*suspicion*". Does the term "suspicion" describe only the founded suspicion in the sense of § 41 para. 1 Austrian banking act (BWG), does it also cover mere suspicion (for example, that from § 39 para. 3 Austrian banking act (BWG)) or does it only describe a subsequently reported subjective assessment by an employee of a financial institution/credit institution? As already demonstrated at another point, a founded suspicion – including that from § 41 para. 1 Austrian banking act (BWG) – is the personal probability assessment necessitated by the objective circumstances. On the other hand, a negligently assumed incorrect suspicion from para. 7 is an assessment which should not be supported at all if proper diligence is applied. The incorrect suspicion from para. 7 can therefore never be, considered objectively, a founded suspicion. If proper diligence is applied, then in most cases of negligent ignorance that a suspicion is incorrect it must even be noticeable that every suspicion is incorrect. A distinction between founded suspicion and simple suspicion is therefore superfluous, because in the cases from para. 7 it is in any case recognisable with proper diligence that the "suspicion" is incorrect. The suspicion from para. 7 can therefore represent no objective standard. It appears probable that the term "suspicion" refers to every subjective assessment leading to a report, irrespective of the probability of correctness.

e) In concrete terms it is the case that ignorance of the circumstance that a reported suspicion is incorrect triggers no damage compensation claims by the customer if the report is due to a negligent *breach of organisational obligations and duties to investigate.* The law does not draw a distinction between an entire omission to perform obligations and other behaviour contrary to duty. Only where the employee has seriously believed it possible that his suspicion is incorrect and accepts this does this liability exclusion no longer exist. Intentional desisting from fulfilling duties will routinely justify intent. Admittedly, such cases will barely have practical relevance. It is, after all, strictly in the interest of the credit institutions and financial institutions not to report their customers incorrectly.

f) In the area of (straightforward) *incorrect assessment* of information gathered according to duty no distinction – as shown above – must and can be drawn from the objective probability of an incorrect suspicion in the sense of para. 7. In other words, no distinction can be drawn between cases in which there is no founded suspicion but there is a suspicion, and cases in which neither a founded suspicion nor even one suspicion exists.

g) If a breach of duties to investigate or organisational obligations and a negligently incorrect assessment coincide, liability exclusion is likewise brought to bear. No distinction is to be drawn between cases in which a report would have been justified according to the subjectively available information, and cases in which no report would have been necessary even according to the subjectively available information. In respect of the differentiation with regard to the objective probability of a suspicion (including on the basis of subjective knowledge) the same considerations are brought to bear as with the straightforward incorrect assessment.

Further, according to the wording of the act the liability exclusion from para. 7 stands only in the event of *negligent ignorance* that the suspicion was incorrect. The liability exclusion would therefore only stand in cases in which it was recognisable that the reported suspicion was incorrect. Cases in which it is recognisable only after the transaction has been delayed that a reported suspicion is incorrect, would accordingly not be recorded. This represents no problem for cases in which credit institutions and financial institutions or their employees, respectively, behave according to duty. In any case, the illegality required for damage compensation claims is lacking here. Cases in which credit institutions and financial institutions or their employees, respectively, behave negligently in contravention of duty, but in which it would not have been recognisable even in with behaviour according to duty that a suspicion was incorrect, would not, however, be covered by the liability exclusion. There is namely no negligent ignorance of the circumstance that a suspicion was incorrect. It should not be assumed that the legislator did not wish to include such cases in the application scope of the liability exclusion. If, even with proper diligence, it is not recognisable that a suspicion is false, credit institutions and financial institutions or their employees, respectively, are at least as worthy of protection as in the event of recognisability of the incorrectness of the report. These cases are therefore to be included in the scope of application of § 41 Austrian banking act (BWG) by means of a significance conclusion.

h) It is useful to assume this broad scope of liability exclusion. It can therefore be prevented that credit institutions and financial institutions proceed excessively cautiously with regard to reporting suspicious transactions.

2.3. Banking secrecy and data protection

In principle, credit institutions, their associates, agency members, employees etc. are obligated not to disclose or exploit secrets arising from business connections with customers (§ 38 para. 1 Austrian banking act (BWG) – banking secrecy). The Austrian banking act (BWG) in § 38 para. 2 no. 2 provides an exemption from banking secrecy for the reporting of a founded suspicion (§ 42 para. 1 Austrian banking act (BWG)) and for the distribution of information to authorities in connection with the prevention or prosecution of money laundering.

The Austrian data protection act (DSG), as well, exempts the forwarding of data on the basis of an express authorisation or obligation to forward data from its scope of protection (§ 8 para. 1 no. 1 DSG).

3. Money laundering in Austrian lawyer regulations (RAO)

Implementation of the second money laundering directive[221] also brought about changes in the Austrian lawyer regulations (RAO). The obligations now standardised in the RAO are similar to the

---

221 Directive 2001/97/EC

regulations of the Austrian banking act (BWG). The differences between BWG and RAO will therefore be dealt with in the following. The profession-specific problems of implementing the 2nd money laundering directive will also be discussed briefly in the following.

3.1. Due diligence obligation

Unlike the banking act (BWG) the lawyer regulations (RAO) do not set down any general *particular due diligence obligation* (§ 8a para. 1 RAO) of the lawyer in the event of transactions whose nature suggests a connection with money laundering or terrorist financing. Particular due diligence obligation only rather arises if the lawyer collaborates in the planning or implementation of purchases or sales of properties or companies, the management of money, securities or other assets, the opening or management of bank, savings or securities accounts, the founding, operation or management of trustee companies or similar structures including the procurement of means necessary to the founding, operation or management of companies, or conducts financial or real estate transactions as a representative of his party (§ 8a para. 1 no. 1 und 2 RAO).

According to the view of the legislator a risk of money laundering may only actually arise in connection with the activity of a lawyer in the above named cases.[222] That these dealings suggest in principle a connection with money laundering or terrorist financing, is not expressed. The extent of the due diligence obligation corresponds to the diligence benchmark already existing for lawyers according to § 9 RAO.[223] The obligations standardised in the following paragraphs put the benchmark in concrete terms. It is contentious whether duties to investigate also arise.[224]

---

[222] See RV 174 Doc. no. 22 GP
[223] See RV 174 Doc. no. 22 GP
[224] See *Maurer/Manhart*, The Second EC Money laundering Directive and the Duty of Discretion of Liberal Professions [German], wbl 2004 [magazine for Austrian and European economic law], p.401; *Lausseger/Likar*, The Money laundering Regulations of the RAO and the Lawyer's Professional Profile [German], AnwBl [lawyers' journal] 2004, p.132

3.2. Duties to identify

a) In the business cases listed in § 8a para. 1 no. 1 and 2 RAO there is a *duty to identify* of the lawyer if a contract is commenced on a permanent basis, the contract sum is at least EUR 15,000.00 or there is the founded suspicion that a transaction is conducted for the purposes of money laundering or terrorist financing (§ 8b para. 1 RAO).

A contract can be assumed to be commenced on a permanent basis if (normally) the conducting of several transactions is anticipated, even if it only comes to the conducting of one transaction in the actual event. As in the Austrian banking act (BWG), it also applies according to RAO that one single transaction can consist of several proceedings. In contrast to the Austrian banking act (BWG), however, the connection between the proceedings need not be obvious. Appearance is sufficient in order to lead to the addition of individual order sums of coherent proceedings; in respect of the founded suspicion that a transaction is conducted for the purposes of money laundering or terrorist financing, a reference should be made to the remarks in the chapter concerning the Austrian banking act (BWG)[225].

b) The opportunities in the RAO for lawyers to comply with the duty to identify are similar when there is direct contact with the party to the requirements of the Austrian banking act (BWG) placed on banking and financial institutions in the event of direct contact with the customer. In principle, identification via official photo ID is necessary. However, if submission of an official photo ID is not possible, according to RAO (§ 8b para. 2 1st line) the identity of a party (or of a trustor) is permissible through an officially documented, equally evidentiary proceeding. In this connection the bodies of law give testimonials issued by the notary public as examples.

The identity of a representative or trustee must likewise be established via the submission of an official photo ID (§ 8b para. 2 RAO). The power of representation must be demonstrated through appropriate certifications. The act does not mention how the identity of the party is to be established subsequently. An analogous application of the regulations of § 40 Austrian

---

225 See from page p.149

banking act (BWG) (particularly with consultation of a copy of an official photo ID) is conceivable.

In the event of long-distance dealings the lawyer must take suitable and evidentiary measures in order to establish the party's identity reliably. The measures necessary in this context are deduced from the individual case.[226] Consultation with other persons having a duty to identify, such as notaries public or credit institutions[227], in particular, appears useful.

c) The establishment of a party's identity can be omitted if the party is a banking or financial institution which is subject to the regulations of the money laundering directive 2001/97/EC or – if based in a third country – corresponding regulations (§ 8b para. 3 RAO).

d) If the lawyer entertains doubts as to whether his client is acting for his own account, or if the lawyer knows that the client is not acting for his own account, the lawyer must apply appropriate measures to obtain information concerning the actual identity of the client (§ 8b para. 1 RAO).

3.3. Organisational obligations

Organisational obligations also concern the lawyer (§ 8a para. 2). It is paramount to remember to instruct aspiring lawyers with regard to combating money laundering and terrorist financing.[228] But training non-legal personnel can also be necessary if it is involved in the conducting of transactions tending towards money laundering.

3.4. Duties to report

a) The Austrian federal criminal police office must be informed if a party does not meet the lawyer's request for information within the context of the required identification (§ 8b para. 1 final line RAO). The lawyer is then strictly not authorised to take over or continue representation of the party.[229]

---

226 See legal regulation 174 Doc. no. 22 GP
227 See RV 174 Doc. no. 22 GP
228 See RV 174 Doc. no. 22 GP
229 See *Tades/Hoffmann*, RAO, p.22

Combating Money Laundering in Austria

b) Further, a *suspicious transaction report* must be made to the federal criminal police office if, in the cases of the transactions listed in § 8a para. 1 no. 1 and 2 RAO there is the founded suspicion (see above on this subject) that a transaction is conducted for the purposes of money laundering or terrorist financing (§ 8c para. 1 RAO).

c) There is an exemption from this duty to report if the lawyer has learned of the facts justifying a suspicion within the context of legal consultation or in connection with representing the party before a court or before an authority upstream of the court (§ 8c para. 1 2nd line RAO). Both the term of legal consultation and that of representing before a court should be understood in the broad sense. Representation before a court also covers, for example, the acquisition of information before and after a court proceeding, including consultation concerning the conducting or avoidance of a proceeding.[230] There is an exemption from the exemption in cases in which legal consultation is recognisably (to the lawyer) sought for the purpose of money laundering or terrorist financing – this is therefore a mixed subjective-objective benchmark [231] (§ 8c para. 1 2nd line 2nd main clause RAO).

A lawyer is strictly not permitted to conduct the reported transaction before and (although not specifically ordered) also after a suspicious transaction report (§ 8c para. 2 RAO). However, if dispensing with the conducting of the transaction is not possible or if prosecution is hampered, the transaction must be conducted and a report must then be made (§ 8c para. 2 final clause RAO). Otherwise, a declaration can be requested from the Austrian federal criminal police office after the report as to whether a transaction may be conducted immediately (§ 8 c para. 2 RAO). The legal consequences ordered in the RAO correspond to those of the Austrian banking act (BWG) in the event of a request by a credit institution/financial institution to the money laundering reporting office.[232]

The lawyer is strictly not permitted to inform the party of the report carried out. However, the lawyer may inform his party of

---

230 See *Tades/Hoffmann*, RAO^8, p.25
231 See *Maurer/Manhart*, The Second EC Money Laundering Directive and the Duty of Discretion of the Liberal Professions [German], wbl 2004, p.401
232 See Austrian banking act (BWG) section from p.166

the conducted report in order to prevent the party from undertaking forbidden acts or omissions (§ 8 para. 1 clause RAO).

3.5. Duties to inform

a) § 9 para. 4 RAO defines as a further exemption from the duty of discretion a duty to inform equivalent to the duty to report according to § 8c RAO of lawyers in respect of the Austrian federal criminal police office.

b) Additionally, the federal criminal police office may order that the implementation of a transaction is to be postponed. The lawyer must be informed of this without unnecessary delay. From the point in time from which the authority must inform the party, the lawyer may also inform the party of the order (§ 8c para. 3 RAO).

3.6. Duties to retain

The lawyer must keep the documents drawn on for the identification of the party in the original as far as possible. If this is not possible or is unfeasible, copies must be prepared and retained (§ 8b para. 4 RAO). For these documents as well as pieces of evidence and records concerning one of the transactions listed in § 8a para. 1 no. 1 and 2 RAO there is a 5-year *duty to retain* (§ 12 para. 3 and 4 RAO). The period in respect of the documents for the identification of a party begins to run on termination of the contractual relationship, the period with regard to the remaining documents on closing of the transaction.

3.7. Legal consequences of a breach

The culpable breach of an obligation for the prevention of money laundering represents a disciplinary delinquency. The potential *consequences* range from a written reprimand through to striking from lawyers' list (§§ 1 and 16 DSt).

3.8. Damage compensation

A similar order to the liability exclusion of § 41 Austrian banking act (BWG) is made in § 9 para. 5 RAO. Communication in good faith to the Austrian federal criminal police office according to

§§ 8a und 8b RAO should accordingly not be deemed a breach of the duty of discretion as well as of other disclosure limitations which are contractual or governed by legal and administrative regulations. Communication in good faith to the Austrian federal criminal police office implies no form of disadvantageous legal consequences. § 9 para. 5 RAO is therefore based on the wording of the directive[233] rather more than § 41 para. 7 Austrian banking act (BWG) and confronts the user with smaller interpretation problems than the corresponding regulation of § 41 Austrian banking act (BWG).

4. Politically exposed persons – PEPs

a) The Austrian banking act (BWG) and the RAO so far make no recognition of the term of PEP. An (explicit) introduction of this term into Austrian law will take place via the implementation of the third money laundering directive.[234] According to Art. 1 of the directive the member states are obligated to rule that the institutions and persons indicated in Art. 2 of the directive (Art 13 para. 4 of the 3rd money laundering directive),

- have at their disposal appropriate, risk-based risk management systems, from which it can be defined whether the customer is a PEP or not;
- must have obtained the consent of the senior management before they commence business relationships with this customer ("senior management approval");
- must take appropriate measures from which the origin of the funds used within the context of the business relationship or transaction can be defined; and
- must subject the business relationship to enhanced ongoing monitoring ("close monitoring").

In terms of content, therefore, the directive implements Recommendation 6 of the "40 Recommendations" of the FATF: for one thing, credit institutions/financial institutions will probably barely get by without suitable computer software for identifying PEP's. For another, senior management approval and close

---

233 See directive 2001/97/EC Art. 9
234 2004/0137 (COD)

monitoring are required on commencement and during the course of the business relationship.

b) According to the directive's definition, PEP's are *"natural persons who exercise or have exercised important public functions and their immediate family members or persons known to them to be closely associated".*

The directive therefore goes beyond the definition of "politically exposed persons" according to the FATF recommendations, which expressly exclude persons of medium or lower rank from the definition.

c) From the current Austrian legal view it can be said that the FMA already currently makes reference to the recommendations of the FATF and draws on these with regard to putting the obligations of credit institutions/financial institutions in concrete terms. For this reason it can be assumed that credit institutions/financial institutions already currently identify PEP's from the recommendations of the FATF and are required to pay particular attention to the transactions conducted by these persons.

d) The textual requirements concerning the manner of proceeding of credit institution/financial institutions with regard to PEP's as customers in accordance with the draft directive and the recommendations of the FATF appear largely clear. On the question as to who is to be qualified as a PEP, the following observations are permitted:

A draft of the directive (2004/0137 (COD)) saw in Art. 3 para. 10 two further cumulative pre-requirements for classification as PEP:

(i) exercising of a public office (currently or in the past) and
(ii) encumberment with complex financial transactions, sometimes with an increased risk of money laundering.

The pre-requirement indicated under (ii) was removed in the final version of the draft. All financial transactions and business relationships with PEP's from another member state of the European Union or a third country are therefore subject to the requirements of § 13 para. 4 of the directive.

e) The circumstance that, in addition to the persons who exercise or have exercised an important public office themselves, their immediate family members are also included in the definition of PEP's is understandable under the aspect of anti-circumvention concerning money laundering prevention. Although delimiting the group of persons coming into question appears to be facilitated by using the term "immediate", it would be advisable to be a little more precise when transposing the directive into Austrian law. More problems are presented by the persons likewise included in the definition of PEP's who are "known to be associated" with public officials. In this connection it appears basically unclear in which form and to whom the close association with the public official must be known.

f) Despite all necessary caution in connection with the topic of money laundering, an interpretation of the definition of PEP's and transposition into Austrian law should take place in a measured manner: on the one hand, a limited interpretation of the term of "public office" should occur. In this connection a limitation, if needs be, as provided by the FATF recommendations (exemption of persons of "middle rank and lower") would be useful. On the other hand, attention should be paid to giving credit institutions/financial institutions instructions that are as clear as possible in respect of their monitoring task, in order to produce the required legal security with regard to the tricky topic of money laundering.

D.
Combating Money Laundering in Germany

Dr. Joachim KAETZLER

1. Legal context / transposition of international measures into national law

1.1. The facts of money laundering

Money laundering is punished with imprisonment or with a fine according to § 261 of the German criminal code (StGB). An extract from the regulations reads:

> *"(I) Somebody who conceals an object which originates from an illegal act indicated in clause 2, obscures its origin or thwarts or jeopardises investigation into the origin, the discovery, expiry, confiscation or securing of such an object will be punished with imprisonment of 3 months to 5 years. Illegal acts in the sense of clause 1 are 1. crime, 2. delinquency* (... a catalogue of preliminary crimes follows).
>
> *In the cases of tax evasion committed professionally or part of a gang according to § 370a of the German contribution ordinance (AO), clause 1 applies for the expenditure saved by the tax evasion and illegally acquired tax reimbursements and credits, as well as in the cases of clause 2 no. 3 also for an object in respect of which payments have been evaded.*
>
> *(II) Likewise punished is somebody who 1. procures for himself or a third party an object described in paragraph 1 or 2. keeps it or uses for himself or a third party when he knew of the origin of the object at the point in time at which he acquired it."*

Everyone will recognise that the facts therefore come in two variants which, for one thing, are of an inherently different criminal nature, and for another, provide clues to the roots of the respective variants of the facts. Whereas the 1st paragraph clearly recalls traditional definitions of receiving stolen goods and is vested as a palpable endangering crime, the real money laundering variant corresponding to a modern understanding of money laundering according to international standards is found in para. 2 as a separate embodiment of the facts in the form of an abstract endangering crime.

Liability to punishment according to §261 para. 1 of the German criminal code presupposes, according to the wording, that a perpetrator (or his accomplice) attempts to conceal a tainted object – or money – from the public authorities in order to prevent its confiscation. Naturally, this is can only be proved with great difficulty, because only in the rarest of cases is an order, for example a money remittance abroad, carried out solely for the purposes of obscuring the origin of assets and without any economic background whatsoever. The great majority of convictions for money laundering in Germany therefore take place for breach of the further defined factual features of the second paragraph (therefore for mere self-procurement, safekeeping or use of incriminated assets). Not only in the legal respect, therefore, does para. 2 represent a subsidiary solution; the further criminal definition also serves in actuality as a "drip tray" for unclear orders where only one thing is clear: that the perpetrator, a bank employee for example, knew or thoughtlessly failed to recognise that the assets originated from a crime. The receipt of a tainted object in thoughtless ignorance of the origin of the asset is therefore punishable on its own, for example, according to § 261 Abs. 2 German criminal code (StGB). Typically occurring acts of money laundering, particularly in bulk transactions – the forwarding of payments, the receipt of cheques or cash, for example – are covered by this regulation.

Particularly striking when drawing international comparisons – as is now the case with many European money laundering facts – is the breadth of the associated preliminary crime catalogue. Although it was a declared legal policy aim of introducing money laundering culpability to actually ("only") combat organised crime by trying in a certain sense to "dry it up at its financial roots", the preliminary crime catalogue was expanded ever further. In addition to assets originating from the primal days of money laundering facts (drug dealing, terrorism or arms dealing) the receipt of objects originating from probably rather unspectacular crimes (compared with organised crime), such as simple theft, simple embezzlement, simple fraud or simple forgery of certificates, is now likewise punishable. This so-called "all-crime principle" has significantly contributed to interpretation uncertainties with money laundering facts, which in some legal regulations have changed from being "a sharp sword in the fight against terrorism" to a big drip tray for problem cases in which it was often impossible to trace the origins of the preliminary crime neatly. In the end, the accusation of money laundering was also suitable for having criminal trial measures such as, for example, a search or telephone monitoring, ordered without legal error even in the case of petty crimes.

It is particularly striking in the international respect that, according to German law, serious tax delinquencies, too, particularly the so-called "professional" tax evasion according to §370a of the German contribution ordinance (AO), are contained in the catalogue of crimes preliminary to money laundering. In other words, somebody who accepts his business partner's assets in thoughtless ignorance of his partner's tax dishonesty, be it for safekeeping, management or be it merely as an acceptance for a service in kind, such as tax consulting, renders himself liable to punishment for money laundering. Also of particular importance in Germany is the fact that not only the gains acquired directly from a tax evasion (therefore, for example, interest gains generated in the context of professional tax evasion), but also the economised expenditure, acquired tax reimbursements or credits come into consideration as objects of the crime. In the area of sales tax criminal law (in particular, therefore, the practice-relevant cases of the so-called sales tax carousel), German criminal law even goes so far that assets acquired completely legally, which, for example, are used to operate a sales tax carousel, can be the object of a money laundering crime. Though such an extensive form of the money laundering facts is expedient owing to the inclusion of tax crimes in the preliminary crime catalogue, compared internationally, however, such a broad understanding clearly goes beyond the customary.

There is discord between individual scholars, the German Federal Supreme Court and the German Federal Constitutional Court over the purpose and the actual objectives of the facts, whereby a number of interpretation difficulties and, not least, unclarities arose when weighing up the legally protected rights concerned. Compared internationally, it can certainly be said that there is a particularly large number of interpretation and implementation difficulties in Germany concerning the punishment of money laundering. For one thing, this is probably due to the low number of convictions and published judgements; there is no firm jurisprudence practice per se. For another, legal dogma errors were committed when money laundering was adopted in the criminal code (originating from 1871) through the act on combating organised crime in 1992; these errors will be dealt with later. In any event, the more detailed form was not sufficiently thought over for facts, which according to the general understanding were to serve as "a central point in the combating of organised crime". It was clear that German criminal law had urgently needed money laundering facts; however, the dogmatic and academic bases had previously been just as thin as the practical ones. Only this can explain why – necessary though money laundering culpability was – the standard commentary[235] by Fischer/Tröndle concerning the criminal code, in harmony with may other scholars, describes the concept of money laundering culpability as *"dubious from the legal policy point of view"*. According to the view of a leading criminologist, the expectation of being able to successfully combat money laundering by means of the present facts was even classifiable *"on a downwardly open scale between naive and absurd"*.

According to the view of the German Bundestag during discussions concerning the draft law, *"state administration of justice"*, *"the investigation interest of prosecution authorities"* was the decisive legally protected right and required priority protection. According to parliamentarians, as regards actual money laundering culpability in the sense of §261 II German criminal code (StGB), the affected legally protected right of the preliminary crime also implies punishment through §261 German criminal code (StGB). There is a widespread opinion that behind a stand-alone money laundering culpability there is the effort to protect the "legal financial flow", while other viewpoints stress the already mentioned [236] "concept of drying up organised crime". The German Federal Court, on the other hand, views money laundering as being endowed with its own illegality, but has not as yet put this in concrete terms. The variety of represented views – which has only been touched on – shows that the real reason why money laundering

---

235 *Tröndle/Fischer*, Criminal Code and Bylaws [German], 52nd edition., publishers C.H. Beck, 2004
236 See for example also from p.52/53

has its own inherent illegality and why punishment of money laundering is necessary beyond punishment of the preliminary crime is unclear even to many lawyers and decision makers. Even the German Federal Constitutional Court has publicly described the whole purpose of specific money laundering culpability as *"vague"* – and hereby opened the floodgates for critics and those with constitutional misgivings.

In addition to culpability of attempt (§261 III German criminal code (StGB)) German law sets down an enhanced range of sentences from six months up to ten years for money laundering in particularly difficult cases (§261 IV). There is generally a particularly difficult case if the perpetrator acts professionally or as a member of a gang which has associated itself with repeated money laundering. Again, if one bears in mind that money laundering laws are designed to combat organised crime and terrorism, the question is raised why money laundering as part of a gang, or done professionally, represents only the qualification but not the basic facts.

As intimated above, a subjective element is also required in addition to the fulfilment of objective factual features; the baker's wife who receives money from an unknown tax evader is of course not liable to punishment. In respect of subjective facts, at least *"thoughtlessness"* is required in German law, § 261 Abs. 5 German criminal code (StGB). This term differs conceptually from the internationally used concepts of "dolus eventualis" or gross negligence. The threshold of thoughtlessness is clearly higher than that of failure to exercise duty. If a perpetrator underestimates the fact that the object originates from a catalogued crime and if the criminal origin virtually comes to his mind given the objective situation, if the perpetrator disregards this at the same time out of particular indifference or gross inattentiveness, he renders himself liable to punishment. In respect of the actual act of money laundering, conditional intent is of course not required; if the perpetrator does not know that he is receiving a tainted asset at all, he is of course exempted from punishment.

The concept of culpability of thoughtlessness is based on the "romantic" preconceptions of money laundering described above. However, a dark figure without a pass, but nonetheless equipped with sunglasses, a briefcase full of money and two bodyguards will appear in front of a bank employee in the rarest of cases. Ideally, acts of money laundering today are barely distinguishable from perfectly normal bulk transactions. Therefore, to accuse a perpetrator, for example a lawyer or bank employee, of particular "thoughtlessness" generally proves to be difficult. Nevertheless, it need not be explained in more detail that prosecution authorities have far better opportunities to gain access through reduced intent requirements than in systems in which only deliberate money laundering is punishable.

Naturally, particular problems arise in profession-specific bulk transactions, for example, therefore, in banking communications, with other financial service providers, or with lawyers. In one spectacular judgement the German Constitutional Court quashed the conviction of a defendant who had merely received the fee of a client accused of investment fraud and placed enhanced requirements on the subjective pre-requirements with regard to defendants. Only with direct intent was the defendant's liability to punishment unproblematic, it said.

The judgement of the German Federal Constitutional Court naturally raises unanswered questions in respect of the subjective facts regarding the handling of other professional and case groups in which neutral activities occur routinely. If one bears in mind that, according to strict theory, even the above mentioned baker's wife who receives money for the sale of rolls from a tennis star accused of a serious tax crime, commits money laundering, this shows up the deficiencies of German regulations. In particular, expanding the facts of money laundering to proceeding thoughtlessly makes it clear that the intention is to avoid frequent past difficulties in providing proof – to the detriment of the clarity and consistency of the criminal facts. On the other hand, it is precisely for this reason that there are clear misgivings in terms of constitutional law against such thoughtlessness, often interpreted as a "hidden rule of evidence", as culpability.

After a few years of discussion in criminal law literature as to whether daily bulk transactions should not be removed from the money laundering scope of application entirely, there is now essentially unanimity that this would not really be expedient. Nowadays, money launderers purposefully hide themselves in bulk transactions. The only corrective for the still excessively broadly interpreted money laundering culpability is probably, according to today's understanding, the subjective side of the criminal facts. Whether there is a need to punish the baker's wife who takes receipt of two euro from the tax evader consciously and in knowledge of the preliminary crime is not, however, explained by this.

Not least due to the uncertainties mentioned above, the criminal facts of money laundering were the object of further decisions by the German Federal Constitutional Court on many occasions, since accused persons appealed against the practical application of the criminal facts through the courts. It is already quite clear today, twelve years after the money laundering facts were introduced, that efforts to combat organised or economic crime effectively may possibly be more successful at the primary crime level and yet only be subsidiarily successful at the money laundering level.

Simply the low number of convictions for money laundering provides food for thought. In total, in 2003 only 140 criminals were convicted for money laundering, the smallest number of them, incidentally, due to suspicion reports by financial service providers. The majority of convictions for money laundering refer to the post-crime behaviour of participants in the crime in the drugs and arms milieu and were effected in the context of criminal proceedings in the area of "blue-collar crime".

Although the retention of money laundering culpability is of course thoroughly desirable from a legal policy view, re-calibration of criminal prosecution, however, seems necessary. Back focusing on the underlying preliminary crimes at least appears worth a lot of consideration, now that, from a practical point of view, the facts of money laundering have not kept their promises in Germany up to now.

1.2. The German money laundering act (GwG)

Obligations according to industrial law for the prevention of money laundering correlate with criminal law. The regulations that are significant for the banking and financial services sector are to be found in the German money laundering act (GwG) of 25th October 1993 ("Act concerning the tracking down of profits from serious crimes"). According to the regulations of the German money laundering act (GwG), banking and financial institutions, as well as financial or insurance companies, must identify the contract partner when closing a contract for the establishment of a new business relationship, document this identification, verify it if necessary and retain the corresponding documents for six years. When accepting cash, securities or precious metals with a value of EUR 15,000.00, or when carrying out financial transactions which have an accumulated value of EUR 15,000.00 or more, the duty-bearer must likewise identify the acting person. This generally occurs via the submission of a passport or personal ID.

Lawyers, if they are active in the transaction and structuring business, auditors, real estate agents and casinos were from now on included in the general catalogue of obligations of the money laundering act through the second EU money laundering directive. The German legislator not only precipitately transposed these and the other stipulations of the second money laundering directive into national law in an unprecedented parliamentary show of strength in the wake of the events of 11th September 2001, but also added certain regulations at some points. Extending money laundering obligations beyond banks and financial service providers has, however, shown practically no political effect so far. No sufficient industry sensibilisation is currently observable among lawyers, tax consultants and real estate agents, in particular. The above mentioned groups of persons are also obligated to identify the contract partner in cases of suspicion below the EUR 15,000.00 threshold. (§ 2 para. 1 GwG). However, they are meeting their obligations only sluggishly. Of the 8,062 suspicion reports to the FIU in Germany, only 11 came from lawyers and one from a notary public; moreover, however, banks alone reported twelve more suspicious transactions on accounts related to notary publics or lawyers, respectively.

The German legislator made use of the discretionary powers set down in the second money laundering directive in the money laundering act and, due to misgivings in respect of constitutional law and due to professional ethical principles, obligated the above named professional groups not to report directly to the so-called Financial Intelligence Unit, but initially to the local professional lawyers' associations, which are already historically responsible for assessing professional ethical matters, conflicts of interest etc. Only when the local professional lawyers' associations are also of the opinion that there is indeed a suspicion of money laundering during the processing of a transaction does it appear justified, according to the view of the German legislator, to break conventional principles of professional ethics. Whether the professional lawyers' associations – as anticipated in the legislative procedure – actually do gradually develop competence centres that participate in anti-money laundering certainly appears more than questionable in the face of the low number of suspicion reports on the part of the bar in the first years following their obligation.

If, in the case of banks or other duty-bearers under the German money laundering act (GwG), facts arise from the circumstances of the transaction which lead to the conclusion that an agreed financial transaction may be for the purposes of money laundering, the transaction must be examined more closely. If, in the course of this examination, a duty-bearer observes that corresponding suspicious facts are at hand, he initiates a report in accordance with § 11 GwG to the Financial Intelligence Unit, established in Germany at the Federal Criminal Police Office.

German law sets down – as do most systems – that the suspicious financial transaction generally must not be executed unless either the public prosecutor's office has given its consent or two working days have elapsed without a response. If it is not possible to postpone the financial transaction, then it may be carried out according to German law; however, the bank employee bears the burden of proof in this case with regard to the urgency of the transaction. If a bank employee meets these obligations, he can no longer be criminally prosecuted in any event. Moreover, the German money laundering act sets down liability exclusion for issuing a suspicion report. If the bank employee (or a bearer of other obligations) has not grossly negligently or deliberately submitted an incorrect suspicion report, he is exempted from liability. However, this liability exemption only applies for the consequences of the suspicion report (such as tax damage, libel etc.) and expressly does not extend to assumption of liability for damage arising from the fact that the bank holds up a transaction for the described two days. This legal matter is simply unclarified in Germany; general state liability for holding up a transaction in aid of criminal investigations – unlike in many other European countries – is lacking.

The German money laundering act also applies for branches and companies abroad. Just like companies at home, these are also obligated to take precautions against being abused for money laundering. Conversely, branches of foreign banking institutions located in Germany are also subject to the money laundering act.

Not only the regulations of the money laundering act (§ 14 para. 1), but also the act concerning banking (§ 25 a para. 1 no. 4) establishes that banking institutions must possess appropriate business and customer-related security systems that are designed to minimise the bank's risks of being abused for money laundering. According to § 14 para. 2 German money laundering act (GwG) and also according to the banking act, banks and other persons are obligated to follow essentially four strands when combating money laundering:

- Appointment of a money laundering commissioner immediately subordinate to the senior management;
- Development of internal principles and regulatory mechanisms in order to prevent money laundering and the financing of terrorist associations;
- Assurance that employees who are authorised to carry out cash and non-cash financial transactions are reliable;
- The regular instruction of these employees concerning methods of money laundering and the obligations existing according to the law currently in force.

Moreover, banks are obligated, since 1st April 2005 in accordance with § 24 c of the banking act, to conduct a file in which they present, on the one hand, the account numbers / custodian account numbers together with the day of set-up and the day of dissolution and, on the other hand, the name and, in the case of natural persons, the date of birth of the bearer, a person with power of disposition or another form of economically entitled person. This national peculiarity, which is often criticised as "the introduction of the transparent bank customer", will be dealt with later.[237]

---

[237] See on this subject for example from p.204

1.3. Administrative practice: Announcements from the German Federal Financial Supervisory Authority (BaFin)

The more detailed placing into concrete terms of the organisational obligations of banks and other affected entities is regulated in Germany by the Federal Financial Supervisory Authority (BaFin) in the form of circulars and announcements (these are irregularly appearing publications, often compiled in the wake of modifications to international stipulations). This practice may appear alarming, because banking institutions are regularly constrained by the circulars to adapt their prevention systems at great expense. The financial burdens for functional money laundering prevention in order to satisfy the respective supervisory authority requirements require millions in financial expenditure by the individual banks. The fact that administration by means of mere administrative acts or a published administrative practice encroaches deeply on the organisation structures of banks and financial service providers appears alarming and is repeatedly reprimanded as being impermissible internationally too, because according to the view of some there is no formally sufficient implementation of the EU directives. In actuality it is more than questionable whether, in the face of legal proviso in the case of encroachments on the ownership rights of companies, effective implementation of the directives can be effected only through mere circulars. A supreme court clarification of this far-reaching legal question is still outstanding.

While banking institutions mostly accept this clear breach of the principle of the legal proviso through gritted teeth in order to avoid conflicts with the financial supervisory authority, the latter points out that the concrete terms contained in the announcements are merely the more detailed form of existing industrial obligations in any case, consequently therefore not measures of administrative, police or criminal law, but original obligations placed on the industrialist. On the other hand – according to the German Federal Supervisory Authority – legislative procedures are often too slow and therefore hardly the right means for reacting to ever more rapidly developing money laundering techniques. While the latter point basically does not appear unfounded, the supervisory authority does not recognise that the facts governed in the money laundering directives themselves are only the long-term vertices of anti-money laundering, which have predominantly remained the same for years. Facts which urgently and immediately require modifications and adaptation to criminals' potentially new money laundering techniques are not regulated by the circulars. For the remainder, the speed of the implementation of the act to modify the money laundering act in the wake of the events of 11th September 2001 shows that an act can definitely be implemented in real time if the necessity of adaptations is also recognised by politics.

The supervisory requirements on the form of money laundering prevention systems are currently (still) governed in the "Announcement of the German Federal Supervisory Authority for Banking concerning banking institutions measures to combat and prevent money laundering" of 30th March 1998 in the version of 8th November 1999. This announcement replaced its predecessor, the announcement of 30th December 1997, and further shaped the 40 recommendations of the FATF (in their version of 26th June 1996). A revision of the announcement has been announced many times, most recently for the second half of 2005, but is not in existence as yet.

In addition to the announcements there is a variety of other administrative circulars which, for one thing, transfer the list of the "non-cooperating states and territories" and other FATF documents into German law. Moreover, the German financial supervisory authority has published individual letters to banking and financial service provision institutions discussing, for example, the more detailed form of internal prevention systems or the minimum requirements on the risk analyses to be drawn up by the institutions.

In order to satisfy the standards of the German Federal Financial Supervisory Authority, banking institutions must fulfil considerable minimum requirements but are of course equally called upon to set down organisational regulations going beyond these. In the above mentioned announcement, for example, it is ruled that natural persons must strictly identify themselves with a valid national passport / ID card and – if the customer is not physically present at the conducting of the banking transaction – identification must take place only through so-called reliable third persons, consequently therefore third banks, Deutsche Post or other certified service providers. In the event that so-called professional bearers of secrets, therefore for example lawyers and notary publics, auditors or tax consultants, act as contract partners to the banking institution, the banking institution must receive a list of economically entitled persons, since, according to German experience, customers with consolidated and borrowed funds, in particular, frequently play a not inconsiderable part in the obscuring of money laundering transactions.

Behavioural obligations in cases of suspicion are also defined in more detail by the announcement. If the transaction has no recognisable economic background and its circumstances or the acting persons are non-transparent, if the type and amount or the origin of the assets or the recipient of the transaction, for the remainder, do not fit the client's life circumstances or, respectively, business activity known to the bank, or if the transaction is simply to be transacted in a circuitous manner or routes are chosen that appear cost-intensive and economically nonsensical, the banking institution is obligated to deposit a corresponding suspicion report. The required standard of certainly is described by the German Federal Financial Supervisory Authority in the following terms:

"there are objectively recognisable clues for the presence of a transaction using which illegal funds are withdrawn from the reach of prosecution authorities or using which the intention is to hide the origin of illegal assets and a background in the sense of § 261 cannot be ruled out."[238]

Clues of this type enable duty-bearers to take the necessary measures to ensure effective money laundering prevention.

At the centre of the obligations of banks, financial service providers and other industrialists and duty-bearers is the so-called suspicious transaction report (STR), which must be made to the prosecution authorities and in copy to the FIU as notification of the suspicion of money laundering. The banking institution does have – like all other duty-bearers – scope of assessment when questioning whether the transaction-related and person-related facts

---

[238] German Federal Financial Supervisory Authority, Federal Financial Supervisory Authority, circular 26/2002

are suspicious. However, a "double primary suspicion" in the criminal trial sense is not required. Even if, therefore, the money laundering consultant arrives at the conclusion that no suspicion report need be deposited, he is obligated to document the investigation and retain the corresponding documents for six years. In this way, a "paper trail" of events should at least be established which should at least give the investigatory authorities the opportunity to undertake an archaeological reconstruction of events.

The behaviour of German banks when submitting suspicious transaction reports is characterised by an increasing sensitivity for money laundering incidents, but also by the view, by international comparison, that reports of a qualitatively high standard are submitted to the Financial Intelligence Unit. If one bears in mind that the number of transmitted suspicious transaction reports amounts to only a fraction of those submitted in the USA or Great Britain, it is clear that the financial sector already puts in considerable criminological groundwork in order not to heap suspicious transaction reports of a qualitatively inferior standard onto the FIU.

Unfortunately, it is often overlooked that the success of money laundering measures is not only evident from the number of money laundering suspicion reports. A look into police criminal statistics reveals that, in the whole of Germany in 2003, for example, more than 6,000, in 2004 more than 8,000, suspicious transaction reports were sent to the German Federal Criminal Police Office, of which, however, in 2003, only 2 % led to investigatory procedures in connection with organised crime and only 5 % to investigatory procedures in connection with money laundering. In the face of the enormous costs of anti-money laundering, this ratio appears unsatisfactory in the opinion of financial service providers.

An offered financial transaction which appears suspicious to the money laundering consultant may not be conducted by the banking institution until it has received the consent of the public prosecutor's office, or the second working day following the day of the report suspicion has elapsed without the conducting of the financial transaction being prohibited by criminal proceedings. Although the banking employee, according to the money laundering act, is able to label a transaction as an "urgent case", as described above, but still carry it out — to deflect damage to the institution or the customer, for example — the Federal Financial Supervisory Authority instructs money laundering consultants in the announcement not to make use of this urgent case regulation of § 11 para. 1 clause 3 German money laundering act (GwG) if the suspicion of an act of money laundering *practically comes to mind*. However, the Federal Financial Supervisory Authority does not mention who is to take over liability for a held-up transaction in such circumstances. If individual transactions should condense into one suspicious situation, according to the view of the Federal Financial Supervisory Authority the business relationship should be subjected to longer-term monitoring by the money laundering consultant until the intervening doubts have been dispelled. If the doubts cannot be dispelled in the long term, the financial provider will break off the business relationship for reasons of risk alone.

Continuing suspicious customer accounts solely for the purpose of criminal investigation is not, of course, among the tasks of the banking institutions. In order not to prejudice investigations by the prosecution authorities, the Federal Financial Supervisory Authority recommends that, before breaking off the business relationship, banking institutions inform the responsible prosecution authorities in individual cases where they have sent a suspicious transaction report according to § 11 German money laundering act (GwG). Nonetheless, the banking institute must justify in the event of conflict why a business relationship was not terminated despite a suspicion; it thus continues to bear sole liability in terms of criminal and civil law for continued existence of the business connection.

The financial supervisory authority further prescribes the use of specific technical measures in the area of conducting transactions. In Germany, for example, a remittance system is now in use during the conducting of international payments which ensures that the name, address and bank number of the commissioning customer, as well as of the beneficiary, are indicated and forwarded in the payment order data record. The intention here is to support a paper trail and place the bank in the position to identify the origin and sender of payments with precision. This technical standard plays a major role in the handling of PEPs.

The function and more detailed form of the money laundering commissioner's area of responsibility are also clearly governed by the Federal Financial Supervisory Authority. Pursuant to § 14 para. 2 no. 1 German money laundering act (GwG) the banking or financial institution must appoint a money laundering commissioner and a deputy. He is responsible for contact with the authorities, processes bank-internal suspicious transaction reports, decides on forwarding to the responsible investigatory authorities, updates the procedures and inspections for the prevention of money laundering, trains employees and creates internal organisation structures.

A link with the international typology papers of the FATF, in which the latest trends and standards in the combat against money laundering are depicted, is also produced in the announcements of Federal Financial Supervisory Authority. The Federal Financial Supervisory Authority instructs the money laundering commissioners of banks and financial service providers to pay particular attention to those transactions which appear suspicious from the banking institution's point of view on the basis of a status report, the typology papers of the FATF or of the joint financial investigatory groups from the federal states, or other indications.

The supervisory authority broadly encroaches upon the planning supremacy of banks and financial service providers at another point as well. Outsourcing of the functions of the money laundering consultant is impermissible. The money laundering commissioner must directly report to the highest management level within the company and is to enjoy extensive independence. The money laundering commissioner and his deputy must also possess the required expertise for the fulfilment of their role; this expertise is checked by the banking supervisory authority.

In the face of this already ample catalogue of stipulations it is only legitimate that continued reference to the not inconsiderable costs of effective anti-money laundering is made by banking institutions and financial service providers. The principles outlined only roughly above provide an idea of the expenditure that banking institutions must put in merely to satisfy the minimum requirements. Although not every banking institution is affected by the catalogue of measures to the same extent (it essentially comes down to the weighting of individual business areas), the measures naturally most affect those institutions which are active in bulk transactions or have far-reaching correspondent relationships.

1.4. The Federal Financial Supervisory Authority letter of 10th August 2000 concerning corruption and misappropriation of state assets

Compared internationally, the German financial supervisory authority expressed itself relatively early on the subject of PEPs. The then BAKred had already addressed itself to all banking and financial service providers in a formal letter on 10th August 2000 in connection with the emergence of assets from known dictators and the influx of considerable sums of money from often dubiously conducted privatisation processes in states of the former Soviet Union. The letter is often overlooked in the discussion concerning the innovations of the 3rd money laundering directive. The letter reads as follows:

"I.
Illegal preliminary crimes of the facts of money laundering in the sense of § 261 para. 1 no. 2a German criminal code (StGB) are also, according to German law, the committing of corruptibility (§ 332 I and III German criminal code (StGB)) and of corruption (§ 334 German criminal code (StGB)).
Through the act on combating international corruption of 10th September 1998 (BGBl.II, 2327) the German legislator placed foreign officials on an equal footing with German officials. Therefore, the receipt of funds which were granted to foreign officials for corrupt purposes can also be an object of the crime of money laundering and therefore punishable irrespective of the place in which the corruption has taken place. This fact likewise falls under the obligation to report suspicion of § 11 para. 1 German money laundering act (GwG) to which the banks are subject.

Funds originating from corrupt sources are in circulation in the international financial system. In the past they were also invested at German banks in Germany or, respectively, transited and forwarded via German banks, which damaged the image of individual banks.

The Federal Supervisory Authority for Banking deems it necessary to point out to banking institutions the connection between the corruption of foreign officials and money laundering. When entering into a business relationship and receiving funds, banking institutions should allow the diligence required according to the money laundering act to prevail in this matter too and take the necessary securing measures in accordance with § 14 para. 2 no. 2 and 4 German money laundering act (GwG).

II.
A similar connection to the one between corruption and money laundering exists for German banks also in the case of funds originating from the misappropriation and abuse of public funds of foreign states. Though these assets, provided that no professional committing or committing as part of a gang of one of the catalogued crimes of § 261 para. 1 no. 4 German criminal code (StGB) is at hand, have not previously been an object of crime in the sense of the German money laundering facts in every case (cf. § 261 para. 8 German criminal code (StGB)), it should be considered that overlaps with such facts or, respectively, corruption, are definitely possible in the individual case.

The German Federal Supervisory Authority for Banking deems it appropriate, for this reason and in the interest of the financial centre of Germany, to apply the same duties of diligence also to persons exercising prominent public functions for a foreign state or, respectively, to natural and legal persons who – recognisably for the institution – are closely associated with these persons, when entering into a business relationship and receiving assets and to desist from forwarding transactions if the institution is obliged to assume that these originate from the embezzlement of public funds of third countries and are therefore in connection with acts of embezzlement.

Breaches of these diligence obligations are moreover liable to cast doubts upon the legal compliance of the senior management."

Although it appears welcome from the point of view of the banks that the financial supervisory authority had taken up the topic of the misappropriation of state assets – and hence the PEP problem – at such an early stage, the content of the letter is somewhat astonishing. Under para. II it is set forth that, in some cases, the misappropriation of state assets is possibly not to be regarded as industrial embezzlement or, respectively, as a crime punishable abroad. Consequently – in formal terms – no suspicion of money laundering would be possible, since the pre-requirements for a preliminary crime according to § 261 para. 1 German criminal code (StGB) would not be in place. As a result – according to the formal view – a banking institution would also have no occasion to deposit a suspicious transaction report because there are no crimes of theft, embezzlement or other crimes according to the preliminary crime catalogue, committed professionally or as part of a gang, at hand. Nevertheless – according to the financial supervisory body – corresponding simple misappropriations or embezzlements, or misappropriations or embezzlements not subject to punishment in the individual countries, are *generally* sufficient preliminary crimes, though, in the sense of the banking supervision law, meaning that the institutions are *generally* urged to deposit a suspicious transaction report.

In actuality the banking supervisory authority's approach is understandable. The money laundering consultant is generally not able to estimate whether a misappropriation is committed as part of a gang or even threatened with punishment at the place of the crime, for example in a developing country, with ultimate certainty. From the theoretical side this letter is, however, barely comprehensible and again appears problematic with regard to the intervention competence of the financial supervisory authority; the administrative briefing requires of the banks a non-justified breach of banking secrecy even in cases in which no money laundering cannot be at hand owing to a lack of a sufficient preliminary crime.

The barely convincing-sounding justification that banks are exposing themselves to reputational risks is definitely not in proportion with the threat openly articulated in the final clause of the letter to withdraw an institution's banking licence if it does not comply with this administrative briefing. Whether the financial supervisory authority in Germany has done banking institutions and the matter of anti-money laundering a favour by this circular remains an open issue here. On the other hand, however, the weakness of the money laundering facts is shown in its conduct, the expressions of which are possibly understood differently in banking supervision law and in criminal law. There can be no other justification for the above mentioned letter.

1.5. Overlaps with tax laws and so-called "automated account querying"

Value is being placed on an interlocking of money laundering and tax law to an increasing extent at the international level. This interplay between the two groups of standards is particularly strongly pronounced in Germany.

It has already been mentioned that, in Germany, the facts of *"professional tax evasion"* according to § 370a German contribution ordinance (AO) can be a crime preliminary to money laundering. Moreover, there are remarkable overlaps in Germany in respect of procedure too. Owing to the introduction of the so-called "Al Capone" principle in the German money laundering act (GwG) as a follow-up to the 2nd EU money laundering directive, the transmitted records may – in so far as a criminal proceeding for money laundering has been initiated against the accused – be communicated by the public prosecutor's office to the financial authority too and used for the implementation of taxation or tax criminal proceedings. Conversely, § 31b German contribution ordinance (AO) enables financial authorities to provide facts leading to the conclusion of a suspicion of money laundering and coming to light in the course of a taxation process to the prosecution authorities in breach of tax secrecy.

Though the modifications of the German money laundering act based on the 2nd EU money laundering directive had been celebrated as a great breakthrough of the "Al Capone" principle, it must be pointed out that in Germany, for example, the duties to identify according to money laundering and tax law had led a parallel existence since time immemorial. How closely associated money laundering prevention and tax law are in Germany is ultimately demonstrated by the regulation of § 154 German contribution ordinance (AO), according to which the identity of an account holder must also be established precisely for the purposes of taxation. Identity checks according to money laundering and tax law can, however, of course be undertaken in one operation. The modifications following the 2nd money laundering directive therefore produced only a link between the two disciplines, which have been anchored in German laws for a long time.

More recently, the so-called "automated account query process" according to § 24c of the banking act has particularly been the focus of – sometimes bitter– discussion. With equal taxation of all individuals in mind, highly extensive access rights of the financial supervisory authority to individual customer master data have been permissible in Germany since 1st April 2005, predominantly in favour of financial and tax authorities. At the tax law level § 24 C German banking act (KWG) corresponds with § 93b German contribution ordinance (AO), which governs the pre-requirements of a request on the part of the tax authorities. The essential principles of automated account query are easy to describe.

On the basis of § 24c German banking act (KWG) the financial supervisory authority now has the opportunity to seek names online in a purposeful way, in order to find out at which banking institute a suspicious citizen is keeping accounts. The data base therefore provides the financial supervisory authority with the opportunity to establish whether an account exists or has existed within the last three years. From the point of view of supervision law this duty to query only exists for the inspection of stipulations according to supervision law. Only the account number can be deduced from the request; transactions, potential credit or the type of account cannot be deduced from the data base query.

However, the financial authorities also have access to this data query according to § 93 para. 7 German contribution ordinance (AO). To this end a special "application order" was created on 10th March 2005, governing the pre-requirements in detail. A query may only take place if a request for information made to the taxpayer has previously failed or promises no success from the start. "Shot-in-the-dark queries", feared by many in the press, should thus be prevented. Neither the banking institution nor the customer may initially be notified of a query. However, this occurs subsequently in the tax statement.

Although a fully automatic account query will probably only be available to the full extent in a few months, owing to not yet fully developed technology, supervisory authorities are already making ample use of their intervention competence right now. Within the first month – according to reports in the German press – 2,000 requests were already registered at private banks alone, which were evidently processed manually. The numbers alone lead to the assumption that it is not – as planned – about individual queries, but that the financial authorities are systematically attempting to improve data quality during taxation.

Although these organisational measures of the "transparent bank customer" appear alarming in respect of constitutional law, the German Federal Constitutional Court rejected one local bank's urgent request aimed against the introduction of automated account querying. In the decision of 22nd March 2005, however, the German Federal Constitutional Court also expressly emphasised that overall, no decision had therewith yet been taken concerning the unconstitutionality of the regulations on automated account querying. It will therefore remain to be seen whether not only the theoretical body of standards, but above all its practical implementation on the part of those entitled to gain access, will likewise take the high benchmarks of the German Federal Constitutional Court into account.

The considerable expenditure which in turn is established for the institutions will probably – that much is at least already clear – lead to a further rise in transaction fees for the end customer. No prognosis can as yet ventured as to the benefit of universal automated account querying – which is really intended to enable queries into individual items of data in individual cases.

2. Sanctions and risks for banking institutions and bank employees

There are risks of culpability or the risk of a fine for the institution, for bank employees concerned with the matter, potentially also for bank management boards or other members of the senior management if a banking institution is brought into contact with acts of money laundering.

2.1. Risks for banking institutions

Unlike other states, German criminal law recognises no responsibility of companies in terms of criminal law. Consequently, criminal law sanctions in Germany concern the employees of the banking establishment who are responsible in each case. According to German criminal law dogma, corporate liability is excluded due to a lack of the possibility to attribute *"personal reproachability"* or, respectively, personal *"guilt"* to a company.

Criminal law liability of a banking company or another financial service provider due to money laundering or participation in another party's money laundering is therefore ruled out; on the other hand, a fine according to administrative law can be levied against a legal person without a second thought. Owing to the fine capped at EUR 500,000.00, the German administrative offences act naturally only has a very limited deterrent effect. The regulation of § 30 para. 5 German administrative offences act (OWiG) also represents a serious obstacle to effective corporate prosecution. If a fine is imposed according to the German administrative offences act, this excludes all possible measures for siphoning off profits according to the criminal code. Although the sense of this regulation can be easily seen – the aim is to avoid double sanctions and a clear delimitation of administrative offence and criminal law – it will probably have fatal effects particularly in the area of combating money laundering. It is becoming clear that the reference to straightforward administrative offence law is only an "emergency solution". The creation of corporate criminal law in the actual sense, on the other hand, is a distant concept owing to dogmatic misgivings of criminal law theory in Germany, meaning that in this regard no systematic improvement can be expected yet, at any rate not in the immediate future.

It is a similar case in the area of breach of obligations arising from the money laundering act, too. Nonetheless, in the 3rd EU money laundering directive, too, whose Art. 35 and 36 demand that member states demonstrate effective punishment mechanisms in the event that banks do not, for example, fulfil their duties to report, the responsibility of banks in Germany is shifted to administrative offence law, governed in § 17 German money laundering act (GwG). Here, maximum limits of EUR 100,000.00 apply.

If serious deficiencies with regard to the internal organisation of a money laundering prevention system can be proven against an institution, this can lead to a revocation of the banking licence on the part of the financial supervisory authority, §§ 35 para. 2 no. 3 in connection with § 33 para. 1 clause 1 no. 7 German banking act (KWG).

Beyond this there are no impending state sanctions for the affected company. The reputational risks[239] which do of course arise due to money laundering activities will be dealt with later at another point.

2.2. Risks of culpability for acting bank employees

If a bank employee or another person concerned in the regulatory scope of the money laundering act behaves in a reproachable, therefore thoughtless, manner by rendering financial services on the illegitimate activities of a criminal, then the bank employee concerned renders himself liable to punishment for money laundering and has to reckon with consequences ranging up to imprisonment of up to five years or with a fine. If the bank employee operates as a member of a gang or conducts money laundering in a professional form, prison terms of up to ten years are even possible.

2.2.1. Thoughtlessness

As described, a bank employee renders himself liable to punishment even by accepting tainted assets, conducting transactions or entering into business relationships with criminals and in so doing acting *thoughtlessly*, therefore not necessarily with intent, i.e. knowingly and deliberately.

Typically, the bank employee acts *"thoughtlessly"* if the criminal origin of the concerned assets from a catalogued crime comes to mind after the circumstance, but the bank employee disregards this out of particular indifference or gross inattentiveness. In the case of bulk transactions – for example when an employee enters bank remittances – the difficulties already mentioned are naturally the result in this connection. The accusation of thoughtlessness

---

239   See from p.273

should therefore, according to current German law, be evaluated against the respective industry standards. If the bank employee has complied with the industry-standard precautionary measures when conducting a transaction, the criminal accusation is easily mitigated. However, if the bank employee omits to make obvious queries, where necessary a further check or investigation of the customer or a transaction, even though this is urgently necessary according to internal or industry-standard benchmarks, he therefore exposes himself to a suspicion of thoughtlessness.

Scholarly efforts to raise the thoughtlessness threshold in individual professional groups, particularly in bulk business, failed. Only in the case of defendants who, where applicable, already expose themselves to risk by merely accepting a fee originating from a serious crime, has the German Federal Constitutional Court placed higher requirements on evidential proof and ordered a reduction of the criminal facts. However, in respect of bank employees the thoughtlessness limit remains.

2.2.2. Exclusion of culpability owing to reporting, and its coverage

In addition to the suspicious transaction report according to the German money laundering act (GwG), criminal law also sets down a specific liability exemption / relief, not harmonised with the money laundering act, owing to the reporting of an act of money laundering to the responsible authorities.

From the point of view of criminal law the bank employee can escape the impending criminal consequences by subsequently reporting in accordance with § 261 para. 9 or 10 German criminal code (StGB).

This possibility of a retrospective notification represents, according to the predominant opinion in Germany, a case of *"active remorse"* after completion of the actual crime and, in any case, has nothing in common with the suspicious transaction report according to the German money laundering act (GwG). Whereas the suspicious transaction report according to the GwG is submitted to the responsible authorities in view of prevention, in the case of the notifications according § 261 paragraphs 9 and 10 German criminal code (StGB) these are genuine charges and a culpability privilege is involved. The proportion of the suspicious transaction report according to § 11 GwG and of the notification according to § 261 para. 9 German criminal code (StGB) or of other measures according to § 261 para. 10 German criminal code (StGB) is not clarified with ultimate certainty.

However, there are no indications of any kind that a criminal ever actually made use of the opportunity to bring a subsequent charge. This in turn makes it clear that the standard of § 261 German criminal code (StGB) is, in terms of detail, constructed in a completely half-baked and dysfunctional manner.

Practically the most important question is of course raised with regard to the consequences of a suspicious transaction report for the bank employee according to the money laundering act. By human estimations a bank employee ought to emerge exempted from punishment if he submits a suspicion notification according to § 11 GwG due to a suspicion of money laundering. However, material criminal law in § 261 German criminal code (StGB) completely fails to make any mention on this point. The legal issue is simply unclarified. Although a number of things speak for the exemption from punishment of a bank employee who reports a transaction in the event of suspicion in breach of banking secrecy, but conducts the transaction nonetheless, it is equally clear that this can only apply to a limited extent in the case of deliberate action by a bank employee who deliberately undertakes money laundering for a customer and hopes that the public prosecutor's office sees no occasion to stop the transaction. However, the act is also completely silent on this subject. Clarification would definitely be appropriate in order to at least give a certain degree of legal certainty to bank employees, who deposit thousands of suspicious transactions reports. This considerable deficiency is, unfortunately, only one of many examples that show how little criminal law and money laundering act are in tune with each other in Germany.

Another very significant deficiency is the restriction of exemption from punishment by means of notification (be it according to the German money laundering act or according to material criminal law) to money laundering culpability. If a bank employee helps an industrial tax evader in securing his assets and if the bank employee has the corresponding intent to do so, then the bank employee possibly renders himself liable to punishment according to § 257 German criminal code (StGB) for aiding and abetting. The suspicious transaction report alters nothing in this case. Subsequent notification according to § 261 para. 9 or 10 German criminal code (StGB) is also not relevant to culpability due to aiding and abetting. With regard to the criminal acts, aiding and abetting and money laundering are very similar in conceptual terms. It possibly appears hardly appropriate in some cases to leave a balance of culpability with the bank employee following a suspicion transaction report or a subsequent notification according to the German criminal code (StGB). However, German law sets this down.

It is clear to everybody that cases exist in which the bank employee was already a participant in the bank customer's preliminary crime. For example, if a bank employee manages the assets of the bank customer and supports the customer in evading taxes, then he is liable to punishment for abetting tax evasion. German criminal law in § 261 para. 9 clause 2 German criminal code (StGB) sets down that a participant in the preliminary crime is not punishable for money laundering. If it is, however, not clarified whether the bank employee who conducts the suspicious transaction has already cooperated in the tax evasion, then in the large majority of cases a conviction for money laundering and not for aiding and abetting tax evasion would take place by way of the so-called *Postpendenzfeststellung*, that is, establishing liability for a subordinate subsequent offence.

2.2.3. Exterritorial effect of German criminal law?

According to § 261 para. 8 German criminal code (StGB) a bank employee is also liable to punishment if the assets concerned originate from a similar crime abroad if the crime is threatened with punishment abroad. In this connection it is not necessary for literally identical culpability to be involved abroad; in any case, the actual proceedings abroad must be sufficient for a conviction. This is essentially the case with regard to most criminal facts for which the facts of money laundering had been created. There are only differences in this context in respect of national peculiarities in Germany, for example in respect of tax evasion conducted professionally or as part of a gang according to § 370a German contribution ordinance (AO). This does not represent a crime, for example, in Switzerland; the facts of "tax fraud", subject to a considerable prison term in Switzerland, are different in terms of definition.

Pursuant to § 3 German criminal code (StGB) the territoriality principle also applies in Germany. There are no exceptions for money laundering. Since according to § 9 German criminal code (StGB) a crime is committed at the place where either the outcome of the criminal act occurs or the criminal act itself is undertaken, connections abroad are only conceivable with difficulty. In the event that a banking institution abroad receives tainted assets, the applicability of German criminal law is generally only actually possible in the event of serious crimes of obscuring according to § 261 para. 1 German criminal code (StGB) because – even if the criminal acts are undertaken abroad – the outcome of the crime, namely the obscuring of the origin, possibly takes place in Germany. If, therefore, a bank employee actively undertakes bogus accounting entries or similar serious breaches of obligation and with the intention to obscure the origin of a criminal's assets, then an application of German criminal law is not impossible provided that there is a sufficient link with German territory.

However, with regard to bulk transactions – such as payments – as described above – culpability generally comes into consideration only according to § 261 para. 2 German criminal code (StGB) (receipt, safekeeping etc. of incriminated objects). In this case, both the criminal act (receiving) and the outcome of the crime (receipt) of the abstract endangering crime occur abroad; generally, the German money laundering act is accordingly not applicable to such straightforward foreign crimes.

2.3. Criminal law risks for the agents of the bank and the money laundering consultant

Liability of company agents is being called for ever more frequently in Germany. However, a look into the law could well confuse readers who are not familiar with German criminal law dogma. § 14 para. 1 German criminal code (StGB) rules that, if someone acts as a legal person's agent with authorisation to represent, criminal law is even applicable to him if *"particular personal qualities, relationships or circumstances"* justify culpability and these are at hand not with the agent, but with the legal person. This is extended to commissioners or department managers in § 14 para. 2 German criminal code (StGB). Strictly, this ought to also include the money laundering commissioners of banking institutions.

Yet the regulation does not mean – and this is incomprehensible for the foreign reader – that the presence of criminal intent or other personal features in the agency member or the senior manager is assumed. § 14 of the German criminal code does effect a general expansion of culpability, but is not intended to break the principle of intent and guilt. § 14 German criminal code (StGB) is merely intended to shift obligations actually concerning the company to the person who is acting for the company.

Consequently, the managing director of a bank only renders himself punishable for money laundering if he realises a criminal act of money laundering in the actual individual case himself and at least thoughtlessly. Since a bank's managing director makes decisions concerning the commencement of a business relationship only in very rare cases and probably only rarely makes decisions concerning individual transactions, a potential risk of culpability is restricted to these cases and correspondingly easier to control.

Culpability of a bank's managing director for money laundering due to omission also does not generally come into consideration if there are organisational deficiencies in the area of money laundering prevention. It is not the aim of German criminal law to render organisational lapses punishable by prison sentences, at least not as long as the actual criminal act is not in concrete form. If, on the other hand, an agent of the bank omits an organisational measure in breach of duty in the knowledge that an act of money laundering is thereby enabled and committed in an actual individual case, then the culpability of the agent is at least not excluded. The planned crime must, however, already be in sufficiently concrete form.

Of course, the institution is then threatened, however, with the administrative law consequences described above, right up to cessation of business operations and considerable fine payments;

further, the company director must confront the question of whether he still possesses the required aptitude for managing a financial service or banking institution.

The liability risk for the money laundering consultant proves to be far more difficult. According to the stipulations of the financial supervisory authority, the money laundering consultant is commissioned in the place of the duty-bearer, for example the bank or the financial service provider, to check transactions and hold them up where necessary, deposit suspicious transaction reports or effect the breaking up of a business relationship.

The money laundering consultant is therefore particularly closely associated with all potential criminal acts of money laundering and, following checks, also realises the implementation of individual critical transactions where applicable, even though a suspicion of criminal behaviour had existed prior to implementation of the transaction. If, contrary to the view of the money laundering consultant, a transaction subsequently turns out to be an act of money laundering, the money laundering consultant has potentially realised all objective factual features of money laundering personally.

Once again, it essentially comes down to the subjective side of the crime. Since in Germany, as described, *"thoughtless"* money laundering also comes into consideration, it is not necessarily required for a criminal accusation that the money laundering consultant acts with intent or even collaborates with the criminal. However, the law does require him to carry out a diligent check on the suspicious transaction and to comply with industry standards in the process. Although it definitely comes down to the individual case when judging whether the efforts of a money laundering consultant were sufficient, it must nevertheless be emphasised that simple failures to fulfil obligations are not sufficient.

The important thing in this connection is neat documentation of the checking procedures – as soon as the money laundering consultant can prove that he has checked obvious facts and complied with internal stipulations in the process, culpability will probably generally not exist if delinquencies, minor misestimations or other failures to fulfil obligations have occurred to him.

There are no indications in Germany to date that a money laundering consultant of a larger banking institution was punished for money laundering.

3. Difficulties when dealing with PEPs in Germany: obligation to contract, data protection and bank secrecy

The special handling of PEPs has already been described nation-specifically in the "Austria section"[240] or from the international viewpoint, respectively[241]. In Germany, too, banking institutions and financial service providers predominantly make use of electronic screening systems in order to check whether politically exposed persons are among their customers. If such a customer is discovered, the money laundering consultant subjects this customer to precise checks; the senior management decides on the commencement or continuation of the business relationship.

Germany is going to translate the stipulations of the 3rd EU directive into practice. It is to be hoped that the regulations concerning PEPs will be effected via a modification to the money laundering act, not via an administrative circular of the type described above. Details of this are not yet known.

---

240 See from p.179
241 See from p.51

Joachim KAETLZER

"Connected with PEPs?"

From the viewpoint of the individuals concerned, the high requirements of the banking supervisory authority on the business relationship with politically exposed persons pose, of course, entirely their own specific questions in connection with national law. The banking institution could – in the extreme case – in view of the considerable and cost-intensive measures associated with a business relationship with a PEP, simply refuse to open up a corresponding business relationship at all. If one bears in mind that, according to the current legal situation in Germany at least, there is no obligation to contract placed on banking institutions according to constitutional or straightforward law, this possibility definitely cannot be dismissed. The question is definitely raised whether it really can be the aim of effective anti-money laundering to make access to the formal banking system considerably difficult for one section of the population – and thereby potentially drive them, in many parts of the world, into informal banking systems or non-transparent trustee companies. The aim of effective anti-money laundering around the world should not be to allow such parallel systems to come into being. However, experience shows that German banking institutions are not very accommodating when it comes to the question of the "whether" of a business relationship; experiences with reputational damage, which a number of German institutions have had after accepting assets from PEPs in this decade, will probably rather reinforce this trend.

From the viewpoint of the PEPs concerned, questions of data protection are naturally also raised. The question whether an individual has a claim to information in respect of the banking institution, whether the individual is recorded on a "black list", is unclarified in Germany to date, at least judicially. In the face of the extensive rights to information and the restrictive handling of data storage according to German data protection law (BDSG), this appears more than doubtful. Legal bases forming the foundations of intervention for financial institutions and which could protect these institutions from pointless court trials do not currently exist. The upcoming modifications of the regulations in respect of PEPs can therefore potentially only be managed by creating corresponding elements of intervention.

The commercial service providers providing banks and financial service providers with automated screening programmes have so far predominantly avoided this problem. Service providers merely bundle pieces of information already available to the public and make these available to the banking institution.

However, in the case of institutions' own black lists, in which institutions' own assessments are reflected, this legal issue turns out to be a little more difficult. How jurisprudence will deal with corresponding claims to information against the background of the right to informational self-determination and of the regulations of the German federal data protection act, remains to be seen.

Consequently, the question is naturally also raised as to what extent the "black lists" are judiciable as such. On this point, too, there is neither established jurisprudence nor an established legal opinion from banks or banking supervisory authorities, respectively. This is of course of little help for effective anti-money laundering.

In any case, complaints have been piling up against banking institutions in recent years in connection with suspicious transaction reports. There is an increasing trend among citizens who view themselves as being violated in their informational self-determination by the suspicious transaction report according to § 11 of the German money laundering law, and who have possibly suffered indirect asset damages as well, to attempt to make banks liable for this. Should this trend continue, it would not be improbable that, one day, classification as a "PEP" could also be appealed against before a court by the individual concerned.

Equally unclarified is the question of who actually assumes liability when a banking institution holds up an individual transaction because, for example, it perceives the payment recipient to be a criminal potentate. Damages are therefore particularly conceivable since the banking institution – barring the urgent case solution – is bound to hold up the transaction for 48 hours initially. Damages arising from delay and arrears are possible in this connection. Whereas, in other European countries, and also outside Europe, subsidiary state liability is under discussion, corresponding questions have not as yet been discussed in Germany. The question should at least be raised as to whether banks, which practically act as the long arm of prosecution and financial authorities, are now supposed to bear the risk for near-sovereign behaviour in addition to the incredible costs.

4. Business or not — The tightrope between business interests and the general public interest

It has already been mentioned briefly that the interests of banking institutions and their owners are naturally in the direction of generating earnings that are as high as possible from the banking transactions on offer. This implies keeping the costs of money laundering prevention as low as possible and possibly also consciously taking justifiable risks, also with regard to individual private customers.

Standing in opposition to this is the bank's function as a custodian of the general public interest. It is certainly accurate that it is not the task of banks to catch embezzling despots or drug dealers; an association of banks as "deputy police officers" would be of as little help as it would be misleading. It is, however, the duty of banks to avoid the perversion of their own services as effectively as possible and to ensure that – should a bank customer abuse the services of the bank for the purposes of money laundering – a suspicious transaction report is dispatched to the investigatory authorities, just as every department store reports a shoplifter. Further, it is indispensable that the bank assists in compiling the paper trail in any case, if the constitutional pre-conditions for breaking bank secrecy are in place.

Portrayals of money laundering often suffer from the fact that the role of "watchman" at the entrance to the legal financial system is attributed to banks, as which they are virtually expected to undertake "public tasks". Mention has already been made of the misgivings against the gatekeeper problem; unlike the case with drug crimes, in the area of embezzlement of state assets, for example, the money has typically already been in the legal cash flow for a long time.

A certain publicly-oriented duty cannot be denied, however. According to the view of the German Federal Financial Supervisory Authority, it is indeed a question of obligations which are associated with the nature of the industry and accordingly are not of a police or criminal law nature. However, principally in the area of PEP handling, it is clear that obligations to cooperate in the identification of despots, for example, who have embezzled state property, are definitely in the public interest; furthermore, that the bank will usually view the obligation not as such, but as a defence mechanism for its own risks. In the past, risk models associated with business management in the area of anti-money laundering collided with inflexible obligations and regulations which encroach upon the conducting of industrial operations.

Owing to the change in dogma from the "rule-based" to the "risk-based" approach, which was recorded in the 3rd EU money laundering directive, both spheres are now combined. From the point of view of risk alone, a bank can potentially have a self-interest in entering into a business relationship that is a little dubious. However, in no event can it have an interest in doing business with an obvious criminal.

According to the formerly predominant Anglo-American "rule-based approach", this conflict of aims between earnings aspirations and effective money laundering prevention was resolved by having a bank operate a more offensive reporting policy. The buzzword "take it, but report it" represented a handed-down view of the financial sector, which ultimately also perverted the regulatory systems with which money laundering was supposed to be prevented. The effect of this "rule-based approach" was an incredibly high number of suspicious transaction reports which were unusable to a far higher extent than is now the case under consideration of individual risk criteria. Contrary to popular opinion, expenditure was not reduced for banking institutions with the radical change from "reporting by steamroller" to the more flexible, institution-dedicated risk-based approach. Customised risk scoring is definitely far more difficult to manage than a broad reporting policy where every transaction above a certain amount is simply documented and reported as suspicious.

5. Conclusions: Risk models as decision aids

The change in dogma which ultimately has banks falling back on the system of risk appraisal well known to them is unreservedly welcome. Banking business is a risky business. Account is taken of this in various areas of supervisory law. Within the context of the equity requirements according to the "Basel II" agreement, the so-called operational risks are likewise decisive for equity costs.

The management of reputational risks in the group therefore integrates itself outstandingly within bank structures. Not a few institutions have begun to shift money laundering and compliance roles from the legal area of responsibility to their risk management departments.

It may be expected that banks' risk scoring systems in the area of money laundering prevention will become equally as refined as the PEP lists of institutions and superordinate organisations. This is also unreservedly welcome. The banking industry has accepted the challenges set to it by a sustainable financial market of the future. Although many open questions remain in terms of detail, the financial service sector is justified in hoping that a change of image will soon come about.

Internally, money laundering consultants must avoid being perceived as pessimistic "business brakes" and will therefore be motivated to shape their risk prevention systems as precisely as possible. Externally, banking institutions should indeed avoid the impression that they are acting as "deputy police officers" to the financial authorities or public prosecutor's office. However, a modern banking institution must make it clear in its public relations that ethical principles influence the business model more and more. Only in connection with successful risk minimisation can the behaviour of financial service providers be sustainable and workable.

E.
Combating Money Laundering in Switzerland

Dr. Peter BOSSHARD

Dr. Peter Bosshard was born in Zurich, Switzerland on 15th May 1942. He studied jurisprudence and economics at the University of Zurich and gained his doctorate as Dr. iur. in 1968. He acquired the lawyer's licence same year. After two years' studying and working in New York he entered the lawyers' office of Wyss & Partner in Zurich, where he specialised in economic and insolvency law. In 1998 he opened the advocacy office Bosshard Rechtsanwälte in Zurich. He is a member of the administrative boards of various Swiss banks and industrial and trading companies. From 1981 to 2002 he was president of Christian Blind Mission International, a globally active organisation for the prevention and treatment of eye diseases.

Dr. Peter Bosshard began to collect contemporary Swiss art in 1970 and today possesses the country's largest private collection of this type. He co-founded the *Zürcher Kunsthalle* art gallery in 1985 and was its president for the following eight years. He chairs numerous cultural foundations.

1. About the term

The traditional definition, dating from 1984, that, "Money laundering is the process by which one conceals the existence, illegal source, or illegal application of income, and then disguises the income to make it appear legitimate" was adopted into the money laundering regulations of the Swiss criminal code in 1990. The money laundering act (GWG) of 1997 is also based on this term.

Naturally, the term "diligence" during financial transactions is still not exhaustively defined even in the Swiss money laundering act (GWG) and the guidelines of the Swiss Federal Banking Commission (SFBC). Although Arts. 3 to 8 GwG put this duty of diligence into concrete terms adequately, a certain degree of individual and profession-specific discretion remains. Due diligence is also based on the actual situation, under consideration of profession-specific characteristics.[242]

Concerning the term PEP (politically exposed person), the guidelines of the SFBC established the definition, "*Person exercising an official public function*". The Wolfsberg and FATF principles[243] supply the concrete terms: heads of government and state, members of a royal family; supreme court judges, party functionaries, military or state-owned industry heads; heads of an international global or religious organisation. It depends on the individual case whether and to what extent closely associated family members or trustees of the above named persons should be classified as PEPs.

2. Evolutionary history

The recommendations of the FATF – to which Switzerland has belonged since the beginning, therefore since 1989 – were applied only tentatively in the banking sector at first, and then in the remaining financial intermediary field. Correcting and completing

---

242   See BBl 1989 II 1089
243   See the international section for further information on the Wolfsberg banks (from p.43) or the FATF, respectively (from p.35)

this was one of the principal tasks of the Swiss money laundering act (GwG) of 1997.

In addition to the FATF recommendations, the EU directive of 1991 (updated in 2001) was also the benchmark and guideline for the regulations of the GwG and its enactment decrees, particularly in the area of duty to report. The "Wolfsberg Guidelines and Principles" were then also taken into consideration from 2000.

3. Regulation and self-regulation

Since individual financial intermediaries, especially banks and lawyers, are subject to strict professional secrecy (Art. 47 Swiss banking act, BankG, Art. 231 Swiss criminal code, StGB), it was useful and necessary, in addition to the sovereign regulation of the facts of the GwG, to annex a self-regulation mechanism in the form of a supervisory authority from intermediaries' own ranks as well. This widespread institution, essential for the Swiss understanding of authority regulations, is expressed, for example, in the professional etiquette of the Swiss bankers' association (VSB 03) or, among others, in the SRO regulations of lawyers and notaries public. There are twelve such self-regulatory organisations in total in Switzerland.

According to Art. 18 GwG, SROs are all subject to inspection by the Swiss Federal Tax Administration. The executive orders are ruled at the money laundering regulations control office as well as in many directives from the control office.

4. Success

The preventive effect of the Swiss money laundering act is predominantly evident in the falling number of suspicious transaction reports made to the reporting office. Whereas 863 suspicious transaction reports were submitted in 2003, these decreased for the first time in 2004, by 5 % to 821. An increase has been seen in reports from the straightforward banking sector (13 % to 340), an indication that banks have been more keen to report and more cautious in general – <u>too</u> cautious, as many groups are expressing during the discussion stage of a package of legal modifications in the course of adapting to the new FATF recommendations. The intention is to reduce the international forerunner's role in anti-money laundering allegedly held by Switzerland to a tolerable extent, i.e. in the service of the financial centre of Switzerland.

With 1311 reports processed in 2004, all of 49 cases resulted in a court judgement. That is 1.8 % of the cases forwarded to the prosecution authorities and 3.7 % of the cases processed.[244]

On the one hand, this ratio indicates the rash implementation of the suspicion report mechanism, on the other hand, how difficult pithy criminal law coverage of money laundering facts is. The shunting of international financial transactions from the financial centre of Switzerland to the known (tax) oases of offshore jurisdictions must probably be evaluated as a "success" of Swiss money laundering regulation efforts.

5. Legal context

5.1. Regulations concerning money laundering in the Swiss criminal code (StGB)

5.1.1. StGB Art. 305bis

This regulation is the actual money laundering article and punishes *"somebody who undertakes an act that is liable to thwart investigation of the origin, the discovery or confiscation of assets which, as he knows or must be aware, originate from a crime"* with imprisonment or a fine, in serious cases with imprisonment of up to five years and a fine of up to one million Swiss francs.

A serious case is particularly at hand if the perpetrator a) acts as a member of a criminal organisation or a gang that has formed for the exercising of money laundering, and b) generates *"a major turnover"* or *"considerable profit"* through professional money laundering.

---

[244] See also at this point the statistics section of this publication from p.313

5.1.2. StGB Art. 305ter

This article also renders punishable the activity of a financial intermediary who, as part of his profession, "*accepts, keeps, invests or helps to transfer*" third-party assets punishable according to Art. 305bis and "*omits to establish the identity of the economically entitled person with the diligence appropriate in the circumstances*". In these cases the punishment is prison for up to one year, detention or a fine.

The right to report, respectively the impunity of a report (and the immediately ensuing blocking of assets) is also expressly stipulated in para. 2 of this article: Financial intermediaries are entitled (but expressly not obligated) to report to Swiss prosecution authorities "*observations that lead to the conclusion that assets originate from a crime*".

5.1.3. StGB Art. 260^{quinquies}

Finally, this regulation places all actions concerning (aiding) terrorist financing under the maximum punishment of up to five years' imprisonment. "Terrorism" is every "*violent crime through which the population is intimidated or a state or an international organisation is forced into an act or omission*".

5.2. Money laundering act with ordinances

5.2.1. Swiss federal act of 1997

The Swiss money laundering act (GwG) is particularly designed, in addition to combating money laundering, to "*guarantee diligence during financial transactions*" (Art. 1).

The regulations of the Swiss money laundering act apply in accordance with Art. 2 for all financial intermediaries (FIs), therefore for

- Banks in accordance with the Swiss banking act,
- Fund management in accordance with the Swiss investment funds act,
- Insurance in accordance with the Swiss insurance supervision act,

- Securities traders in accordance with the Swiss stock exchange act,
- Casinos in accordance with the Swiss casinos act.

However, FIs are also "persons who, as part of their profession, accept or keep third-party assets or help to invest or transfer them", therefore, in particular, trustees, asset managers, lawyers and notaries public (Art. 2 para. 3).

Arts. 3-8 govern duties of diligence, among them the identification of the contract party on the basis of evidentiary documents (Art. 3) as well as the establishment of the economically entitled person(s) (Art. 4).

If, in the course of the business relationship, doubts arise as to the identity of contract parties or economically entitled persons, then the identification / establishment must be undertaken again (Art. 5).

The FI must clarify the economic background and the purpose of a business relationship or an individual transaction, particularly if there clues that assets (could) originate from a criminal activity or be subject to the power of disposition of a criminal organisation (Art. 6).

The FI must compile evidence concerning every enacted transaction and conduct its necessary clarifications, in such a form that an informed third person is able to judge compliance with the Swiss money laundering act (Art. 7).

And, finally, the FI must take organisational measures necessary for compliance with the Swiss money laundering act, namely in respect of staff training and inspections (Art. 8).

Arts. 9-11 govern duties in the event of suspicion of money laundering: in the event of *"founded suspicion"* in the sense of Swiss criminal code (StGB) Art. 305bis or Art. 260^{quinquies} there is the duty to report. The only exceptions from this are lawyers, who are subject to the professional secrecy of Art. 321 StGB (Art. 9) in their traditional forensic or consultancy activity (therefore *not* when undertaking "mere" asset management).

The FI must immediately block the assets entrusted to him that are connected with the suspicious transaction report. The asset block must be maintained for five working days from the report at the longest. Neither persons concerned nor third parties may be informed of the block. (Art. 10).

As already stipulated in Art. 305ter Swiss criminal code (StGB), the FI cannot be made civilly or criminally liable either for the report or for the asset block *"if he has proceeded with the diligence appropriate in the circumstances"* (Art. 11). Here lies the crux: where does the rash suspicious transaction report and block end, where does the "founded suspicion" following diligent clarification begin?

Arts. 12ff. govern supervision. Art. 17 determines that the Swiss Federal Tax Administration sets up a control office if dedicated supervisory authorities are not already deployed for this purpose. Self-regulating organisations according to Arts. 24ff. are subordinate / obligated to report to this control office. The control office notifies the reporting office in the event of "founded suspicion" of punishable acts in the sense of Art. 305bis and 305ter. The reporting office (Art. 23), for its part, which is managed by the Swiss federal office against organised crime, lodges criminal charges with the responsible (cantonal or confederate) prosecution authorities (public prosecutor's offices, federal bar) in the event of "founded suspicion" that assets originate from a crime or are subject to the power of disposition of a criminal organisation.

5.2.2. Ordinances concerning the Swiss money laundering act (GwG)

The executive orders concerning the Swiss money laundering act are contained in various ordinances, for example in the control office ordinance and the reporting office ordinance (MGwV). Business relationships with enhanced (legal and reputational) risks are described in more detail in the ordinance of the Swiss Federal Banking Commission for the Prevention of Money Laundry (GwV-EBK). Such enhanced risks are namely deduced from:
- Place of residence and nationality of the contract party and of the economically entitled person,
- Nature and location of the business activity of the contract party and the economically entitled person,
- Absence of personal contact with contract party and economically entitled person,

- Nature of the requested services or products,
- Amount of the introduced assets as well as their inflows and outflows,
- Country of origin or destination of future payments,
- Deviation from stipulated transaction types, volumes and frequencies,
- Physical delivery of assets and
- Business relationships of/with PEPs.

Among the *"enhanced duties"* of diligence in comparison with the general duties of diligence according to Art. 3-8 GwG are, according to Art. 17ff. GwV-EBK, additional clarifications in the event of increased risks if these can be performed with *"appropriate effort"*. What "appropriate effort" is, however, is not explained.

Arts. 24ff. GwV-EBK govern behaviour in the event of indications of money laundering as follows:

- If the *"founded suspicion"* already appears during negotiations to commence business relationships, then the FI breaks off these negotiations and sends a suspicion report to the reporting office (Art. 24).
- If, within five days of a report, the FI receives no order from the prosecution authorities concerning maintenance of the block, "*he can, at his own discretion, decide whether and in what context he wishes to continue the business relationship*" (Art. 26).

Another crux: if the FI has no "founded suspicion", but has made observations from which it can be concluded that assets (could) originate from crime, he can make use of the right to report according to Art. 305ter para. 2 StGB (exemption from punishment and liability) (Art. 27).

In the event of breaking off dubious business relationships without a report (lacking a founded suspicion), "he may permit the withdrawal of significant assets only in such a form that allows the prosecution authorities to follow the trail (paper trail)" (Art. 28). A dubious business relationship may not be broken off or the withdrawal of significant assets permitted in the event of recognisably "imminent authority security measures" (Art. 28 Abs. 2).

5.3. Self-regulation

5.3.1. Professional etiquette of the Swiss Bankers' Association (VSB 03)

These rules of etiquette, benchmarks in Swiss banking, are contained in an agreement of 2nd December 2002 by the Bankers, Association with the signatory banks. They agree:

- To take anti-money laundering measures by undertaking to identify their contract partners and the individual transactions and, in the event of doubt, to obtain an explanation from the contract partner concerning the person economically entitled to the assets,
- Not to render active assistance to capital migration,
- Not to render active assistance to tax evasion by submitting incomplete or misleading certifications.

Banks must not misuse their foreign branch offices covered by professional etiquette in order to circumvent professional etiquette.

The agreement contains detailed regulations concerning how the identification of contract parties and economically entitled persons is to take place. In marginal note 29 to Art. 3 it determines that in the event of *"serious doubts"* as to the correctness of written declarations by the contract party which are not *"eliminated through further clarifications"*, commencement of the business relationship or conducting of the transaction must be refused.
Pursuant to Art. 6 para. 3 the bank is obligated to break off relations with the contract party if the suspicion comes to mind from the business transactions that the bank has been deceived during the identification of the contract party or of the economically entitled person, or if doubts (continue to) exist even after repeated or supplementary clarifications.

5.3.2. Lawyer SRO regulations

Out of the permitted twelve self-regulating organisations, that of the lawyers is definitely the most prominent. Its regulations, passed in August 1999 and revised in August 2005, contain lawyer-specific executive orders, namely concerning due diligence obligations and special duties to clarify in accordance with Arts. 3-8

Swiss money laundering act (GwG) as well as the duty to report (Art. 10 GwG).

Art. 8 GwG (Special Duties to Clarify) reads as follows:

Using the clues for the existence of money laundering the lawyer, as FI, must decide whether the proposed transaction or business relationship is unusual and/or risky. The lawyer must know his contract party well in order to be able to decide whether a transaction is "unusual". He acquires this knowledge by compiling a profile of the contract party and by continuously observing the nature of the transaction attentively.

The lawyer uses a specially designed reporting form for the suspicious transaction report according to Art. 9 GwG. For the duration of the blockage of the credit according to Art. 10 para. 1 GwG the lawyer need inform neither the persons concerned nor third parties, nor the SRO about the report that has been made. However, the lawyer can let the SRO know about a report that has taken place without naming names.

Art. 41-46 of the new SRO/Swiss Lawyers' Association regulations govern the special duties to clarify, particularly transaction monitoring (Art. 44).

5.3.3. Regulations of other SROs

To date there are twelve SROs, which have all passed their own, profession-specific executive regulations or professional etiquette concerning the relevant articles of the Swiss money laundering act (GwG), for example the Association of Swiss Asset Managers, the "Swiss Leasing Association", the Chamber of Trustees, the Swiss Insurance Association, the Swiss Post Office and, finally, the general self-regulatory association Polyreg, which covers all FIs not accommodated in any other SRO.

5.4. International regulations

The "Global Anti-Money Laundering Guidelines for Private Banking" of 30th October 2000, together with the "Guidelines on Suppression of the Financing of Terrorism" of 11th January 2002 of the so-called Wolfsberg Group are just as much a Swiss banking standard as the Wolfsberg "Anti-Money Laundering Principles for

Correspondent Banking" of 5th November 2002 or the Wolfsberg "Statement on Monitoring Screening and Searching" of September 2003.

"The Forty Recommendations" issued by the Financial Action Task Force on Money Laundering (FATF) on 20th June 2003, containing in particular regulations on international cooperation and the handling of PEPs, also became integrated into Swiss anti-money laundering regulations.

Switzerland has had treaty ties with the EU via the Bilateral Agreements I since 1st June 2002 and via the Bilateral Agreements II since 1st October 2004, without being an EU member.

Although this does not directly bind Switzerland with the actual implementation of the money laundering directives, Swiss money laundering regulations overlap with the regulations of the EU directive to a large extent. This is not least because the EU draws/drew substantially on the expert recommendations of the FATF, which after all had been co-founded by Switzerland.

The problem of international legal assistance from the Swiss point of view in connection with compliance with Swiss banking (customer) secrecy, particularly with regard to tax evasion / fraud, will be returned to later under item 7.

6. Practical organisation by institutions

6.1. Banks

6.1.1. General compliance

The practical executive orders for the prevention of money laundering are governed in the ordinance of the Swiss Federal Banking Commission of 18th December 2002 (GwV-EBK), in the agreement concerning the professional etiquette of the Swiss Bankers' Associations of 2nd December 2002 (VSB 03). According to Art. 10 GwK-EBK, organisation of a bank's prevention mechanism must be assured via internal instructions. These instructions should predominantly govern:
- the criteria for ascertaining business relationships (Art. 7) and transactions (Art. 8) with enhanced risks and

- how these enhanced risks are recorded, restricted and monitored; staff training (Art. 11); (particularly IT-supported) systems for effective transaction monitoring (Art. 12); creation of an internal central money laundering technical office, consisting of one or a number of persons specially qualified for the task depending on the size of the institution (Art. 13).

A Swiss bank having branch offices abroad or leading a financial group with foreign companies must record, restrict and monitor its legal and reputational risks associated with money laundering (Art. 9 GwV-EBK).

6.1.2 "Enhanced Customer Due Diligence"

Additional clarifications in the event of enhanced risks must be carried out in accordance with Art. 17 GwV-EBK *"with appropriate effort"*, particularly in respect of:

- Origins of the introduced assets,
- Purpose of withdrawn assets,
- Plausibility of larger payment entries,
- Origin of the assets of contract parties and economically entitled persons,
- Professional and business activity of contract parties and economically entitled persons,
- The question whether a PEP relationship is involved in the case of contract parties or economically entitled persons.

These additional clarifications may include in particular, according to Art. 18 GwV-EBK:

- Introduction of written and/or oral information from contract party and economically entitled person,
- Visits to the place of business activity of contract party and economically entitled person,
- Consultation of generally accessible public sources and data bases,
- Inquiries with trustworthy third persons such as, for example, (foreign) correspondent banks etc.

The bank must always evaluate the result of these clarifications from the standpoint of plausibility (Art. 18 para. 3). Additionally, the bank must also safeguard the privacy of persons concerned during these clarifications (data protection) (Art. 18 para. 2). It can delegate these clarifications to third persons – naturally under the responsibility of the bank; however, documentation must be conducted at the bank itself (Art. 19).

Clues for carrying out enhanced customer due diligence are contained, for example, in Annexe A to the professional etiquette of the Association of Swiss Asset Managers[245] of 20th August 1999.

6.1.3. Senior Management Approval

The commencement of business relationships with enhanced risks requires the consent of a senior person or function (Art. 21 GwV-EBK). According to Art. 22 GwV-EBK the commencement and, where applicable, continuation of business relationships with PEPs must be decided by the highest senior management.

"Allow me – My name is PEP(pino)"

---

245 Web address of the Association of Swiss Asset Managers: http://www.vsv-asg.ch

6.1.4. Close Monitoring

Business activity and the individual transactions of a relationship with enhanced risks are of course subject to a bank's close monitoring.

According to Art. 6 VSB 03 the procedures to establish and document according to Art. 2-5 must be repeated with every change with regard to the identity or signature authorisation of contract parties or economically entitled persons. The same also applies when deficiencies are observed or when doubts arise.

The relationship must be broken off if such deficiencies or doubts cannot be dispelled or if there are indications that the bank has been deceived with regard to identification of contract parties and economically entitled persons and with regard to business purpose or a transaction.

6.2. Lawyers

Lawyers are not subject to a duty to report and hence also to revise according to Art. 9 para. 2 GwG if they act in their actual professional activity subject to banking secrecy according to Art. 321 Swiss criminal code (StGB). The lawyer is active in his own professional sphere – and is therefore strictly bound to the professional secrecy protected according to Art. 321 StGB – if he carries out financial transactions in the context of his forensic or advising (i.e. contractual) activity.

However, as soon as lawyers have taken receipt of, managed and forwarded assets, for example as a management board consultant of a company specifically created for the purpose, in execution of a *"non profession-specific, accessory business activity"*, they as FIs in the sense of Art. 2 GwG are obligated to report and inspect.

The valid due diligence obligations are retraced in the regulations of SRO lawyers of August 2005 in Art. 22ff. The special duties to clarify, document, monitor, retain and report are explained in detail there.

Close monitoring is a particular responsibility of lawyers; they must conduct a transaction list for incoming and outgoing amounts (Art. 44). Lawyers must undergo further training each year and compile an annual report to the SRO/Swiss Lawyers' Association.

If the number of persons conducting a subordinate activity, or the complexity of the mandates requires special organisational regulations, it is necessary to approve internal guidelines (Art. 59) and internal training (Art. 57).

Agents of the SRO (who are themselves lawyers for reasons of safeguarding professional secrecy) revise the dossiers to be kept from time to time.

7. Conflicts

7.1. Banking secrecy

Swiss banking (customer) secrecy according to Art. 47 of the Swiss banking act, in which the bank customer, and not for example the bank, is the bearer of the secret, by no means applies definitively but is cancelled by criminal law (e.g. through Art. 305bis and 305ter) and now also by the Swiss money laundering act in respect of criminal investigation and reporting authorities.

7.2. Professional secrecy

Lawyers' strict professional secrecy concerning duty to certify and inform according to Art. 321 Swiss money laundering act only does not apply against authorities according to item 3 of this article if confederate and cantonal laws cancel this official secrecy. This is applicable in the case of relevant criminal law regulations as well as of Swiss criminal law regulations in respect of criminal investigation authorities.

Lawyers may, as mentioned, only refer to professional secrecy with regard to actual *"activity as a lawyer"*, not, however, as an FI in the context of money laundering facts.

7.3. Data protection

Customer protection in the area of data transfer is guaranteed to a limited extent in the case of banks and lawyers. Art. 18 GwV-EBK records that clarifications must be conducted with enhanced due diligence obligations whilst safeguarding the privacy of the persons concerned.

Lawyers must not inform the reporting office of the name of the person concerned when making a suspicious transaction report.
In the event of opening criminal investigations, data protection is, however cancelled, likewise in cases where Switzerland grants legal assistance to foreign authorities. According to Art. 19 of the ordinance on data protection, the confederate data protection commissioner must be informed in the event that data are delivered to foreign authorities.

7.4. Legal assistance, particularly in tax matters

Official assistance to foreign authorities is always granted by Switzerland if delinquencies or crimes of (Swiss) criminal law are <u>rendered credible</u> (therefore not proven).

Accordingly, tax evasion[246] does not fall under the liberal state interpretation predominating in Switzerland, but qualified tax fraud[247] does (therefore, for example, in the case of tax evasion in connection with certificate forgery etc.).
In order to handle the cancellation of bank secrecy in this area, Switzerland agreed to the so-called EU interest taxation from 1st July 2005, which subjects the earnings of EU citizens in Switzerland to an automatic 15 % (from 1st July 2011 35 %) tax. In return, Switzerland received a permanent exemption with regard to legal assistance in the case of direct tax crimes from the EU on 19th May 2004 (there is a separate anti-fraud agreement for indirect taxes).

8. Weak points or room to manoeuvre?

Various regulations of the Swiss money laundering act (GwG) and the corresponding profession-specific regulations are (deliberately) formulated in a way that needs interpreting. They will probably also be responsible for ensuring that the success of the GwG reports is extremely modest:

---

[246] Definition is found in the Swiss federal act concerning direct federal tax, Article 175.1
[247] Definition is found in the Swiss federal act concerning direct federal tax, Article 186.1

- When, for example, is a suspicion a founded suspicion, as this is required in the GwG Art. 9 or in Art. 24 GwG-EBK the FIs <u>duty</u> to report?
- How long is the effort <u>appropriate</u> that the FI must apply according to Art. 17 GwG-EBK if he is required to recognise "enhanced risks"?
- According to Art. 9 GwG-EBK the FI is not only to globally record and monitor money laundering and terrorism financing in foreign branch offices or foreign financial companies, but to <u>restrict</u> them. What does that mean (according to what law) in concrete terms, beyond establishment and reporting?
- How can the <u>privacy</u> of the person concerned be <u>preserved</u> if the FI needs to undertake clarifications in the area of the enhanced due diligence obligations according to GwV-EBK Art. 17/18?
- The FI must check the plausibility of the results of the (special) clarifications (Art. 18 para. 3 GwV-EBK). When are results of this kind sufficiently <u>plausible</u>, so that a suspicious transaction report can be refrained from?
- And when are transactions <u>unusual</u> in the sense of lawyers' SRO concerning Art. 8 GwG, so that they give rise to extended clarifications and, if the need arises, a suspicious transaction report?

While the *"necessary diligence"* in the sense of Art. 3ff. GwG – always referring to the individual case – can still be defined in concrete terms to a certain extent, these are terms lying within the discretion of the individual FI and mark the weak points, but also the appropriate rooms to manoeuvre, within legislature all about the subject of money laundering.

9. A question of reputation

It must be said that a large amount of <u>personal discretion</u> is asked of the individual FI, the reporting authority and finally the criminal investigation authority in all of these cases. Therefore, Art. 26 GwV-EBK opens the floodgates for the use or abuse of the FIs "personal discretion" when he is asked to decide at his own discretion "whether and in what context the business relationships" are to be continued in the absence of an authority decree.

The question comes to mind of whether every FI and every controlling authority applies this discretion, for its part, <u>in a responsible manner</u> on the one hand or, on the other hand, also in a manner <u>appropriate to the circumstances</u>. In all places where "personal discretion" comes into play it ultimately becomes a question of the reputation of the institution or individual FIs of whether and when which money laundering regulatory agents are applied.

F.
Money Laundering Law and Fundamental Rights

Dr. Wilfried Ludwig WEH

As a lawyer, Wilfried Ludwig Weh is managing director of Weh Rechtsanwalt GmbH with its head office in Bregenz/Austria and consultation facilities in Vienna.

Born in 1952 as the son of a lawyer, he graduated from the humanistic high school in Bregenz. After achieving a High School Diploma in Norwalk, USA, he studied legal sciences and languages in Innsbruck, Dijon, Santander, Strasbourg and Madrid. In 1976 he gained a doctorate in canon and civil law after already achieving his appointment as a court interpreter for English, French and Spanish. This was followed by employment as a university assistant, a court practice for a total of nine months, a three-year internship at the European Human Rights Commission and, on 1st January 1980, entry into the lawyers' office in which he is active to this day.

His focus is on matters of constitutional law, human rights and Community law – and above all on their implementation in everyday legal practice. He regularly represents private clients before the Supreme Courts and both European Courts in Strasbourg and Luxembourg. He is the author of a monograph concerning implementation of Community law in national legal regulations and of multiple publications concerning matters of his specialist areas nationally and internationally. He also has a varied role as a lecturer.

He is married and has two sons at university.

A basic rule in chess says: "Be wary of obvious moves". There is a similar rule for human rights encroachments. It many cases it would be logical to forbid something, and the individual fundamental rights encroachment would even be defensible, but its overall effects – viewed integrally – can no longer be so.

The intention at this point is to describe the stipulations of International and European law, together with the basic features of the constitutional laws of the authors' countries of origin, and undertake a few basic considerations concerning the human rights conformity of anti-money laundering measures.

1. The Council of the European Union

Founded as Europe's community of nations after the Second World War and arising from experiences of human rights violations during this war, the Council of the European Union set itself the goal of promoting democratic and constitutional developments in Europe.

Today, nearly all the countries in Europe are members of the Council of the European Union, just as democratically elected governments are in exalted positions in almost all countries in Europe.

Important agencies of the Council of the European Union are the Minsters' Committee and the Deliberative Assembly, whose delegates are parliamentarians from the Member States. The members of the Deliberative Assembly are therefore not directly elected to their European role. The Deliberative Assembly of the Council of the European Union meets, like the totally different, democratically elected European Parliament (of the European Communities), in Strasbourg.

The Council of the European Union set itself the goal of finding cooperative solutions for various legal fields in Europe. The Council of the European Union's conventions are international law agreements holding the rank of international law regulations in the Member States.

Many of these conventions are only directed towards the Member States that subsequently implemented them. Such conventions are often extremely effective and have accomplished a lot in Europe, the European Social Charter, for example. However, implementation also sometimes turns out to be tough and sluggish, sometimes it even going on "eternally".

However, the flagship of the Council of the European Union is the

2. European Convention for the Protection of Human Rights and Fundamental Freedoms

In short, the European Human Rights Convention (EHRC).

Whereas many of the people born at the time the EHRC was being elaborated and decided on have now retired or are about to do so, the European Human Rights Convention continues to look young and unspent. Every citizen in Europe having a grievance against a high court decision by a member country (even by another country) can turn to the European Court of Human Rights (ECHR) if he has exhausted all national legal means in vain. The ECHR conducts a complex process of legal formalities, at the end of which it decides whether the Member State has breached the European Human Rights Convention.

The former division into the European Human Rights Commission and the European Court of Human Rights was abandoned in the second half of the 1990s in favour of an integrated Court of Justice, at which private individuals' unrestricted right to appeal also stands. Everyone can appeal to this Court of Justice, and will be awarded damages and redress at the end of the process if the Court of Justice has established a breach of human rights.

Some of the human rights are of great importance for this book's theme.

Art. 6 of the Human Rights Convention guarantees a fair process in civil and criminal matters. There is a legal claim to a decision by an independent and non-partisan court within a useful period.

The presumption of innocence applies for every person suspected of a crime; only after guilt has been legally proven can somebody be described as being guilty of a crime. The presumption of innocence not only provides protection in respect of state agencies, but also in respect of private individuals. Therefore, for example, § 7b of the Austrian media act renders a media breach of the presumption of innocence punishable by strict sanctions ranging up to considerable fines.

Every accused person has the right to certain procedural minimum guarantees in a criminal trial. These also include being informed in comprehensible language, within the shortest possible time, of all details of the grounds for the criminal charge that has been raised. Art. 6 EHRC also firmly guarantees the right to be able to defend oneself sufficiently and sufficiently prepare the defence, and the right to pose questions to witnesses for the prosecution. The ECHR checks these requirements strictly – almost half of convictions take place owing to a breach of this fundamental right.

According to Art. 8 EHRC everybody has a claim to respect for his private and family life, his home and his correspondence.

This regulation is broadly applied in practice. Moreover, the decisive factors are not the German translation of the Human Rights Convention, but its two original versions in English and French, which have the following wording:

> *"Everyone has the right to respect for his private and family life, his home and his correspondence."*

or, respectively,

> *"Toute personne a droit au respect de sa vie privée et familiale, de son domicile et de sa correspondance."*

Many aspects that become relevant in connection with anti-money laundering fall under this regulation.

The scope of meaning of the term "home" is much broader than that of the German term *Wohunung*; it guarantees the protection of a home as a place of personal retreat, the focus of life interests, intimacy.[248] Art. 8 EHRC also protects, among other things, against unjustified house searches.[249] The collecting of personal

---

248 See ECHR judgement *Gillow* of 24th November 1986, no. 9063/80
249 See ECHR judgement *Chappell* of 30th March 1989, no. 10461/83

data in secret must be restricted to cases of unconditional necessity and strictly controlled.[250]

The scope of meaning of the English and French "correspondence", respectively, "correspondance" goes much further than the German term, *Briefverkehr*. It denotes every type of person-related data exchange and naturally covers all types of communication via telephone or electronic data carriers of whatever kind, from fax and the exchange of e-mails, internet queries, through the calling up of account management data, right up to the data exchange of personal data material. Therefore, for example, the recording of telephone numbers is also included in the protected scope of Art. 8 EHRC.[251]

According to the Human Rights Convention, individual fundamental rights should not be viewed for their own sake, but in association with other fundamental rights. Art. 10 EHRC, the fundamental right of freedom of opinion, also plays a role here. The fundamental right of freedom of opinion not only includes the right to exchange information and opinions, but also the right not to have information *circulate*.

A multiphase examination procedure must be conducted in the event of encroachments upon the fundamental rights of private and family life or freedom of opinion, respectively. It should first be examined whether a state sanction encroaches upon a fundamental right.

If the existence of an encroachment is affirmed, this encroachment must be based on a legal standard that is precisely described and publicly made known. Every state intervention must therefore have a recognisable, clearly described legal basis. Standards that do not fulfil these requirements of determination and notice form no suitable basis for a fundamental rights encroachment.

Every intervention must also be in aid of a goal recorded in a catalogue of goals. Only when an intervention is suitable for achieving the goal is it goal-compliant. Of particular interest here are the

---

250 See ECHR judgement *Klass* of 6th September 1978, 5029/71 concerning monitoring act "G 10"
251 See ECHR judgement *Malone* of 2nd August 1984, no. 8691/79

legitimate goals of anti-crime measures and the protection of the rights of others.

Finally, an encroachment upon one of these fundamental rights – as fundamental rights with the proviso of material intervention – is only permissible if it is unconditionally necessary and proportionate in a democratic constitutional state. In turn, an intervention is only proportionate if it is appropriate and if milder forms of intervention are not sufficient for achieving the goal. There must be "a pressing social need".

The two fundamental rights to private and family life and to freedom of opinion are, in addition to Art. 6 EHRC, among the most frequently judged fundamental rights regulations of the Human Rights Convention. It has been decided that telephone number records fall under the protected scope of these fundamental rights.[252] Many of the interventions described in this book go beyond the intervention intensity of such telephone number records in any case.

The Human Rights Convention also expressly guarantees the right to chose a defence lawyer. There is compulsory defence in the case of serious criminal matters. Absolute confidentiality of information between defence lawyer and client is standard. Complete guarantee of confidentiality of conversations with defence lawyers is an indispensable pre-requirement for the accused person's being able to plumb every opportunity for defence in the criminal trial. For this reason, correspondence between lawyers and accused persons in custody must be kept absolutely free of censure, as the Court of Justice had to rule many times before Austria, too, believed it.[253]

In addition to this are the fundamental rights, not so directly decisive for the object of the examination, to personal freedom and safety,[254] the right to form associations that serve legal purposes,[255] and the basic right to property.[256]

---

252 See ECHR judgement *Malone* of 2nd August 1984, no. 8691/79
253 See ECHR judgement *Pfeifer and Plankel* / A. of 25th February 1992, no. 10802/84
254 See Art. 5 EHRC
255 See Art. EHRC
256 See Art 1 additional protocol concerning EHRC

According to the EHRC, the state is not only obligated not to encroach upon fundamental rights, it can also be obligated to actively protect fundamental rights. It must therefore also guarantee a protective framework against private encroachments.[257] As the bearer of exclusive authority, the state must ensure that its citizens are protected against encroachments and are also placed in the position to have corresponding legal defence opportunities against encroachments. Every Member State is therefore obligated to create courses of law so that every person affected can also assert the breach of his fundamental rights up to court level.[258]

In any case, in all four of the states to be discussed here there is the opportunity to appeal to a court that can then examine the legality of the action with more or less comprehensive powers of decision in the event of fundamental rights encroachments.

3. European Community law

The European Economic Community has been in existence since the end of the 1950s. While the European Economic Community was originally founded by six continental states with similar legal traditions, it now covers 25 members which, in some cases, have completely different legal traditions. The linchpin holding this complicated construct together is a nonetheless observable common European history and a nonetheless existing European background of the adoption of Roman law and Greek philosophy.

One of the goals of the European Community is the creation of the so-called Single Market.[259] This is intended to guarantee a uniform legal sphere for market matters in the Community region. This Single Market appears to be implemented to a certain extent in the area of free movement of goods, while the services directive is currently being hotly contested.

A Community constitution was rejected by the population of France and the Netherlands in a referendum last year. The Constitution was intended to render the Fundamental Rights Charter

---

257 See ECHR judgement *Plattform Ärzte* of 21st June 1988, no. 10126/82
258 Art. 13 EHRC provides a comprehensive course of law guarantee
259 Starting from the Single European Act in the 1980s

of the European Union binding, create various simplifications and merge the Union treaty with the EC treaty. However, it does not merit the term "constitution" even by the most modest of standards, meaning that discussions are underway to fillet the "Constitution" draft and decide on the usable sections elsewhere.

The European Community predominantly acts in two legal forms, namely through directives and through ordinances. Ordinances have a direct effect in the Member States, replacing all forms of opposing national law. However, there is routinely the need to supplement the ordinances with procedural regulations by means of national law. Directives, by contrast, are aimed at Member States, therefore not obligating individuals directly. The Court of the European Communities (European Court of Justice, ECJ) decided that directives may only be directly applicable if a directive is not implemented.[260] However, this applies only in favour of private persons, not, though, to their detriment and particularly not for the area of criminal law.[261]

If a directive is not implemented through national law, a person cannot be brought to court for a "breach" of the directive. This principle has been questioned many times, but firmly confirmed in this form by the European Court of Justice in each case.

Therefore, the money laundering directives can have no direct effect as criminal law standards on account of breach of duties to act of economic participants or private persons. A breach of a money laundering directive alone cannot therefore lead to a punishment; the pre-requirement for a punishment can always only be a breach of a national criminal law associated with its implementation. There must be a national penal provision in order for a criminal sanction to be imposed. In so far as directives are not implemented nationally by means of legal regulations, they do, however, apply as an aid to interpretation in the event of doubt. The laws must then be interpreted as broadly as possible using the example of the directive (principle of directive-compliant interpretation).

---

260 See ECJ judgement *Santillo* of 22nd May 1980, Case 131/79
261 See ECJ judgement *Pretore di Salò* of 11th June 1987, Case 14/86; *El Corte Ingles SA* of 7th March 1996, Case C-192/94

The three consecutive money laundering directives are already described in more detail in other articles[262] and therefore require no further analysis. European Community law fundamentally differs from all other international law in one respect. Community law is more than an agreement between the peoples of the individual Member States. It stems from its own legal source. Its law applies on the basis of its democratic decision making structures generally without implementation and ratification by the Member States. The European Court of Justice formulated this precisely at an early stage:

> *"By contrast with ordinary international treaties, the EEC treaty has created its own legal system which, on the entry into force of the treaty, became an integral part of the legal systems of the Member States and which their courts are bound to apply.*
> *By creating a community of unlimited duration, having its own institutions, its own personality, its own legal capacity and capacity of representation on the international plane and, more particularly, real powers stemming from a limitation of sovereignty or a transfer of powers from the states to the Community, the Member States have limited their sovereign rights and have thus created a body of law which binds both their nationals and themselves.*
> *(...)*
> *The law stemming from the treaty, an independent source of law, could not because of its special and original nature, be overridden by domestic legal provisions, however framed, without being deprived of its character as Community law and without the legal basis of the Community itself being called into question."*[263]

The states therefore effected a definitive restriction of their sovereignty rights by reserving rights and obligations which had previously been governed in their domestic legal systems for regulation by Community legislation. The term is therefore "supranational law". This supranational law takes precedence over the law of the Member States and can therefore oppose the application of na-

---

262 See for example the history of the EU directives from p.37
263 ECJ judgement *Costa / E.N.E.L.*, 15th July 1964, Case 6/64

Money Laundering Law and Fundamental Rights

tional law. In other words, the Community law applies directly and is higher ranking than its national law counterpart.

The vocation of the European Court of Justice is to interpret the law of the European Community alone. The Member States may not have Community law disputes decided by their national supreme courts; the courts are rather obligated to submit such legal questions to the European Court of Justice for preliminary decision.[264] The Court of Justice can also declare ordinances of the European Community null and void if they are not in compliance with human rights. The most famous example is the cancellation of the first version of the students' directive.[265]

It can therefore not be ruled out that the European Court of Justice will one day declare excessive stipulations of the money laundering directive null and void. The legal rules of the European Court of Justice accordingly hold the rank of priority Community law.

The European Community has no formal catalogue of fundamental rights to date. The European Court of Justice has already been ruling for years in permanent jurisdiction that no decision can be community compliant if it breaches fundamental rights, with the following justification:

"In fact, respect for fundamental rights forms an integral part of the general principles of law protected by the Court of Justice. The protection of such rights, whilst inspired by the constitutional traditions common to Member States, must be ensured within the framework of the structure and objectives of the Community..."[266]

In the process, in practice, the European Court of Justice applies the European Human Rights Convention, which defines important legal principles for the European Community.

So far, there are no serious and profound contradictions between the fundamental rights jurisdiction of the European Court of Human Rights (ECHR) and the European Court of Justice (ECJ). It is

---

264 See ECJ judgement *Foto-Frost*, 22.10.1987, Case 314/85, Mtg. 1987, 4199
265 See ECJ judgement *EP / Rat*, 7.7.1992, Case C 295/90
266 ECJ judgement *Internationale Handelsgesellschaft*, 17.12.1970, Case 11/70

rather the case that the European Court of Justice is attempting to adapt itself to the fundamental rights jurisprudence of the Court of Human Rights (ECHR).

This is also thoroughly proper, since in the majority of cases the European Court of Justice rules in the preliminary decision process, therefore in connection with domestic legal procedures. If such a domestic process is later completed on the basis of its preliminary decision on the decisive issue, the respective person concerned can raise human rights complaints. Therefore, the Court of Human Rights ultimately carries out a Community law inspection concerning preliminary decisions as well once the domestic course of law is completed. Thus, for example, the European Court of Human Rights ruled that a regulation declaring that the residents of Gibraltar were not permitted to vote in the European Parliament elections was contrary to human rights.[267]

Though the recent European Fundamental Rights Charter of the European Union is not formally binding, it does provide interpretation assistance when legal questions arise and so is definitely effective.

The European Fundamental Rights Charter already has very far-reaching importance in the practical respect, namely as an interpretation benchmark of the ECJ, even though it is not intended to become obligatory until the European Constitution comes into effect. In the *Christine Goodwin*[268] judgement the European Court of Human Rights (ECHR) even consulted the fundamental rights charter as an interpretation benchmark for contemporary interpretation of the EHRC for the first time, even though, theoretically, it would have been inconsequential for it.

Another important directive of Community law of interest here is the currently highly underestimated opposite number of these money laundering directives, namely the data protection directive,

---

267 See ECHR judgement *Matthews* of 18th February 1999, no. 24833/94
268 See ECHR judgement *Christine Goodwin* of 11th July 2002, App. no. 28957/95, l. 100

which ensures the secrecy of private data[269] and which will therefore be described in more detail.

4. Data protection directive

In justificatory consideration 3 of this directive it is postulated that the *fundamental rights* of individuals must be safeguarded when personal data are used. According to justificatory consideration 6 modern telecommunications facilitate the transnational circulation of personal data. According to Justificatory consideration 10 data protection guarantees the respect of fundamental rights and freedoms, particularly of the right of privacy also recognised in Art. 8 of the European Convention for the Protection of Human Rights and Fundamental Freedoms and in the general principles of Community law. It is the declared task of Community law, says the consideration, to ensure a *high level of protection*. In justificatory consideration 11 the Community legislator refers to the Council of the European Union agreement of 28th January 1981 on the protection of personal data, which is thereby indirectly recognised as a general legal standard of the Community.[270] Justificatory consideration 24 emphasises that the directive is not intended to affect the protection regulations for legal persons during the processing of data referring to them. Justificatory consideration 68 emphasises in turn the protection of the rights and freedoms of individuals and the respect of privacy.

The Member States must pass data protection laws on the basis of this directive and set up a data protection commissioner and a supreme data protection agency.

The fundamental rights charter already contains fundamental rights regulations which are largely reproduced from the Human Rights Convention, including a special guarantee of a fundamental right to data protection, with the following wording:

---

269 See directive 95/46/EC of the European Parliament and Council of 24th October 1995 concerning the protection of natural persons during the processing of personal data and concerning free circulation of data

270 On the indirect reception of legal protection standards, see also in particular *Weh*, Vom Stufenbau zur Relativität, chapter 10.3.

"Article 8, protection of personal data: (1). Everyone has the right to the protection of personal data concerning him or her. (2). Such data must be processed fairly for specified purposes and on the basis of the consent of the person concerned or some other legitimate basis laid down by law. Everyone has the right of access to data which has been collected concerning him or her, and the right to have it rectified. (3). Compliance with these rules shall be subject to control by an independent authority."

In a still thoroughly current judgement[271] the ECJ emphasised that the behavioural code of the Community agents provides for the protection of the individual and his privacy as much as the protection of business and industrial secrecy and the preservation of the confidentiality of documents provided by natural or legal persons. It expressly orders the Commission to check *in every individual case* whether the pre-requirements for the publication of private data are in place.

In a judgement that met with no compliance in the scientific community as a judgement in a British agricultural matter, the ECJ clarified the fundamental principles of Community law for data protection as follows:

"31 In order to answer the question whether certain information contained in the database may be disclosed, the competent authority must balance, on the one hand, the interest of the person who provided the information and, on the other, the interest of the person who has need of that information in order to meet a legitimate objective.
32 However, the respective interests of the persons concerned in regard to data of a personal nature must be assessed in a manner which ensures protection of fundamental freedoms and rights.
33 In that connection, the provisions of Directive 95/46/EC of the European Parliament and of the Council of 24th October 1995 on the protection of individuals with regard to the processing of personal data and on the free movement of such data (OJ 1995 L 281 p.31) (the Directive) provide criteria that

---

[271] See ECJ judgement *NL und Gerard van der Wal / Komm,* 11th January 2000, Case C-174/98 P and C-189/98 P

are suitable for application by the competent authority in making that assessment.

34 Even though the Directive had not yet entered into force at the material time in the case in the main proceedings, it is clear from the 10th and 11th recitals in its preamble that it adopts, at Community level, the general principles which already formed part of the law of the Member States in the area in question.

35 With regard, in particular, to the disclosure of data, Article 7(f) of the Directive authorises such disclosure if it is necessary for the purposes of the legitimate interests pursued by a third party to whom personal data are disclosed, except where such interests are overridden by the interests or fundamental rights and freedoms of the data subject which require protection."[272]

The protection of freedoms and fundamental rights must always be kept in view in matters of disclosure. These fundamental rights principally also include the fundamental right to protection of economic data, which are, after all, routinely personal data as well. The ECJ therefore expressly arrives at the conclusion that the data protection directive comprehensively establishes the criteria for data protection, therefore not only in its direct scope of application. The ECJ emphasises that the directive has merely adopted general legal principles at the Community level which had already been recognised as a European standard in the legal systems of the Member States.

In Austria the question needed to be decided as to whether the publication – with names – of the salaries of top politicians and other leading civil servants in the public sector and the public economy, set down in the Austrian salary limitation act (*Bezügebegrenzungs-BVG*), was compatible with data protection law. The Austrian constitutional court submitted the question to the ECJ for a preliminary decision.

The European Court of Justice then decided[273] that it intends to see the data protection directive applied exactly according to the

---

272 Judgement of 14th September 2000, Case C-369/98, Trevor Robert Fisher and Penny Fisher
273 See *Rechnungshof / ORF* among others, Case C-465/00, or *Neukomm und Lauermann* Case C-138 and 139/01; decision reproduced in GesRZ 2003,

criteria that the European Court of Human Rights (ECHR) has always drawn on when applying Art. 8 European Human Rights Convention (EHRC).
In detail these are: the clear determination and predictability of intervention pre-requirements; orientation towards a legitimate intervention goal; the pressing social need; the necessity of the intervention in a democratic society; and the appropriateness of the means applied. All this would not actually be new, but can*not*, however, be found in Supreme Court verdicts on the disclosure directives to date.

Article 8 says that the term "personal data" requires broad interpretation, because the protective scope of Art. 8 EHRC is to be broadly interpreted overall and the intervention pre-requirements are to be narrowly interpreted in each case. It is strictly not the intention to exclude professional activities from the term of private life. On this matter the ECJ cites the judgements of the ECHR in the legal matters *Amann*[274] and *Rotaru*[275]. It is not a matter of whether the information conveyed is sensitive (marginal note 75). Under marginal note 85 the European Court of Justice poses the question, which is central for recourse applicants too, whether the purpose of disclosure could not be achieved equally as effectively by having the corresponding data *made accessible to inspection agencies only*.

The ECJ explicitly names economic disadvantages as one reason *against* disclosure. The ECJ expressly emphasises that the prejudicial standards of the directive are directly applicable.

The ECJ also expressly affirmed the authority to keep data confidential in a current Austrian case.[276] In its ensuing finding[277] the Austrian constitutional court then decided in summary that the salary data of public company employees may not be generally published with the naming of names.

---

338. See also the essay by *Weh* in GesRZ 2003, 322 Protection of Economic Data in European Data Law [German]

274 See ECHR judgement *Amann / Switzerland* of 16th February 2000, no. 27798/95
275 See ECHR judgement *Rotaru / Romania* of 4th May 2000, no. 38341/95
276 See ECJ judgement *Glawischnig* of 12th June 2003, Case C-316/01
277 See Austrian Constitutional Court Finding of 28th November 2003, KR 1/00-33

In two judgements that had already been confessed[278] the ECJ expressly pronounced that no company must be forced to incriminate itself. This, it said, did not only apply for the immediate scope of a criminal proceeding in the sense of Art. 6 EHRC, but also for other procedures which could lead to unfavourable results for the company.

Not much later the ECHR also pronounced in a judgement[279] that the right to remain silent and not need to incriminate oneself arises from the fairness principle of Art. 6 EHRC. In another judgement shortly afterwards[280] the ECHR confirmed that *"the right not to incriminate oneself cannot reasonably be confined to statements of admission of wrongdoing or to remarks which are directly incriminating"*. In the end the Court of the First Instance of the European Communities[281] in turn expressly emphasised the right to remain silent.

Concerning the fundamental right to data protection of companies, the Austrian constitutional court[282] pronounced, for example:

"A comprehensive duty to publish (see § 2 para. 2 Austrian federal statistics act BStG) the result of statistical surveys is incompatible with the regulation of § 1 Austrian data protection act DSG in the rank of federal constitutional law, since inferences concerning data which are under the constitutional law protection of § 1 DSG are possible from such publications in certain combinations that in no way occur in individual cases only."

For the time being, therefore, it may be doubted whether all money laundering law sets down interventions that are appropriate to the fundamental right to data protection.

---

278 ECJ judgements *Orkem SA / Komm*, 18th October 1989, Case 374/87, and *Solvay*, 18th October 1989, Case 27/88
279 ECHR judgement *Funke,* 25th February 1993, no. 10828/84, EuGRZ (European fundamental rights magazine) 1989, 461, E
280 ECHR judgement *Saunders,* 17th December 1996, no. 19187/91, Z. 71
281 See EuGeI judgement *Mannesmann,* 20thFebruary 2001, Case T-112/98
282 Finding Constitutional Court Mtg. (VfSlg.) 12228 of 30th November 1989, G 245/89 and many others

5. International organisations

All other international organisations and other international law instruments such as treaties apply only because the respective Member State has undertaken to behave in a certain manner.

International law treaties can be immediately applicable in individual Member States, but it can also be declared that the treaty is not immediately applicable domestically, but is aimed at the legislator only (so-called execution proviso).

In order to judge the effectiveness of money laundering regulations in international stipulations, it therefore needs to be tested in the individual case whether it is a question of European Community law taking precedence over all opposing law, or whether it is a question of international law obligations having more or less direct significance domestically depending on the circumstances.

The negligible forcefulness of international instruments and their implementation provisos often largely stand in the way of effective legal standardisation. On the other hand, though, states are often not willing to hand over more than is agreed in an international treaty.

6. National fundamental rights guarantees

A large number of European states have set up constitutional courts in one form or another, granting fundamental rights protection. The legal situation is different in each of the four German-speaking countries under discussion.

The Republic of Austria and the Federal Republic of Germany are members of the European Community, the Principality of Liechtenstein is associated with the European Union in the European Economic Area agreement; the Swiss Confederation, on the other hand, is connected with the European Union via bilateral agreements establishing Switzerland's association status. This also means different responsibilities of the European Court of Justice in Luxembourg.

The scope of validity and formal grounds for application of the Human Rights Convention is also different. Whereas the European Human Rights Convention has formal constitutional ranking in Austria and can therefore be asserted by anyone before the Austrian constitutional court, this does not apply to the three other countries to the same extent. The Federal Republic of Germany has standardised its own fundamental rights catalogue in the Basic Law, which came into being at about the same time as the European Human Rights Convention and contains sometimes further-reaching, sometimes less far-reaching rights guarantees.

The Swiss federal court's and Liechtensteinian state court's handling of the EHRC is rather uninhibited and cannot be described in more detail here. All four states are essentially bound by the human rights convention, because appeals can be made to the European Court of Human Rights against every one of their final-instance decisions. All four countries already permitted individual appeals long before the human rights appeal became obligatory for all Member States.

In addition, all four member states protect many of the rights described above domestically as well, to a greater extent in some cases. This includes, for example, the defence lawyer guarantee, the fundamental right to data protection and the principle of appropriateness.

7. Money laundering and fundamental rights

The combating of money laundering, together with the siphoning off of criminal gains and therefore also, indirectly, the more extensive combating of crime, are no doubt at all among the legitimate tasks of every constitutional state.

The figures appearing in this book, however, raise the strongest doubts as to whether anti-money laundering methods so far are really suitable, not to mention in proportion, for achieving their goal.
After all, the accusation of money laundering represents a very serious indictment, and if the conviction figures fall within the marginal percentage range (presumably, generally only the most clumsy get caught with minor offences) the question already arises about the suitability of the elements of intervention for achieving the goal, to say nothing of the appropriateness of such

a juggernaut-style collection of personal data, compared to which the STASI data bases look like bungled efforts.

The deterrent effect of existing money laundering prosecution systems would especially need to be examined, for now that the money laundering apparatus cannot be justified from the convictions only a provable solid deterrent effect could justify the expenditure described in this book. The tightening of the money laundering bans probably has a certain preventive effect; the only thing that would need to be examined is how far it goes and to what extent it justifies the expenditure. Doubts about appropriateness appear justified here as well.

The question against the background of the appropriateness principle is whether one could not achieve better results with the same amount of concentration and same energy and same deployment of resources using different methods.

The European Community should therefore carry out a thorough efficiency inspection before stacking up further directives, the cost of which is ultimately borne by consumers (who else?).

Each of the main areas indicated in this book which result in flight capital could also be tackled via different measures.

Overall, one is permitted to assume that the majority of flight capital originates from five areas, from drug crime, human trafficking, organised crime in general, corruption and tax evasion.

In the case of drug dealing, the question arises as to whether a clearer distinction between softer and harder drugs would not lead to a decline in illegal drug dealing. Advocates of the legalisation of soft drugs (hashish, marijuana) argue that these drugs are less harmful than socially accepted or downright courted drugs such as alcohol. Alcohol prohibition in the United States was actually a real "elixir of life" for the coming into being of organised crime there. A change in the sometimes miserable conditions in the producing countries could be more effective.

Human trafficking, too, is flourishing on the basis of the state's dishonest basic social attitude in respect of prostitution. Legally prohibiting prostitution many times over, but practically tolerating it because it is virtually not opposable, creates precisely the right breeding ground for illegal structures from human trafficking right up to the money laundering in question. Legalising prostitution with corresponding control of prostitutes and taxation of their income could no doubt reduce human trafficking and black money flows in this area.

The question arises even more blatantly with corruption. Corruption can be committed in the public sector area, but also by employees in the private economy.

The opportunity for corruption is practically institutionalised in various national rules of law, not only in Austria. Every overlong decision period by an authority, every opportunity for discretion given, for example, to a town planning office, every margin of allocation granted to a public allocations office practically means an invitation to the respective applicants or complainants to influence or accelerate the decision process by means of "favours" (who greases well, drives well). A rigorous time constraint for authority procedures, the elimination of free authority discretion, comprehensive courts checks on the facts of authority decisions and reinforced personal liability of civil servants for official breaches could force back corruption considerably. Overlong decision periods, further room for discretion and escalating authorities to act are the quagmire on which bribe money really flourishes.

It is possibly the case that neither the legislator nor the general public are aware that anti-money laundering should also precisely be in aid of anti-corruption, and right in the middle European countries described here as well.

In Bregenz, Austria, a few years ago, a middle-ranking civil servant was able to shift 35 million Austrian shillings (approximately EUR 2.5 million) onto his private accounts[283] without it occurring to anybody at the local government offices or the bank. This true story is all the more incomprehensible for the fact that, on top of it all, the perpetrator invested the money embezzled by him in real estate in Vorarlberg, so in the immediate vicinity, in which process he also had to work his way through all the financial and land register procedures.

Opinions appear to differ on the issue of tax-evasion money. While Germany intends to add this to the area of traditional money laundering, the Principality of Liechtenstein recognises the fiscal

---

283 Process 22 Vr 545/98 of Feldkirch local court

proviso, therefore the favouring of pure black funds by money laundering law.

One occasionally encounters the argument that the best methods against tax evasion are of a preventive nature. Some believe that a tax rate viewed by the population as being fair would reduce tax evasion. These people are historically backed by experiences wherein tightening the tax screw sometimes led to lower tax results – and not to higher ones. In addition, those who believe that tax evasion would decline if the population were of the opinion that tax funds were being used purposefully are possibly right as well.

In terms of fundamental rights policy, including tax evasion in anti-money laundering represents a fundamental problem. If intervention measures need to be proportionate, then the intensity of permitted interventions must depend on how grievous the breached legally protected right is. It is now definitely a European standard that taking part in human trafficking or serious corruption is more grievous than paying a cleaning lady who cleans the house twice a week cash-in-hand.

From the standpoint of appropriateness, serious encroachment upon personal rights should only be justified in the case of serious crimes. The broader the scope of crimes preliminary to money laundering and the facts of money laundering themselves, the more everyday facts the scope is held to include, the more critical appropriateness in relation to fundamental rights becomes.

8. Legal resources against anti-money laundering

Every person affected by an anti-money laundering measure must have the opportunity to defend himself against this measure in a process under the rule of law. The protection requirement can collide with the necessities of money laundering measures in the process.

It is obvious that many measures need to be applied using surprise tactics, house searches for example, because house searches announced two weeks in advance have seldom yielded evaluable results.

On the other hand it is standard, for example, that the results of a house search must be sealed if the person concerned requests this. This gives the person concerned the opportunity to appeal against the legality of the house search afterwards, with the consequence that the sealed documents must be returned without delay if the illegality of the house search is established.

Exploiting the documents before an opportunity to appeal has been checked legally would be illegal in normal house search law.

The question arises as to how far such principles should not also be transferable to anti-money laundering.

For example, it is questionable why the person suspected of money laundering cannot be made aware of the existing suspicion as soon he is incapable of causing more damage owing to nature of the case.

The justification for surprise measures without prior questioning of the person concerned is routinely based on the fact that the official action would not otherwise be possible. In the case of house searches or impounding of chattels, the objects would disappear if the person concerned were warned in time. If a money laundering suspect can no longer conduct his transaction, however, it is questionable why one is not obliged to inform him about the existing suspicion immediately and give him the opportunity to organise his rights of defence as early as possible.

An account seizure or account block may be indispensable as an immediate measure, but in that case it is all the more appropriate that the corresponding information should be provided to the suspect as soon as possible. A fair balance between the two interests should accordingly be struck by allowing non-deferrable measures to be applied without questioning, but having the person concerned informed as soon as possible.

The Austrian security police act also recognises the term of delayed access, which is designed to enable the police to reach the persons behind a crime. In so doing, it expressly rules that every person experiencing an encroachment upon his rights through such access must be compensated appropriately.[284]

There is an obvious objection to assessment during the processing of money laundering suspicion reports. It cannot be comprehended why, for example, § 41 para. 7 Austrian banking act

---

284   See § 23 para. 2 Austrian security police act (Sicherheitspolizeigesetz)

(öBEG)[285] also expressly exempts from punishment an indefensible, incorrect money laundering suspicion report submitted in a grossly negligent manner. Why (even gross) negligence should be expressly exculpated here is incomprehensible from the point of view of fundamental rights. If the suspicious transaction report has taken place according to the principle of businessmanlike due diligence, there is no negligence, and if it is not compiled according to the principle of businessmanlike due diligence, the question arises as to why it should nonetheless be favoured. The presumption of innocence of Art. 6 para. 2 EHRC provides protection against unjustified suspicions. The regulation of § 41 para. 7 Austrian banking act therefore appears contrary to fundamental rights.

In many areas of legislation there is a distinction between immediate measures that need to be quickly applied ad hoc and other measures to be taken after carefully considered examination of the circumstances. Their correctness must consequently be calculated differently as well. That is why there is no uniform judgement automatically following every Interim Order and not every criminal law accusation leads to sentencing.

It is incomprehensible why no reference can be made to official responsibility criteria, according to which an indefensible act triggers an obligation to pay damages. It is incomprehensible why it cannot be asked of a money laundering suspicion report that it be defensible in the light of all circumstances.

This calculation also applies, for example, for doctors' treatment methods, lawyers' consultancy requirements etc. Professional malpractice liability is also occasionally mentioned in the process. That a professionally negligent suspicious transaction report should nonetheless exculpate the person submitting the report is absolutely incomprehensible and in no way compliant with human rights. Switching two patients is indefensible, but it would still be negligent. Nonetheless, no hospital law in the world would dream of exculpating the hospital if a patient receives a new heart instead of an upcoming tonsillectomy.

The legitimacy of a suspicious transaction report should therefore be assessed using defensibility criteria instead of on the basis of

---

285 See for example the "Austria" article from p.169

the inappropriate criminal law criteria of intent and negligence. If the suspicious transaction report, for example, is in the wrong name because the bank employee incorrectly copied the name from the passport or mixed up two passes, though it only occurred negligently, it is of course indefensible.

Reference will have to be made to the actual situation in the case of the defensibility of textual comments. The emergency doctor called to a road traffic accident cannot take a blood sample from the accident victim – he has to apply immediate ad hoc measures. Ad-hoc measures may even be involved in a major operation, while continued treatment is only permitted to take place on the basis of corresponding examinations.

Under certain circumstances, therefore, the essence of suspicion reporting is inherently the recognition that no conclusive examination of the facts has taken place. On the other hand, there is also of course the possibility of describing in the suspicion report the underlying elements of the suspicion and to what extent examination measures were applied. Every appraiser must describe the bases of his finding in his appraisal.

It also appears more than questionable whether the withholding of a payment is appropriate, proportionate and to be regarded as the mildest method in every case. In the case of remittances with deadlines, which may be associated with loss of rights if delayed, there may be the possibility of carrying out the transaction and obligating the recipient bank under money laundering law to the effect that the transaction is carried out but the remitted amount is not cleared by the recipient bank until the money laundering suspicion is settled. Without question, therefore, it is not the mildest method of achieving the goal of anti-money laundering in every case if payments are withheld even though they could also be withheld at the recipient's end but would thereby enable the payer to meet his civil law obligations.

Overall, there is currently the impression that – cost what it will – the main attention for the time being is on increasing the dubious efficiency of anti-money laundering. It is natural that during efforts of this type to increase efficiency, less attention is paid to other aspects than that of appropriateness, indeed that attentiveness can be lost altogether in the process.

A strategy of this type can, however, also have repercussions.

9. The duty of discretion of liberal professions

It is obvious that effective criminal defence is impossible if the defence lawyer is unable to guarantee absolute discretion of his information. It is obvious that a defence lawyer cannot defend an accused person if he is obliged to report all facts that he learns from the accused person to the authority. Even somebody who collaborates in a crime preliminary to money laundering or has only realised money laundering must unconditionally have the right to effective self-defence – that is guaranteed by the EHRC. The duties of defence lawyers must therefore not be diluted under any circumstances, including in the context of anti-money laundering.

This principle must apply for every criminal defence, in whatever process it takes place, in financial criminal law for example. It must also be possible for a defence lawyer to take the legal fee without risk even in a financial criminal case.

On the other hand, it cannot be denied that not every type of lawyer activity is worthy of protection to the same degree:

Naturally it is out of the question that the lawyer can instruct his client on money laundering opportunities with impunity. According to Art. 17 EHRC nobody is permitted to abuse his rights in order to encourage fundamental rights encroachments. Also not subject to the absolute protection of defence lawyer secrecy is the case where a lawyer carries out cash transactions for a client in the name of non-specific services. In this case it is possible to request the corresponding due diligence from him.

However, it is not possible to request that he forward information that has been entrusted to him as a lawyer which he requires for his representative activity in his professional role. Essentially, the local lawyers' regulation described in the Liechtenstein chapter, for example, takes good account of the difference, the chapter on Austrian law, for instance, as well.[286]

---

[286] See for example Art. 16 (FL) SPV or the "Liechtenstein" article from p.112; a similar solution is also shown in the "Austria" chapter from p.176

It should therefore be requested that the core of real legal consultancy activity and defence lawyer activity must remain absolutely protected, while other services further removed from consulting also performed by lawyers may be made answerable to the money laundering act. The debate appears to run in this direction by and large.

10. Closing remarks

The author's intention with this article was to create awareness and highlight problems. Naturally, the issue cannot be dealt with conclusively in such a small space.

All persons concerned should be aware that anti-money laundering, too, must respect fundamental rights as comprehensively as possible. Anti-money laundering is legitimate and serves to assert fundamental rights, namely the protection of personal safety, property and freedom of income. However, all this must not alter the view that anti-money must not breach the tested principles of European fundamental rights protection.

In international competition, Europe has no less to offer than this standard of human rights that was created under the influence of European constitutional traditions and the European Human Rights Convention. The standard must not fall victim to a current phenomenon.

A current press statement from the leading specialist and president of an Austrian professional lawyers' society gets to the heart of the problem as follows:

> *"Under the pressure of current attacks, bugging operations and computer searches have been introduced in the past and money laundering regulations approved, even though no perpetrator was caught by these means. The risk of abuse can never be ruled out. We hope that the legislator takes account of lawyers' misgivings and will refrain from further encroachments upon fundamental rights."*[287]

---

287 Sepp Manhart in the newspaper *Vorarlberger Nachrichten* of 04./05. February 2006, D1

II.
The "Ivanov" Case Study – In the Crossfire of Due Diligence Obligations

A.
Reputation
–
The Underestimated Factor

Dr. Andreas INSAM

> "It takes many good deeds to build a good reputation, and
> only one bad one to lose it"
> (Benjamin Franklin)

"Money laundering" – as can be deduced from the extensive regulations at both the national and international level, be they legally binding standards or only recommendations, from the hitherto theoretical part of this publication – is an extremely complex topic.

One aspect which has already been outlined here and there but still requires a somewhat more focused look is the *reputational risk* in connection with money laundering occurrences – the frequently underestimated factor.

Successful money laundering requires one thing: a stable bridge to legality for dubious capital. It is the task of legislation in interplay with the most-frequented bridges, i.e. predominantly with financial institutions and intermediaries, to prevent this migration as best it can. Banks in particular stand in the crossfire at the same time and view themselves as being exposed to several risks. For one thing, to a criminal law risk if they do not combat money laundering proceedings with all means at their disposal, ranging from high fines right up to withdrawal of their licence and thus to the forced closure of the bank.

Any involvement with money laundering – be it wittingly or unwittingly culpable – brings a further risk with it: the reputational risk, which jeopardises banks' existence.

Bank transactions are transactions based on trust. Trust, for its part, can only be claimed by somebody whose reputation is intact. For banks – even more than for other businesses – it is accordingly the case that good renown, the reputation as a trustworthy partner with integrity in a business relationship, must always be interpreted as a central value of one's own business.

A bank's business success is based both on credible conveyance of its core values as well as on its core competencies. If core values such as "trust" show only the beginnings of damage, not even qualitatively outstanding services, for example "asset management", can be offered convincingly any longer. A previously barely perceived aspect of a single business relationship can therefore – via media attention in the case of an unwanted involvement in money laundering, for example – inflate to an existence-threatening risk overnight.

As Benjamin Franklin already got to the heart of it, the value of "reputation" is difficult to build up and at the same time very easy to lose. Or to put it another way: who aims at transactions without a basis of trust? There is no second chance for a good reputation! Particular caution is therefore necessary when dealing with potentially reputation-jeopardising transactions. In this connection the term is "due diligence obligation", which was already discussed in the first part.

Analogously, due diligence obligations are aimed not only at ensuring a tidy financial centre by fending off criminal customers, but equally serve the purpose of the bank's own maintenance of its painstakingly acquired reputation, a traditional basis of trust and honourable business conduct.

Good reputation is simultaneously effective and also at risk at several levels. From the insignificant employee, through the local bank branch, right up to the supraregional banking association or even the respected financial centre, many tiny cogs interlock, each of which can quickly dampen its own and others' reputation. Mutual dependencies render it impossible to fix the risk on one single wheel, just as a functioning machine is dependent upon many correctly operating individual components.

From the viewpoint of the small state of Liechtenstein the reputational risk gains even more significance than for other financial centres. The geographical concentration on the most restricted of spaces and the media perception as an attractive tax location brings with it heightened public interest. Liechtenstein's reputational risk as a financial centre lies in the discovery of dishonest business relationships by the world's press. Possible inconsistencies in the market are quickly processed into clichés by the media and permanently damage the "Liechtenstein" brand in the financial world. For this reason, over recent years the Principality has passed one of the strictest acts for combating money laundering and abuse of the financial centre, taking care of the maximum possible diligence both in the case of new and already existing business relationships.

From the viewpoint of the banks the reputational risk lies in the loss of customer funds due to the association with crime. One single case in the public eye can be sufficient to ruin the good reputation of an individual institution, possible parent institutions or subsidiaries or otherwise associated banks, respectively, and, in the example of Liechtenstein, even of the entire financial centre due to geographical concentration. Binding banking association directives on the one hand, and bank-internal directives on the other, expand the statutory regulations concerning duty of diligence, in order to provide optimum protection. Within the industry, "corporate governance" as the buzzword of modern corporate culture encompasses the safeguarding of good reputation.

A personal reputational risk is run by the acting customer representative, who is responsible as the final link in the "duty of diligence" chain for the correct implementation of all regulations. If a representative accumulates a series of less conscientiously conducted checks, he risks his own reputation as a qualified employee at the branch and thereby his professional career. Additionally, he jeopardises the repute of his employer through improper behaviour. True to the motto, "better one suspicion too many, than one too few", the customer representative has the major responsibility of finding a balance between the interest of business customers and the bank. The crucial factor is the evaluation of the customer's risk potential in relation to the banking institution, i.e. whether a "mistake" could subsequently prove fatal or rather, negligible. Benchmarks in the process are the size of the foreseeable business in relation with the bank's overall transactions, the customer's exposure ("prominence factor") and both the bank's size and its status. The customer representative's cultural proximity with the customer (language, roots) makes overall estimation and examination of the economic background considerably easier. Nevertheless, the one-to-one principle must always be a pre-requirement in duties of diligence.

Optimum safeguarding of reputation is consequently in the interest of every link in the chain, of the financial centre, the bank and the individual employee.

International examples from practice underline the importance of reputation and the dangerous threat posed by money laundering. For example, a renowned New York bank entered dire straits in 1999 after two members of the senior management supported a Russian money laundering network by opening accounts in return for high commission fees. More than 7 billion US dollars flowed to third parties via the Bank of New York in the few years under consideration.[288] It is hard to put the damage done to the bank's image in figures, but millions of US dollars can no doubt be assumed.

In Switzerland, too, there have been accounts with embezzled public assets in recent years – invested by state representatives[289] or their powers of attorney. The professional etiquette of Swiss federal banks was tightened, not least owing to the ensuing reputational damage due to the acceptance of these embezzled funds or corruption profits, respectively. Since the last update in 2003, transactions of this type must no longer be accepted and business connections with politically exposed persons must be examined particularly closely.

It becomes obvious how easily one single dishonest transaction can inflict major damage on the entire surroundings. Liechtenstein's reputation as a customer-friendly capital market, promising the greatest discretion, is very attractive for customers. If it does not succeed in preventing the abuse of the banking centre by undesirable customers in a screening process within the context of statutory and internal requirements, then the good reputation of the financial centre and of its service providers will very quickly be wrecked.

---

[288] Transcript of the court trial in New York of 16th February 2002, http://russianlaw.org/grant.htm

[289] Primarily by leaders of dictatorial regimes, who abused their power to accumulate and move assets

"I've just come from a successful business closure and am interested in securities investments"

For this reason, investors are checked particularly thoroughly in Liechtenstein and examined for suitability as business partners. In many cases banks go beyond statutory requirements in order to do justice to the special exposure of Liechtenstein in the focus of international observers. It must be said that even with the most conscientious checks, acceptance of "black sheep" can never be completely avoided, since the partner's entire background is sometimes not obvious in a first-time business relationship. Personal commitment and ongoing critical inspection in the case of existing business relationships fortunately allow even subsequent corrections to the customer portfolio or, from time to time, give rise to suspicious transaction reports to the national security agency.

One thing becomes obvious from these accounts, which have been kept short:

Andreas INSAM

Money laundering and reputational risk are closely associated with each other. Without a good reputation, particularly in banking circles, no business can be done. It is correspondingly in the interest of all acting partners to "keep a financial centre tidy".

A bank cannot afford a failure in legal regulations – that is why Hypo Investment Bank (Liechtenstein) AG entrusted "Pros" with the material. Using the example of an extremely striking, suspicious case study, *"Boris Ivanov"*, they demonstratively dispel the uncertainty that can arise from similar business relationships and point the way through the legal jungle that is not easy to fathom for the layman.

The case is solved by our legal experts according to the national law applying in each case:

- Dr. Erek Nuener —— Principality of Liechtenstein
- Mag. Johannes Trenkwalder, LL.M —— Austria
- Dr. Joachim Kaetzler —— Germany
- Dr. Peter Bosshard —— Switzerland

B.
"Boris Ivanov"

"The new Russian Doll – more parts than ever!"

The Fictitious Case Study

The following case study has no connection whatsoever with current or past customers of Hypo Investment Bank (Liechtenstein) AG. The facts of the case to be legally appraised employing a wealth of techniques were woven around the varied experiences of the authors Dr. Andreas Insam and DDr. Vladislav V. Mudrych. In the process, the former was the ideas provider for the due diligence obligations aspects and the latter was the expert for social law constructions in Russia, which are known to be complicated, and together they constructed the "touchstone".

Particular thanks are due to Dr. Joachim Kaetzler, who as a legal expert crucially sharpened many a formulation in order to provide the appraisers with as much scope for interpretation in the national regulations as possible.

1. Making contact

Fifty-year-old Russian citizen Boris Ivanov approaches the bank in June 2001.[290] The motive for making contact is a specialist article appearing in the "Kommersant Daily", combined with an interview with the CEO of the bank. When it emerges that Mr. Ivanov wishes to claim the bank's asset management services as a new customer and transfer a payment of 15 million US dollars for the purpose, the bank employee conducts a customer due diligence process that reveals the following:

Mr. Ivanov indicates that he is acting not for himself, but for SUNSHINE Ltd. (a company with its headquarters in Nicosia/ Cyprus). However, since, he says, he is the 100 % owner, he is not acting in the legal sense, but nonetheless in the economic sense in his own interest. He presents a valid passport and a valid driver's licence.

In addition to personal details such as place of residence, marital status and date of birth, the bank's customer advisor learns that Mr. Ivanov had reportedly been active in the army during Soviet times, first as a high-ranking staff officer right up to a simple general. Later, however – following interim studies in banking – Mr. Ivanov reportedly founded a small-but-successful holding company, SIBINVEST, with other private investors, which is now apparently in the 80 % ownership of Mr. Ivanov. This company apparently holds, among other things, 51 % of the shares of a small Russian bank (ABC BANK), at which Mr. Ivanov is reportedly chairman of the supervisory board and at the same time, its financial consultant. Additionally, he has reportedly been exercising a state supervision mandate for a number of years, later exercising a supervisory board mandate, at the formerly state-owned diamond extraction group SIBIROMANT. Mr. Ivanov is also apparently active in several public offices, albeit only at the local government level.

---

290 The facts are to be judged under the respective national viewpoint of the appraiser. The bank therefore has its headquarters either in FL / A / D or CH. All subsequent aspects, too, if not expressly to be understood otherwise, should be read from the national standpoint

The Fictitious Case Study

As part of the privatisation of Russian operations, ABC BANK, as credit provider in the context of so-called deposit auctions, apparently became the holder of a right of deposit on the former state diamond operation SIBIROMANT at the initiative of Mr. Ivanov in the mid-1990s. After the claim against the Russian state failed, ABC Bank was apparently able to exploit the pledged property favourably and pay Mr. Ivanov in advance a generous, but still appropriate commission, previously agreed in writing, of 15 million US dollars, which is now to be invested at the bank.

2. Red Flags / enhanced due diligence

The bank employee carries out a sufficient identity check. During the bank's money laundering scoring it turns out that the potential customer Ivanov is deemed to be particularly high-risk owing to the high country risk (Russia has been on the list of "non-cooperating states" since 2001). As a precaution, due to his personal history the bank employee classifies Mr. Ivanov as a PEP and carries out – according to internal instructions – a so-called enhanced due diligence check in order to verify the origin of the assets to be transferred in more detail. This check brings to light the following additional information:

ABC Bank in Russia exists and has a state banking permit. The two trade register entries confirm, on the one hand, that Mr. Ivanov is chairman of the supervisory board of ABC Bank and, on the other hand, that he is a member of the supervisory board at SIBIROMANT. With regard to ownership it emerges that Mr. Ivanov holds no shares in SIBIROMANT and SIBINVEST has a 51 % holding in ABC Bank. In respect of SIBIROMANT the bank employee establishes on the basis of reliable documents that ABC Bank's loans to the Russian state really had failed and ABC Bank had exploited the pledged property. Mr. Ivanov presents him with documents that show that the commission payments by ABC Bank to himself were made in connection with the SIBIROMANT business as part of his performance-related pay arising from the consultancy contract. The company SUNSHINE Ltd. exists and runs three hotel complexes in Cyprus. Mr. Ivanov says that he does not need the 15 million US dollars to be invested, but intends to make smaller medium-term real investments in his hotels.

OVERVIEW

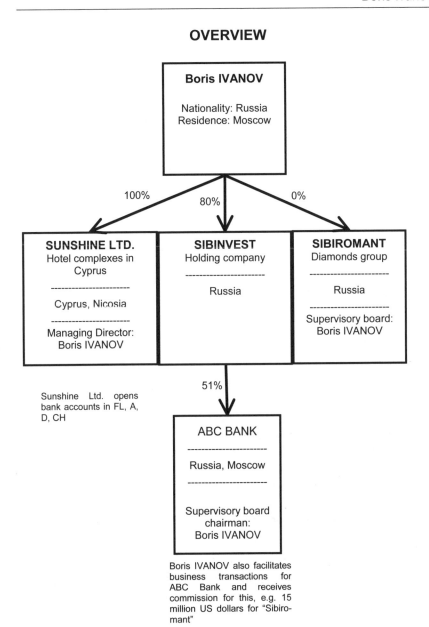

3. Course of the business relationship / close monitoring

The result of the enhanced due diligence is positive, the origin of the funds is plausible from the viewpoint of the bank. There is no form of indication of money laundering. Following approval by the bank's board of management the employee opens a EUR account for Mr. Ivanov as economically entitled person and sole senior manager with power to represent the company SUNSHINE Ltd. and grants his business partner power of attorney over the account. Furthermore, a merchant account and internet access are set for the company SUNSHINE Ltd. The 15 million US dollars are initially invested according to instructions in annuity bonds and first-credit rating corporate loans; the securities orders are charged to the current account and credited. Mr. Ivanov's wife also receives power of attorney for all accounts.

The bank employee monitors Mr. Ivanov's transaction with particular diligence in the subsequent period too. The funds of 15 million US dollars dwindle to a considerable extent in the subsequent months. Hardly any inflows are recorded.

In summer 2001 the account monitoring reveals that the outgoing payments are used to settle invoices for automobile spare parts, confectioners' equipment, hotel beds and other hotel equipment. Documentary credit transactions are also completed in individual cases. For the bank employee, this is proof that transactions really are forming the basis of the cash flows. The customer representative visits Mr. Ivanov at the ABC Bank building in Moscow at the beginning of 2002 and establishes that the latter is still acting as chairman of the supervisory board and consultant.

In March 2002 the customer buys a transportation aircraft from old Russian army stocks for 1.2 million US dollars. A purchase agreement and appraisal report are presented at the bank employee's demand. The bank employee decides to execute the transaction.

An amount of 2.4 million US dollars arrives from a Nigerian account in May 2002. At the bank employee's demand he is informed that the Nigerian head of state had reportedly acquired the aircraft for a high price. A purchase agreement and handover protocol are presented again.

4. New information / Ivanov's tax problems

In July 2003 Mr. Ivanov phones the bank and reports a house search (private residence) on the part of the Moscow tax authority. At the bank employee's demand Mr. Ivanov explains to him that the tax investigation body is alleging that other parts of his assets (so not the transferred 15 million US dollars) are the gains of a serious tax crime. The bank employee learns via his Russian correspondent bank that the process against Mr. Ivanov had been wound up a number of days after the search.

In November 2003 the public prosecutor's office in Moscow raises a complaint against Mr. Ivanov following a prior renewed house search and accuses him of having committed a particularly serious tax crime, which is apparently in the Russian catalogue of crimes preliminary to money laundering, within the context of the privatisation of state assets, particularly in connection with the SIBIROMANT transactions. In addition he is reportedly accused of embezzlement to the detriment of ABC Bank. The bank employee learns of the accusation only by accident.

Mr. Ivanov is arrested for questioning for danger of absconding in December 2003.

In February 2004 Russia requests the bank's home country for legal assistance due to the suspicion of money laundering in connection with the aircraft transaction. This is granted. The bank documents are confiscated by the national state authorities in the course of a house search.

Mr. Ivanov is cleared of all charges in January 2005.

C.
Questions to be Analysed

a) Was the bank permitted to open a customer relationship with Mr. Ivanov at all, according to national regulations? Which instances of suspicion must the bank employee take into consideration in this connection, according to national regulations?

b) When should the bank have deposited a suspicious transaction report, according to national regulations? Is there the obligation to deposit a suspicious transaction report, retroactively if necessary, for transactions that have already been completed?

c) What legal resources does the bank have against a confiscation of bank documents? What legal resources does Mr. Ivanov have?

d) What risks of prosecution do the employee, the bank and its senior management see themselves exposed to, assuming that money laundering has been committed with parts of the deposited funds and the bank employee has acted thoughtlessly, according to the view of the courts, when carrying out the transactions?

e) What risks of prosecution does the bank employee see himself personally exposed to, assuming that he had taken receipt of the gains of a serious crime?

f) What legal possibilities does Mr. Ivanov have in order to defend himself against the suspicious transaction report?

g) What risks of prosecution does the bank expose itself to with regard to the suspicious transaction report that has been made, since Mr. Ivanov was cleared of the charges?

D.
The "Ivanov" Puzzle is Solved

1. "Boris Ivanov" according to Liechtenstein's legal position

Dr. Erek NUENER

Concerning a)

According to the presented facts, the bank employee carried out a sufficient identity check. Assuming that this "sufficient identity check" referred to the contract partner and the economically entitled person, the bank was permitted to open a customer relationship with Mr. Ivanov.

The simple clarifications in the sense of Art. 15 para. 1 due diligence act (SPG) and Art. 1 para. 22 due diligence regulations (SPV) in aid of the plausibility of facts or transactions were unable to bring to light any instances of suspicion in the sense of Art. 16 due diligence act (SPG).

As part of the special clarifications according to Art. 15 para. 2 due diligence act (SPG) in connection with Art. 22 para. 2 due diligence act (SPG), the duty provider must procure, evaluate and document such information as is appropriate to eliminate or harden possible instances of suspicion according to Art. 16. para. 1 due diligence act (SPG). In the objective case, owing to the bank employee's special clarifications specific risk factors in accordance with Art. 16 due diligence act (SPG) were able to be ruled out.

Pursuant to para. 5.1. "FMA guidelines 2005/1 Monitoring the business relationship", business relationships can be continued as before if the facts of transactions clarified in accordance with Art. 15 due diligence act (SPG) are explained plausibly. If duty providers continue the business relationship despite doubts, but without having a suspicion in the sense of Art. 16 para. 1 due diligence act (SPG), they must monitor the course of the business relationship more closely. This is what the bank employee in the objective case has done.

Concerning b)

There is a duty to report to the FIU immediately in accordance with Art. 15 due diligence act (SPG) as soon as the suspicion arises from the clarifications in the sense of Art. 15 due diligence act (SPG), or by another manner in connection with non-permanent relationships, that there is a connection with money laundering, a crime preliminary to money laundering, organised crime or terrorist financing. In this regard it is unimportant whether the corresponding transaction was made in the past.

Pursuant to Art. II A 5 of the annexe to "FMA guidelines 2005/1 Monitoring the business relationship", transactions that cannot be reconciled with the duty provider's knowledge and experiences of the customer and the purpose of the business relationship contain risks with regard to money laundering.

In the objective case, the clarifications revealed that the company Sunshine Ltd. exists and runs three hotel complexes in Cyprus. The introduced funds are essentially not required by Mr. Ivanov as economically entitled person for Sunshine Ltd. However, he intended to make smaller medium-term real investments with these funds.

Since the purchase of a transportation aircraft from former Russian army stocks is not profile-compliant and basically cannot be reconciled with the purpose of the business relationship, there is certainly an indication of money laundering with regard to this transaction. A further indication for this was that the business partner was a politically exposed person from a "non-cooperating state".

However, living up to indications of money laundering does not in itself justify a suspicion for triggering the duty to report, but does occasion background clarifications in the sense of Art. 15 due diligence act (SPG).

The bank employee fulfilled his duty to carry out background clarifications in the sense of Art. 15 due diligence act (SPG) by having two purchase agreements, an evaluation report and a handover protocol submitted to him. Though the background information did not confirm the suspicion of money laundering, there was an enhanced duty of diligence owing to the various indications.

However, pursuant to para. 5.3. FMA directive 2005/1, duty providers, if they have doubts but no suspicion in the sense of Art. 16 Abs.1 due diligence act (SPG) and therefore break off the business relationship are permitted to withdraw assets only in such a form that allows the prosecution authorities, if need be, to follow the paper trail. In this case they are not permitted to pay out funds in cash or physically issue securities and precious metals.

The same must apply if a business relationship is continued despite doubts at hand because the suspicion in the sense of Art. 16 due diligence act (SPG) was not confirmed on the basis of the background clarifications. Should this have been the case with the bank employee, he had to pay attention to ensure that the paper trail was traceable. He was not obligated to report in the sense of Art. 16 due diligence act (SPG).

Concerning c)

The bank and bank customer are entitled to the legal resources according to criminal code (StGB) and criminal procedure code (StPO) in order to act against investigatory measures that are unjustified in their view.

Concerning d)

In the case of legal persons or fiduciary agents the criminal regulations of Art. 30ff. due diligence act (SPG) apply, according to Art. 33 due diligence act (SPG), for persons for whom they have acted or for whom they should have acted, however, under solidarity liability of legal persons or the pledged assets for fines, penalties and costs.

The delinquencies listed in Art. 30 due diligence act (SPG) are punished with imprisonment of up to six months or with a fine of up to 360 daily earnings. The misdemeanours listed in Art. 31 due diligence act (SPG) are punished with a fine of up to 100,000.00 Swiss francs. Culpability on the basis of other criminal standards is reserved according to Art. 32 due diligence act (SPG).

Concerning e)

Pursuant to Art. 165 para. 2 criminal code (StGB) somebody who takes receipt of or keeps asset components originating from a crime, a delinquency according to 287d or according to §§ 304 to 308 criminal code (StGB) or a delinquency according to the narcotics law committed by another person, be it in order merely to keep safe, invest or manage these asset components, transforms, exploits or transfers such asset components or transfers them to a third party, is punishable with imprisonment of up to two years or with a fine of up to 360 daily earnings. The fact alone that the bank employee has, according to the view of the courts, acted thoughtlessly is not sufficient for a sentence in the sense of Art. 165 para. 2 criminal code (StGB). However, if the bank employee seriously deemed it to be possible and has taken it into account that the assets originate from one of the delinquencies or crimes mentioned above, depending on the actual circumstances he is liable to punishment according to Art. 165 para. 2 criminal code (StGB) should the need arise. According to general damage compensation law the bank employee is liable for the damage arising from his illegal and culpable behaviour.

Concerning f)

The bank customer is not entitled to any legal resources against the suspicious transaction report, unless a case of deliberate reporting is at hand.

Concerning g)

Somebody who reports to the FIU in accordance with Art. 16 para. 1 is, if it emerges that the report was not justified, cleared of all civil and criminal law responsibility provided that he has not acted with intent. The bank therefore exposed itself to no risks with regard to this.

2. "Boris Ivanov" according to Austria's legal position

Mag. Johannes TRENKWALDER, LL.M

Concerning a)

Yes. Though the establishment of identity and examination led to a classification as a PEP and as a result to an enhanced duty of diligence of the bank when examining the customer in accordance with § 40 para. 3 banking act (BWG), no instances of suspicion concerning money laundering arose in the course of this examination. Another link for a particular duty of diligence of the bank would have been the circumstance that the Russian customer has no permanent residence in Austria and the transactions carried out provide no logical link with Austria.

Banking institutions must check a transaction particularly carefully if *"its nature [...] particularly suggests"* that it may be in connection with money laundering (§ 40 para. 3 banking act (BWG)). Types of transactions / combinations occasioning particular diligence are described n marginal notes 19 and 20 of the FMA circular of 23rd April 2004 concerning inspection procedures and suspicious transaction reports in connection with money laundering and terrorist financing ("circulars"). Furthermore, regular looks at the FATF homepage are recommended in order to include the money laundering transaction typologies published by the FATF in the examination of transactions.

Concerning b)

Transactions for which the client or recipient is a person located or residing in a non-cooperating state or which are conducted to or from an account at a foreign banking or financial institution located in a non-cooperating state must, if the total amounts to EUR 100,000.00 / euro equivalent, be reported to the authority immediately (§ 78 para. 9 item 5 banking act (BWG)).

The documentary credit transactions completed via ABC Bank in summer 2001 basically fulfil these requirements and would – in the event of exceeding the relevancy threshold – have had to be reported by the bank. The purchase of the transportation aircraft from Russian army stocks meets all pre-requirements and would therefore have had to be reported. The purchase and sale of the transportation aircraft would have had to be examined more closely by the bank, i.e. not exclusively via submission of the purchase agreements, since these transactions do not match the customer's business profile (No. 5 of the FATF Recommendations).

Suspicious transaction reports must also be deposited by banking institutions for transactions that have already taken place, in respect of which a founded money laundering suspicion has resulted (§ 41 para. 1 banking act (BWG)).

Concerning c)

A judge's confiscation order is strictly required for confiscation of objects. In exceptional cases (e.g. in the event of exposure while delayed or if there is also an arrest warrant against the person), security agents are permitted to temporarily secure such objects on their own authority. The court must then decide on confiscation. For an unlimited period, both Mr. Ivanov and the bank are entitled to the legal resource of complaint to the review chamber in accordance with § 113 criminal procedure code (StPO) against the examining judge's decisions. Searching / examination of documents may only be ordered against the owner's will by the review chamber (§ 145 para. 2 criminal procedure code (StPO)).

Concerning d)

Somebody who negligently breaches the obligations according to § 40 and § 41 para. 1-4 banking act (BWG) as a responsible person from a credit institution is punishable with a fine of up to EUR 20,000.00 (§ 98 para. 2 item 6 banking act (BWG)). Pursuant to § 5 VStG negligence is assumed if the perpetrator does not render it credible that no fault can be attributed to him in the breaching of obligations. All members of the management board of the banking institution are responsible persons of this type provided that they have not appointed one or more persons (from their circle or – for objectively distinct areas – third parties) as responsible agents. The bank itself is not liable to punishment, since money laundering can only be committed with intent and therefore the intent of an employees / decision maker of the bank is the pre-requirement for criminal responsibility of the bank according to the association responsibility act (VbVG).

Concerning e)

Pursuant to § 165 para. 2 criminal code (StGB) somebody who knowingly keeps, invests, manages, transforms, exploits or transfers to a third party, asset components originating from money laundering is punishable with imprisonment of up to two years or a fine of up to 360 daily earnings. There are no clues from the facts that the bank employee acted knowingly, which is why the employee's liability to punishment is ruled out provided that he was not appointed as responsible commissioner.[291] According to general damage compensation law the bank employee is liable for the damage arising from his illegal and culpable behaviour, while he, as an employee of the bank, is privileged with regard to the bank by the Austrian service recipient's liability act (DNHG) in his damage compensation law liability arising from his occupation.

Concerning f)

The bank customer has no opportunity to defend himself against the bank's suspicious transaction reports.

Concerning g)

Pursuant to § 41 para. 7 banking act (BWG) no damage compensation claims can be raised from the circumstance that a banking institution or a person working there has delayed or not carried out a transaction in negligent ignorance that the suspicion of money laundering was incorrect. A suspicious transaction report could only bring about the employee's responsibility according to criminal law if the employee is aware that no money laundering is at hand. The facts of credit damage in accordance with § 1330 ABGB are fulfilled if the suspicious transaction report was deposited by the employee in awareness of its incorrectness.

---

291 See also the remarks "Concerning d)"

3. "Boris Ivanov" according to Germany's legal position

Dr. Joachim KAETZLER

Concerning a)

According to the FMA's circular the bank has discretionary powers following checks on the person of the business partner, the origin of the assets and on the transaction profile. If instances of suspicion remain following intensive clarification, then the bank *"should"* reject the business relationship, item 30, para. 3 of the BAKred announcement of 30th March 1998. There is no statutory duty to break off a business relationship. Nonetheless, the bank *must generally* stop an actual transaction if money laundering is suspected, § 11 para.1 clause 3,4 German money laundering act (money laundering act (GwG)), until the prosecution authorities provide corresponding clearance or if they have not provided it owing to the lapse of time (48 hours). Nonetheless, in Germany, in cases of non-transparent privatisation earnings from the area of the former Soviet Union the BAKred circular of 10th August 2000 must be observed. According to the circular, with regard to the financial centre of Germany, the taking receipt of assets which are not necessarily the gains of an embezzlement or misappropriation but which are possibly in connection with such crimes *within the scope of privatisation* should be *generally understood as subject to reporting*. In view of the circular, therefore, it is preferable not to open a bank account, while at the same time the general administrative regulations do not replace the bank employee's individual discretion.

Concerning b)

The institution must submit a suspicious transaction report *"when facts are established that lead to the conclusion that a financial transaction is for the purposes of money laundering"*, § 11 para. 1 German money laundering act (money laundering act (GwG)).

There is no binding catalogue of facts. The banks must base themselves on the stipulations of the German Federal Financial Supervisory Authority (BaFin) in the announcement of 1998 and on the recommendations of the Central Credit Committee as much as on instructions from BaFin itself. In this regard BaFin regularly refers to the publications of the FATF: already according to item 24 of the announcement of 30th March 1998 particular attention must be paid to transactions which either do not match the *customer's business profile, reveal no recognisable economic background* or are *completed via a circuitous route*. The FATF criteria apply in supplement to this. Under reservation of a duty to report which will probably arise owing to the classification of the assets from "privatisation" the following therefore apparently applies: whereas the transactions in 2001 could still have continued as part of the business activity of Sunshine Ltd., the first suspicion criterion would definitely have been fulfilled with the acquisition of the aircraft and a suspicious transaction report would have had to be deposited. Reporting of the transaction in May 2002 would probably have been compulsory, among other reasons, owing to the *deviation from the business profile*, the business partner in a so-called "*non-cooperating state*" and owing to the clear identification of the *payee as a PEP* according to the announcement of 30th March in connection with the 40 FATF recommendations in 2003.

Institutions in Germany are now obligated to identify all existing customers retrospectively as well. Suspicious transaction reports for transactions that have already been carried out need not, however, be handed in *even if the suspicion arises subsequently*.

Concerning c)

If the confiscation is ordered by the public prosecutor, then the bank and the accused are entitled to the right to insist on a decision by the judge, § 98 para. 2 clause 2 criminal procedure code (StPO). Both the bank as the entity concerned and the accused are entitled to appeal against the confiscation of documents according to § 304 criminal procedure code (StPO). The German federal constitutional court made it clear that the appeal to establish legality can also be conducted once the confiscation has already taken place.

Concerning d) + e)

In the event of thoughtless committing the bank employee is threatened with imprisonment of up to two years or a fine, § 261 para. 5 criminal code (StGB). In the event of (conditionally) deliberate acting he is threatened with imprisonment of three months up to five years, § 261 para. 1 criminal code (StGB), in the event of *serious organised money laundering or money laundering as part of a gang* the sentencing ranges up to ten years' imprisonment. Additionally, expiry of the assets acquired due to the criminal act may be requested of the state treasury.

In Germany, companies – like all non-natural persons – are essentially not punishable owing to the particular characteristics of the principle of guilt. A reform of corporate criminal law has been under consideration for decades. There is indeed responsibility of the senior management based on § 14 criminal code (StGB); there must be personal culpability and intent or thoughtlessness on the part of the partner, chairman etc., which is generally not the case. However, in the case of organisational deficiencies, regulatory fines of up to EUR 500.000.00 are impending according to § 130 para. 1 OWiG. Additionally, nonetheless, the bank is liable in the course of civil law in respect of persons potentially damaged by the preliminary crime, provided that actual asset damage is accrued to these persons due to the act of money laundering.

Concerning f)

The bank customer is entitled to no form of legal resource against the suspicious transaction report. The bank customer also has no claim to acquittance of a – textually groundless – suspicious transaction report.

Concerning g)

The German money laundering act sets down *partial release from liability* of banks in § 12 if the bank has not acted *with intent or grossly negligently* when compiling the suspicious transaction report. Whether there is a right to recourse to state liability in the event of a negligently incorrect suspicion report is unclarified to date, since in Germany the *bank's behaviour cannot be described unequivocally as "sovereign"*. The question of who bears the damage of a stopped financial transaction is equally not clarified.

4. "Boris Ivanov" according to Switzerland's legal position

Dr. Peter BOSSHARD

Concerning a)

Yes. The proper money laundering clarifications in the sense of Art. 3-8 Swiss money laundering act (money laundering act (GwG)) as well as Art. 2 and 3 of VSB 03 brought to light no instances of suspicion in the sense of Art. 9 money laundering act (GwG). Even an "enhanced customer due diligence clarification" in the sense of Art. 17 money laundering regulations (GwV-EBK) was able to rule out specific risk factors.

Concerning b)

Only when a founded suspicion in the direction of a punishable act according to Art. 305bis or Art. 260^{quinquies} is at hand *must* a suspicious transaction report be compiled to the reporting office according to Art. 23 money laundering act (GwG) (Art. 9 money laundering act (GwG)). In accordance with Art. 23 para. 4 money laundering act (GwG) the reporting office "*immediately*" reports the case to the responsible public prosecutor's office.

A suspicious transaction report according to Art. 9 money laundering act (GwG) *can* be compiled if doubts concerning the clarifications according to Art. 2 and 3 professional etiquette of the Swiss bankers' association (VSB 03) arise or persist. Nonetheless, according to Art. 27 money laundering regulations (GwV-EBK) a report is also already possible if the FI has no "*founded*" suspicion but "*made/makes observations leading to the conclusion that assets originate from a crime*". He can then – supported by the *right* to report of Art. 305ter para. 2 criminal code (StGB) – compile a report directly with the prosecution authority.

Retrospective checks on existing customers can take place at any time, particularly if doubts emerge concerning earlier money laundering clarifications. The duty to submit a suspicious transaction report retrospectively for transactions that have already taken place only exists if a money laundering act (GwG)-relevant business relationship continues or transactions repeat themselves.

A suspicion in the sense of the money laundering act (GwG) body of regulations is appropriate if a transaction does not match the customer's business profile or no economic background can be documented and/or is recognisable (which in our case study lies within the discretion of the bank in the course of the business relationship).

Concerning c)

The bank and the bank customer are entitled to the legal resources permitted according to criminal code (StGB) and criminal procedure code (StPO) (appeal) in order to proceed against investigatory acts that are unjustified in their view, or, respectively, to have these cancelled or reversed.

Concerning d)

The fallible bank employee or an immediately involved member of the senior management are threatened according to Art. 305bis criminal code (StGB) with imprisonment or a fine, in serious cases in accordance with Art. 305bis para. 2 criminal code (StGB) prison of up to five years and a fine of up to 1,000,000.00 Swiss francs if the money laundering was conducted professionally or *"high sales"* and/or *"considerable profits"* were achieved via the act of money laundering.

Concerning e)

Pursuant to Art. 100^{quater} criminal code (StGB) the bank as legal person is liable according to criminal law if it negligently or deliberately operates or facilitates money laundering during the course of business and if this crime cannot be attributed to any particular natural person owing to an organisational deficiency within the bank. In such a case the bank can be punished with a fine of up to five million Swiss francs. The amount of the fine is based on the seriousness of the crime, the seriousness of the organisational deficiency and the damage that has been caused. The bank is punished independently of the culpability of natural persons if it can be accused of not having taken all *required* and *reasonable* organisational precautions to prevent money laundering (Art. 100^{quater} para. 2).

Both the bank employee and the bank as legal person are liable according to civil law for actual asset damages caused by money laundering.

Concerning f)

The bank customer is entitled to no legal resources in order to defend himself against the suspicious transaction report. Whether and when he is informed of the suspicious transaction report lies within the discretion of the bank. Pursuant to Art. 10 para. 3 money laundering act (GwG) the person concerned must namely not be told of the suspicious transaction report during the asset block imposed against him.

Concerning g)

According to Art. 11 Swiss money laundering act (money laundering act (GwG)), in the event of a suspicious transaction report in accordance with Art. 9 money laundering act (GwG) or Art. 305ter para. 2 criminal code (StGB) and in the event of an asset block effected on the basis of these regulations in the sense of Art. 10 money laundering act (GwG), both exculpation on account of breach of professional or business secrecy and liability exclusion according to criminal and civil law exists "*if (the financial intermediary) has proceeded with the diligence necessary under the circumstances*".

5. Summarising comparison of the solutions

When the solutions are viewed together, one thing becomes clear: despite the commonly encountered opinion that some of the four jurisdictions represented here supposedly have less regulation density in the area of money laundering prevention, the basic structures and also the regulatory mechanisms (money laundering act, liability to punishment, administrative instructions) are very similar.

As was not to be expected otherwise, the national regulations concerning money laundering prevention take regional peculiarities into consideration; therefore, special regulations for "school savings" are contained in Austria (§ 40 para. 2a banking act (BWG)), while the small life insurance investment, typical in Germany, is privileged there (§ 4 money laundering act (GwG)). The regulations' differing range of punishment should probably also be viewed against the background of a generally different level of sentencing. The more expansive regulations in Switzerland concerning alternative self-regulating organisations are probably predominantly founded on a different self-perception by the respective organisations.

A number of further differences in the details are to be found in the raised case under the following aspects:

5.1. Handling of "privatisation cases"

Basically, the strands of argument and the techniques of money laundering prevention are very similar in the individual states. All legal regulations implement the risk approach and combat the problem using a clear evaluation of the facts, which – as shown – has also led to different notions of whether and when a suspicious transaction report would need to be deposited. In terms of form, the fact that proceedings in the case of many privatisations in the states of the former Soviet Union may potentially approached in an only insufficiently regulated manner and, in some cases, unfairly as well, is probably not sufficient for liability to punishment for embezzlement or corruption. Of course, as a result – in terms of form – a suspicion of money laundering would also not be conceivable. This dichotomy is reflected in the selected case study.

The commentary on the case in the country reports from Liechtenstein, Austria and Switzerland takes account of this formal approach, while the German financial supervisory body took up a clear position.

It is very striking that the Federal Republic of Germany handles these "privatisation cases" more restrictively from the point of view of money laundering control – as the BAKred circular of 28th August 2000 shows. Whereas in all other states there are no "special regulations" in terms of responsibility in order to deal with cases of largely unregulated privatisation, the German bank supervisory authority has simply disregarded all formal barriers and – against the terms of the law – referred to the fact that a duty to report on the basis of largely unexplained circumstances could also come into consideration precisely if no attribution of an asset to a case of corruption or embezzlement of state assets is at hand. One case in 2005, in which the financial supervisory body went public in connection with the assets of a Russian PEP arising from privatisation transactions leads to the conclusion that this politically fixed intention does not exist only on paper.

From a systematic point of view, Swiss law with Art. 27 money laundering regulations (GwV-EBK) also has a remarkable standard to hand which also suggests a suspicious transaction report to institutions if there is "no founded suspicion of money laundering", but "observations are made that lead to the conclusion that assets originate from a crime". Parallels are striking if one compares the Swiss regulations with the circular from the German BAKred.

5.2. Moment of submitting a suspicious transaction report

Particularly restrictive from an international point of view are the notions of the Swiss federal banking commission in respect of the reporting of non-customers. A bank or financial intermediary must compile a suspicion report concerning a non-customer even if he totally rejects the opening of a business relationship (Art. 24 money laundering regulations (GwV-EBK)). This obligation takes effect far in advance of a potentially punishable transaction and goes far beyond what is required on the part of a banking institution as "self protection" according to the international understanding. All other considered legal regulations justify a duty to report with regard to a suspicious business relationship only when a business relationship is also to be commenced on the part of the financial intermediary.

5.3. Notions concerning corporate liability law

When comparing the national answers to the case study it is particularly striking that, internationally, no unity has yet been found on the creation of effective corporate liability law. Admittedly, the clear goal of creating the pre-conditions for adequate culpability of legal persons throughout the European economic area had been clearly articulated in the course of the 3rd EU money laundering directive.

As is evident from grounds for consideration 41 and from Art. 39 of the directive, all Member States of the EU are urged to provide sanctions mechanisms for legal persons as well. In the course of the legislative process, this point had been discussed many times in the face of questions of legal dogma in Germany; not least because of this, the European Community has moved away from requiring the introduction of a uniform corporate criminal law.

Nevertheless, international pressure on Germany to continue to envisage corporate criminal law in the medium term with the aim of promoting the integrity of the economic location of Germany has increased, not only through the recommendations of the EU directive, also due to the legal position in Liechtenstein and the modifications in October 2003 owing to the introduction of the new Articles 102 and 102a into Switzerland's criminal code as well as due to the coming into force of the association responsibility act in Austria on 1st January 2006.

5.4. Expression of the bank customer's rights

In Liechtenstein and Switzerland all assets of the affected bank customer are frozen for five days following submission of the suspicious transaction report – an extremely long period when compared internationally (for comparison: Austria: end of the following business day, Germany: two banking days following the suspicious transaction report). If one bears in mind that the affected bank customer must not be informed of the stopped transaction immediately (and damage possibly arises due to this), the five-day period seems unusually long; it is not even conditioned by differing practices in national cash flows, for example. However, this period is compensated for by more relaxed handling of bank customers concerning the suspicious transaction report; in Liechtenstein, for example, there is a right to inform the person concerned after 20 days (Art. 16 para. 5 due diligence act (SPG)); in Switzerland the law merely makes it clear that the bank customer must not be informed during the five-day asset block and places further proceedings in the discretion of the bank.

These regulations stand in opposition to the 3rd EU directive. According to their Art. 28 institutions shall not be permitted to provide any form of information to the bank customer at all in connection with the suspicious transaction report.

In Germany it is already the case today that the bank is not permitted to inform the bank customer of the suspicious transaction report even retrospectively (§ 10 para. 5 money laundering act (GwG)). A highly pragmatic solution is offered by the Austrian law: as soon as an order to confiscate has been made, the FIU is urged to inform the bank customer immediately; the bank herewith has a correlating right to refer the customer to the investigatory authorities.

In all considered legal regulations the bank – in different formulations – is released from the consequences of the suspicious transaction report provided that the bank does not deliberately submit an incorrect suspicious transaction report. In Germany and Austria, exemption from liability applies in the event of grossly negligent behaviour, in Switzerland at least as long as the suspicious transaction report took place in compliance with the law.

With regard to the protection of the bank customer's interests, however, all exemptions from liability have the same dogmatic weak point. The question of who must reimburse the bank customer's damage in the event that a negligent interruption of a transaction is unclarified in all states.

5.5. Conclusion

On closer inspection the differences between the considered legal regulations – with the exception of corporate criminal law – prove to be relatively small. For one thing, this is a clear indication that the goal of international harmonisation of anti-money laundering appears to be bearing fruit even beyond EU boundaries. The legal regulations of the German-speaking regions looked at here have essentially implemented international stipulations; no considerable deficiencies with regard to the FATF stipulations can be recognised. Beyond this, not even the regulations of bank secrecy stand in the way of effective anti-money laundering in any of the states under consideration.

E.
A Question of Statistics

Theoretical discourse on a constructed case study shows "how it would be decided at a given time according to the applicable legal situation". Unfortunately, this does not permit a conclusion on jurisdiction decisions that have really been taken concerning real cases. Therefore, what would theory be without a matching practice-related overview?

Precise figures are the statistician's extra something, succinct contexts the analyst's daily bread. Both – at least partially – can be viewed in the annual reports of the national money laundering reporting offices (Financial Intelligence Units). Without intending to deliver a copy of the reports, the primary interest in connection with this publication is the number of suspicion reports that have taken place to the FIUs, in this context the proportion of reports deposited by banking and banking institutions, the number of cases forwarded to the prosecution authorities by the FIUs etc., or, respectively as far as obtainable, the ultimate results of the long investigatory process in the form of convictions or acquittals.

For this reason there follows a consciously restricted brief statistical report[292] from the national FIUs from the Principality of Liechtenstein, Austria, Germany and Switzerland, complete with contact addresses and a summarising commentary.

---

292 The annual reports of the FIU's should be consulted for more detailed information concerning the suspicious transaction reports (see internet addresses at the reporting offices); the conviction statistics originate either from the FIUs themselves or were requested from the national public prosecutor's offices

1. Principality of Liechtenstein

Financial Intelligence Unit
Äulestraße 51
9490 Vaduz
Principality of Liechtenstein

Tel. secretary's office (+423) 236 61 25
Fax (+423) 236 61 29

WWW http://www.llv.li/amtsstellen/llv-sfiu-home.htm
@ info@sfiu.llv.li

Statistics from FIU Liechtenstein:[293]

Year	2001	2002	2003	2004
Reported cases	158	202	172	234
of which banks	81	96	82	133
in %	51.3	47.5	47.7	56.8

"In the reporting year 79 % of the suspicious transaction reports made were forwarded to the prosecution authorities. Compared with the previous year this means an increase of just under 7 % (2003: 72.1 %; 2002: 61.4 %)."[294]

---

[293] Financial Intelligence Unit Liechtenstein, Annual Report 2004, p.11f.
[294] Financial Intelligence Unit Liechtenstein, Annual Report 2004, p.25

2. Austria

Bundesministerium für Inneres
Generaldirektion für die öffentliche Sicherheit
Bundeskriminalamt
Meldestelle Geldwäsche
Josef Holaubek-Platz 1
1090 Vienna
Austria

Tel. [295]	(++43) - (0)1-24836-85298
[outside office hours	(++43) - (0)1-24836-85027]
Fax	(++43) - (0)1-24836-95 1305
[outside office hours	(++43) - (0)1-24836-85099]
WWW	http://www.bmi.gv.at/meldestellen
@	BMI-II-BK-3-4-2-FIU@bmi.gv.at

Statistics from FIU Austria:[296]

Year	2001	2002	2003	2004
Reported cases	248	215	288	373
of which banks	---	---	---	349
in %	---	---	---	93.6

*"Criminal / subsequent accusations were submitted by the A-FIU to the responsible public prosecutor's offices in 147 cases. [...]
In the period under observation, in Austria as a whole 100 criminal accusations were submitted due to suspected money laundering. The processing of 31 court applications and 32 account opening decisions and the 69 account evaluations carried out on the basis of this led, in addition to the results of 33 interrogations and nine house searches, to the submission of 43 more subsequent accusations, which are already included in the overall number of 147."*[297]

---

[295] Daily Mon. to Fri. from 8 a.m. to 6 p.m., excluding public holidays
[296] Financial Intelligence Unit Austria, Annual Report 2004, p.4
[297] Financial Intelligence Unit Austria, Annual Report 2004, p.5

3. Germany

Bundeskriminalamt
Referat OA 14
Zentralstelle für (Geldwäsche-)Verdachtsanzeigen
65173 Wiesbaden
Germany

Tel. (++49) – (0)611-55 18615 or
      (++49) – (0)611-55 14545
Fax (++49) – (0)611-55 45300

WWW http://www.bka.de

Statistics from FIU Germany:[298]

Year	2000	2001	2002[299]	2003	2004
Initial indications	4,818	8,214	9,050	7,196	8,764
Reported cases according to money laundering act	4,401	7,284	8,261	6,602	8,062
of which banks	---	---	1,940	5,229	6,406
in %	---	---	85.4	79.2	79.5

"In 2004 criminal law investigations were abandoned / abandonment were suggested in 40% of the procedures by the responsible state criminal police offices in respect of the 8,062 suspicious transaction reports according to the German money laundering [...]. In 23 % of the procedures, processing at clearing offices had not yet been completed at year's end. In respect of 33 % of the procedures the suspicion of money laundering / of a crime listed in § 261 German criminal code had hardened to such an extent that the procedures were submitted to a relevant specialist police department for further processing. The suspicion of other crimes including possible tax crimes hardened in respect of a further 4% of the cases. The suspicion therefore hardened in more than one third (37 percent) of the reports."[300]

---

298 Financial Intelligence Unit Germany, Annual Report 2003, p.46 / Annual Report 2002, p.26 / Annual Report 2004, p.47
299 Reports to the FIU from August 2002 only (total: 2,271, of which banks: 1,940)
300 Financial Intelligence Unit Germany, Annual Report 2004, p.8

4. Switzerland

Bundesamt für Polizei
Meldestelle für Geldwäscherei
Nussbaumstraße 29
3003 Bern

Switzerland
Tel. Hotline (++41) – (0)31 - 323 40 40
Fax (++41) – (0)31 - 323 39 39

WWW http://www.fedpol.ch/d/themen/geld/i_index.htm
@ mros.info@fedpol.admin.ch

Statistics from MROS Switzerland:[301]

Year	2000	2001	2002	2003	2004
Reported cases	312	417	652	863	821
of which banks	230	261	271	302	340
in %	73.7	62.6	41.6	35.0	41.4

"From 1st April 1998 to 31st December 2004 a total of 2,708 suspicious transaction reports were forwarded to the prosecution authorities.[302] Of these, 1,311 reports (48.4 %) had led to a ruling by the end of 2004[...]:

-- 49 cases resulted in a judgement.[303]
-- Criminal proceedings were opened in 692 cases, but abandoned again due to findings arising from the corresponding judicial police investigations.
-- In 453 cases no criminal proceedings were opened following completion of the preliminary investigations. Decisions not to open were taken predominantly in connection with money-transmitter reports.

---

[301] Reporting Office for Money Laundering Switzerland (MROS), 7th Annual Report, 2004, p.22
[302] Remark: going by the overall number of reported cases 1998-2004 (3,493) this results in forwarding in 77.5 % of the cases
[303] Remark: 47 convictions, 2 acquittals (cf. Reporting Office for Money Laundering Switzerland (MROS), 7th Annual Report, 2004, graphic on p.48

-- Criminal proceedings were suspended in 117 cases because criminal proceedings were already opened abroad.

Around one half of the forwarded suspicious transaction reports, namely 1,397 or 51.6 % of the cases are still pending."[304]

---

304 Reporting Office for Money Laundering Switzerland (MROS), 7th Annual Report, 2004, p.47

5. Due diligence and success rates

The presented statistics can only be directly compared with each other with difficulty. For one thing, the available information differs both in terms of time and of facts, for another thing, attention needs to be paid to national peculiarities, such as the respective position of the FIUs in the investigatory process.

Judged according to the bare figures – over a number of years – a marked increase in due diligence reports can be seen in all of the states under consideration. For the major part this can be attributed to the tightening regulations, in other points also to the generally increased awareness of the problem among acting parties or, respectively, external effects such as the terror attacks of September 2001.

However, the number of suspicious transaction reports alone does not yet indicate anything about their quality. In the United States, for example, for many years it has been the case not so much of qualitative, but more the case of quantitative reports[305], since a suspicion report was already triggered by a certain transaction threshold value. With this the Americans intended to live up to their view that money laundering can most effectively be thwarted by making it impossible to smuggle the contaminated capital into the financial systems. In this connection there were thousands of reports every day which had nothing in common with money laundering and which unnecessarily burdened the investigating institutions with additional work. For this reason, the Europeans chose the qualitative approach from the start, in which the banks (or other concerned parties) already carry out "investigations" in accordance with the due diligence laws and therefore only forward cases to the national FIUs that promise corresponding success in the sense of "culpability". The Americans also associated themselves with this approach at the end of the 1980s in the course of the founding of the FATF (however, the lower threshold values continue to exist).

In Germany the FIU Annual Report 2004 establishes that on average for the year, a suspicion of a crime could be entirely eliminated in only just under 15 % of the cases forwarded to the FIU, in

---

305 See also Dr. Kaetzler's "international chapter" from p.52 of this publication

order to finally show that in 2004 a full 27 % of cases (2003: 25 %) had to be completed without "*a residual suspicion being able to be eliminated from the point of view of the police*"[306]. Critics will presumably leap on the approximately 40 % of abandoned procedures (whether with or without a residual suspicion) and therefore brand the effort put into diligence duties as exaggerated. However, after subtracting the as yet uncompleted cases of 2004 the Annual Report clearly records an attractive success rate of a bit more than one third. According to the report, the suspicion hardened in 37 % of the cases and (presumably) further investigations and potentially a court decision will follow. Unfortunately, the FIU report does not deliver a final conviction rate. Nevertheless: with its high rate of suspicious transaction reports, the European qualitative approach shows certain strengths in comparison with the (old) American quantitative approach.

Reports are likewise on the rise in Liechtenstein and Austria. It is expected that newly obligated professional groups above all, such as lawyers, for example, will be able to be made more aware of the statutory duties of diligence in coming years so that even more reports take place from this sector. In Austria the reports result almost exclusively from banks,[307] in Liechtenstein approximately one half. The Principality is known for its intensive use of trustee constructions, which is why an almost equally high number of suspicious transaction reports come from trusteeships.

Unfortunately, there are no meaningful conviction statistics available for Liechtenstein and Austria. However, a respectable forwarding rate of suspicious cases to the responsible prosecution authorities can be deduced from the reports. In Liechtenstein this is an extremely impressive 79 %, in Austria, however, 28 %[308]. In this connection, in the Austrian case Mag. Josef Mahr, head of the FIU, points out there are often several suspicious transaction reports concerning one case, meaning that the forwarding rate appears statistically smaller than it is in reality.

---

306 Financial Intelligence Unit Germany, Annual Report 2004, p.4
307 Mag. Josef Mahr, head of the FIU Austria confirms by telephone the 90 % (or more) suspicious transaction reports from banks for previous years too – precise figures are not available
308 Calculated from 104 suspicious transaction reports (147 forwardings minus the 43 subsequent suspicion reports) to the overall pool

In its Annual Report by the MROS (Swiss FIU) Switzerland provides the most expressive statistics of the states under consideration, thereby putting itself in the front line for criticism at the same time. As in the other jurisdictions, an increase in reports can be seen in Switzerland over the years. The marked decline in bank reports in terms of percentage from 2001 can be explained conclusively by the fact that so-called "money transmitters" (companies such as, for example, Western Union, which offer fast cash transfer for a fee) were included in the reporting.

The interesting factor in Switzerland is primarily the published conviction statistics covering several years. According to the figures, rulings were made concerning just under half (48.4 %) of the cases forwarded (a respectable 77 % of the original suspicious transaction reports) to the prosecution authorities since 1998, numbering 2,708.

On the other hand, the next aspect – the judgement rate – is quite disappointing. A judgement was arrived at in only 49 cases, of which a conviction was arrived at in 47 cases. This corresponds, going by the number of forwarded reports with a decision (1,311) to a feeble rate of 3.5 %.

Ms. Judith Voney, lawyer, head of the MROS, kindly informed us at our request that the 47 convictions would only apply to certain facts, and indeed with regard to Art. 260 item 1 (criminal organisation), Art. 305bis (money laundering) and Art. 305 Swiss criminal code (absence of diligence in financial transactions), whereby the MROS only conducted statistics on "money laundering convictions" / received the statistics from public prosecutor's offices. She told us that the statistical indications in respect of convictions carried out, based on the suspicious reports that had arrived at the MROS, should be assumed to be considerably higher for that reason and could not be directly deduced from the published number of convictions (e.g. non-covered judgements for fraud, embezzlement etc.). Additionally, the prosecution authorities met their statutory obligation to make statistical reports to the MROS only insufficiently, meaning that statistical discrepancies had to be expected.

It must be mentioned at this point that there is a considerably higher number of money laundering judgements in Switzerland than just the 49 MROS cases. So-called "autonomous" criminal proceedings for money laundering, which originate directly from the police or the judiciary or which, for example, are initiated by reports from private individuals, do not run through the MROS. Therefore, in the same period (1998-2004) – with 120 acquittals – an additional 537 guilty verdicts resulted according to Art. 305bis Swiss criminal code, and 7 guilty verdicts according to Art. 305ter Swiss criminal code. This multitude of judgements is impressive, but originally the cases do not primarily arise from due diligence obligations, but must probably be classified more as a traditionally police-related success than as the result of efforts by financial intermediaries.

It remains to be noted that the major cases of suspicion generally require a lengthy investigation and are not decided within the first year. The report by MROS Switzerland additionally emphasises that cases of suspicion not forwarded to the prosecution authorities have no notable share of the assets concerned (amount of damage). Out of 772 million Swiss francs in 2004, 760 million Swiss francs were forwarded for further investigation, whereby 24.8 % of the cases, but only 1.5 % of the assets were not examined any further.[309]

The special circumstances of the incompleteness of the statistics, as well as the as yet undecided cases, must also be taken into consideration for Switzerland's conviction rate. Particularly cases with a foreign reference or major assets are frequently drawn out over several court instances and that is why, presumably, the majority of them can still be found in the pool of pending cases. An improvement in the conviction rate is accordingly highly probable.

Despite everything the statistics also show that judgements specifically with regard to money laundering (initiated by due diligence providers via the MROS) are currently still rare. A number of striking major cases presented by the media with particular effect do not hide the fact that the large majority of money laundering suspicion cases, even if the assets are not concerned as well, do not lead to a conviction with reference to money laundering. The reason for this probably lies in the complexity of the evidentiary situation – it is only a shame that a proven preliminary crime in

---

[309] Reporting Office for Money Laundering Switzerland (MROS), 7th Annual Report, 2004, p.13

interplay with documented "proofs of due diligence" is frequently not sufficient, as can be deduced from the figures for a money laundering judgement. The argument that although many cases lead to no conviction with regard to money laundering facts, but at least with regard to the preliminary crimes, is certainly no consolation for due diligence providers. On the contrary: at most it proves that the banks and other duty providers – against all predictions – often do not, as planned, contribute only to anti-money laundering, but also rather play a part against crime in general (preliminary crimes). The perceived existence of the authorities actually being responsible as an "involuntary police deputy" thereby receives a certain amount of confirmation.

Even if the large majority of money laundering convictions, as explained, originate from the traditional police or judicial area, it remains to be hoped that the proportion of MROS cases leading to a judgement will increase in future. The success of due diligence obligations, seen in this light, must in many cases be sought in their preventive effect and not in the conviction statistics.

III.
Russia Undergoing Change
–
Solutions Required

Dr. Andreas INSAM

The 1990s in Russia saw the economic system transformed from a planned economy to a capitalist-based system. According to the Western perception, the planned economy was lacking in efficiency: the inflated administration in the state apparatus was not in the position to always get the maximum out of the Russian economy. Only a few areas were pushed (for example, armament and space travel technology, extraction of raw materials) while many others were neglected. There were inefficient employers in terms of planners who believed themselves to be "cleverer than the market" on the one hand, and unmotivated employees in terms of plan fulfillers on the other. The now infamous saying by a Soviet worker that "they pretend to pay us, we pretend to work" was symbolic for an artificially restricted economic system.

It would be presumptuous to absolutely concur with this Western notion that the central economy never functioned correctly, since in the end it grew faster in some decades than the Western, capitalist market economies. Nonetheless the economic engine began stuttering in the 1970s when the information age began and central offices were no longer able to execute the processing and forwarding of information without a time delay. In the Soviet state operation every product was planned with state prices. A popularly recorded example in this connection is the planning of a modern passenger aircraft which has about three million different parts – which need to be priced in turn.

After the system fell into crisis and gradually disintegrated in favour of non-centralised structures, Russia found itself as the former Soviet Union superpower in the position of a technologically and economically backward giant. The redistribution of state property to private investors did indeed promote corporate efficiency and also attracted foreign investors owing to many entrepreneurs' Western orientation; on the other hand, the ensuing meteoric rise of the new Russian entrepreneurial cadres was not without its jealous onlookers and critics.

The criticism primarily referred to the often somewhat dubious acquisition of the formerly state-owned enterprises at non market-standard, ludicrously low prices. Secondly, in many cases the profits generated by the now privately managed companies now no longer remained in Russia itself, but migrated abroad out of the reach of taxes. Due to (illegal) capital flight[310] and (legal) construction of company networks in order to move profits into less tax-intensive states, the Russian state lost out on EUR billions of income – estimates range, calculated from 1992, up to EUR 300 billion of flight capital.[311]

> "When Russia carried out privatisation, the idea was that private property was more efficient than state property. It was not the idea, however, that property would be sold to the USA and that Khordokovsky would rake in the profit for it."[312]

At this point it must be considered how things should continue with the Russian economy in times of growing uncertainty – mainly politically induced in contrast to the economic crisis of 1998. President Putin practically declared war against the oligarchs and their companies with the arrest of Mikhail Khordokovsky in 2003. The question arises of what, from the economic point of view, would be an optimum solution to the problem of "assets accumulated, in many cases, under somewhat dubious circumstances" by nouveau riche Russians and their leaders, the oligarchs. Several parallel problem areas in the Russian state are urgently crying out for a solution:

- A stop must be put to capital flight to countries abroad;
- The "1990s privatisation story" needs a definitive ending;
- International investors are demanding legal certainty and stability.

A discussion of amnesty as a potential point of departure opens up numerous perspectives. Without trying to raise a claim to completeness, a number of statements for and against amnesty settlement as well as already known effects of amnesties shall be touched on briefly. The reflection will be completed with a brief overview of the latest amnesties in Italy and Germany. A summary of factors that promise success, combined with the current situation in Russia, ultimately provides the input for a recommended course of action for or against amnesty in Russia and a possible organisation scenario.

---

310 Common examples of capital movement from p. 365
311 See Alfa Bank, "Inside and Upside: Monthly No.42", www.alfabank.com
312 Analyst Sergei Markov on Russian basic rules with regard to the oligarchs, Moscow Times, 30th October 2003

A.
Amnesty
–
Bridge to Tax Honesty

"Scents don't come sweeter"

1. General remarks about the term

Amnesty comes from the Greek word "amnestia" and means "forgetting, forgiving". Amnesty is used in the pardoning of criminals. In the financial field it is found in the form of tax amnesties, which on the one hand aim at being able to re-integrate a part of the evaded taxes in the state budget, and on the other hand aim at escorting tax offenders into legality without the negative consequences of criminal prosecution. As an accompaniment to an amnesty other conditions such as minimum supplementary taxes or investment conditions are imposed on "remorseful returnees".

Advantages for the state granting amnesty are clearly obvious. Revenues can be increased in the short term, declared capital can be taxed as normal again in the future and, in terms of administration, amnesty is considerably more simple than a determined search and prosecution of tax offenders. Advantages for the persons granted amnesty lie in the subsequently considerably reduced tax burden and an end to the impending discovery of the tax evasion by financial investigators. Additionally, domestic banks benefit when evaded capital is returned from abroad.

The other side of the coin is revealed in the disadvantages of a tax amnesty. Honest taxpayers pay dearly for their legal compliance – they have no enjoyment of privilege – and tax morale is undermined. The question arises for every taxpayer whether evasion and waiting for the next "amnesty period" would not be more favourable, weighing up the possible risks of such an action, than complying with tax contribution ordinance. The law as an absolute is consequently now only perceived to be relative.

In addition, an inherent problem is the legalisation of illegal funds. Amnesty regulations can be abused by money launderers in order to launder profits from crimes – camouflaged as evaded (legal) capital.

One instrument with a similar effect is the possibility of a voluntary declaration which can be made at any time at the responsible fiscal office, though a voluntary declaration is generally more offputting than accepting an amnesty settlement due to penalty interest and higher tax back payments. Viewed in this light, voluntary declaration is more a final-instance resource for tax evaders if they are already acutely threatened with discovery by investigators.

In the context used in the following a distinction will be drawn between two amnesty possibilities. On the one hand, amnesty on capital (legal origin, not taxed); on the other hand, personal amnesty (illegal origin, not taxed).

Amnesty on capital: i.e. capital returns to the country of residence and/or declaration of assets kept secret / capital not taxed to date (e.g. invested in offshore centres) are not legally prosecuted within a period to be defined. The tax evasion that has taken place is thereby granted amnesty, the available capital declared and taxed as normal in the future.

Personal amnesty: i.e. personal misdemeanours in connection with generated capital are no longer investigated. This form of amnesty guarantees extended protection for persons concerned, since not only the illegal earnings invested (also abroad) and their fiscal non-declaration, but possibly dubious earnings are granted amnesty as well. Earnings amnesty would need to be defined narrowly in this connection, in order, for example, to prevent the amnesty of capital crimes[313].

Personal amnesties are predominantly known to a broad public as "Christmas amnesties" (pardoning and release of criminals by national presidents at Christmas). Personal amnesty would not be implementable within the scope of a tax amnesty, since it would annul the criminal code and render any unlawful gainful act as a crime preliminary to tax evasion exempt from punishment. Personal amnesties can therefore only be narrowly associated with certain persons and not in direct connection with a tax amnesty unrestricted to persons. For this reason it appears more appropriate to devote ourselves to amnesty on capital.

2. Amnesty on capital – tax amnesty

An amnesty on capital takes place either with a view to launching a "recall measure" on flight funds deposited abroad, which subsequently flow back into the domestic capital market, declaring as-

---

313 Particularly serious crimes such as, for example, murder

sets kept abroad and adding them to the tax basis, or bringing capital misappropriated domestically to future taxation.

There was a vivid settlement in the recent past in Italy, which hoped for a capital return from neighbouring Switzerland. Topically, an amnesty settlement expired in Germany on 31st March 2005. These two last major amnesties – Germany 2004/05 and Italy 2002/03 – proved to be very different in their effects. While the declaration of relevant tax offences in Germany failed by far to achieve the hoped-for proportions, the Italian budget was able to rejoice over considerable "earnings on the side".

The cornerstones of Italian and German settlements and their revenues are illuminated in the following. Complementary to this, a judgement of their efficacy will attempt to highlight the narrow dividing line between success and failure.

2.1. Germany 2004/05

In the form of the Tax Amnesty Disclosure Act (StraBEG), the legislator in Germany created an act for the encouragement of tax honesty in order to impose favourable subsequent taxation on assets which were incompletely taxed or not taxed at all in a simple and quick way by means of an exemption from punishment. The legislator sweetened the return to tax honesty by waiving reduced taxes and imposing, in their place, the payment of a favourably flat-rate contribution by the tax offender. Additionally, use of the amnesty was driven by means of announcing stricter controls after the timeframe set forth for voluntary declaration expired. Banks' reinforced duty to inform in respect of fiscal offices (from 1st April 2005), in particular, was designed to make holders of foreign black money accounts uneasy and motivate them to tax honesty.

2.1.1. Structure of the settlement

The statutory basis, the German Tax Amnesty Disclosure Act (StraBEG), published on 29th December 2003, entering into force on 31st December 2003 and supplemented by special instructions on the application of the StraBEG, published on 3rd February 2004, together with further supplementary information (last modified on

16th September 2004), formed the basis of the amnesty in Germany.

The temporal scope of validity (submission period) of the exempting declaration was limited to 1st January 2004 until 30th March 2005. The objective scope of validity concerned the amnesty of ...

Tax crimes according to
§ 370 German contribution ordinance (AO) (tax evasion),
§ 370a AO (tax evasion professionally or as part of a gang) and
§ 26c German sales tax act (UStG) (profession-related or gang-related damage to sales tax revenue) together with
Tax regulation offences according to
§ 378 AO (thoughtless [= grossly negligent] tax evasion),
§ 379 AO (tax exposure),
§ 380 AO (withholding tax exposure) or according to
§ 26b UStG (damage to sales tax revenue),
...

which were committed in the period from 1st January 1993 until 31st December 2002. Settled by the compensation payment were debts arising from income or corporate tax, sales tax, wealth tax, trade tax, inheritance tax and gift tax as well as from additional taxes on income tax (solidarity supplement, church tax).

The temporal limitation to the end of 2002 made it possible to avoid potential nullity declarations and belated amnesty requests. In order to prevent a declaration of funds for the purpose of laundering arising from other crimes, the exempting declaration required an explanation of the funds' origin; though close examination of this origin was generally bypassed, the investigation of origin serving only to secure the submitting person in the event of possible subsequent checks. This in itself was a main reason for the first rejection of the amnesty settlement by the German Bundesrat in September 2003; word was even of a "state-tolerated form of money laundering"[314]. A firm inquiry with the German Federal Ministry on the problem of declaring incorrect life circumstances yielded no further information.

---

314 "Bundesrat rejects tax amnesty" [Bundesrat lehnt Steueramnestie ab] of 26th September 2003, report by the German Bundestag press department, www.bundesrat.de

(Financial) incentives to accept the settlement came in two respects, in reduced evaluation bases depending on tax classification:[315]

Income / corporate tax:	60 %
Sales tax:	30 %
Inheritance / gift tax:	20 %
Trade tax:	10 %

and in reduced lump-sum tax rates:

1st Jan. 2004 – 31st Dec. 2004:	25 % of declared revenues
1st Jan. 2005 – 31st Mar. 2005:	35 % of declared revenues

2.1.2. Revenues

The initially optimistic expectation aimed at tax revenues of approximately EUR 25 billion. The government downwardly revised the figures as early as January 2004 and speculated with EUR 5 billion which, however, just 10 months later – as can be seen from the 2005 budget – was in turn estimated as too optimistic. The revenues were estimated at only just over EUR 1 billion and actually landed up at EUR 1.4 billion.

By the end of December 2004 the state's additional income still amounted to only EUR 889.7 million, in which process the last month in particular was crucial with EUR 333 million declared capital. A very pronounced West-East divide was recognisable on disclosure of the evaded capital. For example only 1.7 % of the payments overall originated from the new German federal states (former East German states).[316]

2.1.3. Appraisal of the efficacy of the amnesty

With just under EUR 1.4 billion of additional income for the German budget the 2004/05 tax amnesty lay far behind the initial high expectations. The exact cause for the relatively low use of the amnesty offer can be traced back to several factors.

---

[315] If an evasion crime concerned several types of tax, the percentage rates were added up to the upper limit of 100 %

[316] See *German Federal Ministry for Finance*, "Act for the encouragement of tax honesty: report on tax amnesty", [Gesetz zur Förderung der Steuerehrlichkeit: Bilanz der Steueramnestie], monthly report of the German Federal Ministry for Finance, September 2005, p.41-43, www.bundesfinanzministerium.de

For one thing, German tax evaders who deposited their capital in neighbouring countries continue to feel very safe against possible prosecution. The foreseeable alignment of capital taxation in the EU region and associated mutual control notifications between tax authorities are not yet fully supported by the most important havens for presumed illegal earnings. These havens include Austria, Luxembourg and Belgium, but also the important non-EU members Liechtenstein and Switzerland. As long as, for example, Swiss banking secrecy does not prescribe information in the event of suspicion of tax evasion[317], source tax for foreign bank balances [318] – in comparison with the occasionally considerably high German income tax tariff – does not deliver a resounding argument for returning to legality, either. Additionally, source tax concerns only interest earnings from cash accounts, fixed-interest securities and pension funds (of private individuals in each case), and dividends, appreciations, certificates, derivatives etc. are therefore not covered. The partial transfer of source tax to the country of residence is therefore only effective until the underlying asset structure is regrouped.

The same line is taken by criticism of the German legislator for not having linked the tax amnesty with reformed capital taxation. An interest withholding tax in the example of Austria, which switched from the declaration of capital earnings in the income tax statement to automated withholding tax with a very successful amnesty in 1993, has been debated for a long time and was originally going to be introduced in parallel with the amnesty, but concrete steps in this direction were not taken. The potential returnee to tax legality is therefore confronted with the problem of the original grounds for flight which continue to exist as before: the high taxation of income. The apparent advantage of the amnesty thereby continues to be merely the gentler taxation of the years covered by the amnesty; not, however, the sought-for lower future taxation.

Furthermore, the initially apparently high remorse rate of 25 to 35 % above the true remorse charge in the event of a report was

---

[317] However, the suspicion of "tax fraud" very likely breaks through Swiss bank secrecy, see on this subject Dr. Bosshard's remarks on the legal situation in Switzerland from p.239

[318] See EU interest directive: Directive 2003/48 EC of the Council of 3rd June 2003, in force since 1st July 2005

misleading. Unlike the Italian amnesty, which required a simple remorse rate of 2.5 % of the declared sum of illegal earnings (or alternatively an assessment in bank annuities amounting to 12 % at non market-standard low returns), the German amnesty became entangled in varyingly high evaluation bases for the respective tax types and assessment according to capital gains instead of original capital. Without closer attention the impression was therefore given of a deterrently high surcharge, although on consideration of the finer points the additional payments that were actually due were in the range of the Italian reform. With declared assets of EUR million, invested in shares, a remorse charge of only barely 2.6 %[319] resulted. The nominal burden of 25 % was therefore more of an unsuccessful marketing policy than a real obstacle.

2.2. Italy 2002/03

The present Italian government had already announced during the election campaign that it would pass a comprehensive tax amnesty for tax evaders. Since the Berlusconi government it is difficult to shake off the impression that comprehensive tax amnesties have become the rule rather than the exception. In order to bring down the state budget's deficit rate, there were generous tax amnesties both in 2002 and in 2003, which were extended in each case.

2.2.1. Structure of the settlements

Tax amnesty I ("scudo fiscale I")

The Italian act concerning the tax-privileged return of flight funds from abroad[320] prescribed exemption from all administrative, tax, contribution and criminal law sanctions if assets illegally sent or retained abroad were declared in Italy or brought back to the country in the submission period from 1st November 2001 until 28th February 2002. Declaration was sufficient in the case of fixed assets such as real estate; movable assets such as cash or share deposits had to be transferred to Italy at the same time.

---

319 See *Hans Flick*, "The Tax Amnesty in Practice" [Die Steueramnestie in der Praxis], Frankfurter Allgemeine Zeitung of 3rd February 2004
320 Statutory basis: Act 35/2001

In parallel as a (financial) incentive an insignificantly small remorse charge of 2.5 % of the declared amount[321] had to be paid or alternatively 12 % of the amount had to be invested in special Italian bank annuities with low interest. The actual asset transfer took place on repatriation to the coffers and on repatriation via credit institutions, thanks to the simultaneous introduction of strict bank secrecy, largely anonymous. In the event of suspicion of non-fiscal misdemeanours underlying the statements banks and financial intermediaries were obligated to deposit a report to the corresponding authorities. The promotion was extended in February 2002 to May 2002 (declared assets only), respectively June 2002 (repatriated assets), even before the declaration period expired.

Tax amnesty II ("scudo fiscale II" and residual variations)

The great success of the 2002 tax amnesty prompted the Italian legislators to extend and expand the existing amnesty model (act 289/2002 and decree 282/2002). Now the tax shield was not only applied to private individuals, but companies were included in the modified model as well. The declaration period from 1st January 2003 until 30th June 2003 was extended in June 2003 up to 16th October 2003, again by decree.

The Italian conditions of Amnesty II – continuously supplemented and repeatedly partially modified – objectively referred both to direct and indirect taxes and were essentially open to all taxpayers. In terms of time, adjustments were generally possible for the years 1998 to 2001 (value added tax), respectively 1997 to 2001 (remaining taxes). Several different amnesty variations (subsequent declaration of concealed income, amnesty procedures concerning tax procedures already introduced, amnesty for individual taxes and periods or overall amnesty procedures etc. ...) covered practically all possible types of tax evasion. In this respect the Italian amnesty went beyond the German regulations, since it offered more room to manoeuvre in the choice and volume of the evasion to be declared owing to the different procedures.

---

321 Unlike the German settlement, though, without reduction of the evaluation bases to the full capital (e.g. in the case of deposits) instead of on the capital earnings as in Germany

Calculation of the remorse charge to be paid differed depending on the choice of procedure. In the area of repatriation of assets from abroad it was based on Amnesty I (private individuals: 2.5 %, companies: 6 %), but higher penalties were implemented in the case of other amnesty procedures, though the penalty tax could now only be paid in cash and no longer completed by purchasing bond annuities. Despite an increase in the penalties there was still a financial incentive to accept the offers.

2.2.2. Revenues

The result can definitely hold its head high, specifically in comparison with other European countries. The first amnesty ("scudo fiscale I") delivered an overall sum of just under EUR 60 billion[322] in newly declared or repatriated capital, a majority of that from neighbouring Switzerland. As a result, due to the small remorse charge an estimated EUR 1.5 billion remained in the Italian state coffers.

The second – considerably expanded – amnesty produced approximately EUR 0.5 billion from the "scudo fiscale II" and a further EUR 8.8 billion[323] in additional income from the remaining amnesties (value added tax crimes etc.) in the Italian finance minister's coffers. Despite the impressive return the overall coverage rate of the repatriated foreign capital corresponds, according to the estimate by the Italian national bank, to only somewhat more than 10 % of the presumed "black money" abroad.

2.2.3. Appraisal of the efficacy of the amnesty

The first amnesty settlement served up extremely minor conditions for tax offenders willing to return. The remorse charge of 2.5 % was not crucial in comparison with the evaded amounts, it has even reportedly been taken over in some cases by Italian banks for customer acquisition. Unlike the German settlement, Italy required the return to Italy in the case of movable assets (specifically in the case of bank accounts and deposits abroad),

---

322 See *Organisation for Economic Cooperation and Development*, "OECD Report: Italy: Phase 2", 2004, http://www.oecd.org
323 Information from Prof. Walter Großmann, expert in Italian tax law and lecturer at the universities of Innsbruck and Bozen

whereby a "bank war" for the investment support of the returning billions was preordained. The second settlement, too, enjoyed minor conditions, though it was more crucial that all taxes were affected in several amnesty variations – covering practically all possible tax misdemeanours – even in the case of procedures already introduced against tax evaders.

The state revenues of both amnesties are impressively high. Nonetheless it should not be forgotten that these also include amounts which would have flowed into the state coffers in any case, therefore specifically amounts from pending tax procedures. It may be assumed that the amnesty was particularly noticed by those who were already involved in a procedure by the tax investigators or for whom this was foreseeable. It also cannot be ruled out that in the course of the largely anonymous utilisation of the amnesties illegal funds flowed into the market via the presentation of false earnings circumstances. Individual checks on the plausibility of the origin of all declarations cannot be presupposed.

Optically speaking the 2.5 % of the penalty tax of the first amnesty wave looked considerably better than the 25 % in Germany. The incomparably larger Italian evaluation basis and obligatory repatriation of assets to their own country were overlooked by many in the process.

The future effect of the Italian amnesty will be better than the German counterpart. Although, owing to the low taxation of declared amounts, no high amounts – viewed proportionately – flowed into the state coffers in the short view, in the long view the declared capital can now be subjected to normal annual taxation amounting to billions. The first amnesty alone brought in an additional EUR 60 billion of taxable volume; the second amnesty added at least more than EUR 100 billion.[324] In the process it should be considered that a proportion would have been fed into the tax basis in any case (amounts from ongoing procedures etc.),

---

324 According to Prof. Walter Großmann only the declarations from the scudo fiscale II (approximately EUR 20 billion) can assumed to be secured. It is not feasible to raise the estimate from the revenues of the remaining amnesty owing to the many forms of calculation, and there are also no official figures available. HIB assumes at least EUR 80 billion of residual declarations at a (probably excessive) remorse rate of 11 %

but an impressively expanded tax basis can nonetheless be assumed.

Brief overview of tax amnesties in Germany and Italy

	Germany	Italy
(Principal) statutory basis	Tax Amnesty Disclosure Act (StraBEG) of 29th Dec. 2003	Act 35/2001 Act 289/2002
Aim	Declaration of evaded capital	Repatriation of evaded capital to Italy, declaration of evaded capital
Submission period	1st Jan. 2004 to 31st Mar. 2005	1st Nov. 2001 to 28th Feb. 2002 (30th Jun 2002) 1st Jan. 2003 to 30th Jun. 2003 (16th Oct. 2003)
Duration in months	15	8 / 10
Period under amnesty	1993 - 2002	1998 - 2001 (sales tax) 1997 - 2001 (remaining taxes)
Objective validity	Crimes acc. to § 370 AO, § 370a AO, § 26c UStG, § 378 AO, § 379 AO, § 380 AO, § 26b UStG concerning corporate tax, sales tax, property tax, trade tax, inheritance tax, gift tax, additional taxes on income tax	Amnesty I: Crimes when declaring assets abroad (private individuals only) Amnesty II: Crimes during tax assessment in the case of both direct and indirect taxes
Remorse charge	25 % until 31st Dec. 2004 35 % until 31st Mar. 2005 (relating to a reduced evaluation basis depending on the tax type) Effective rate: approx. 2-10 %	Amnesty I: 2.5 % of the declared sum, alternative investment of 12 % of the evaluation basis in low-interest state securities Amnesty II: separate rates depending on amnesty procedure
Tax revenues	EUR 1.4 billion	Amnesty I: EUR 1.4 billion (scudo fiscale) Amnesty II: EUR 0.5 billion (scudo fiscale) EUR 8.8 million (residual variations)
In % of GDP	0.06 %[325]	0.41 %[326]

---

325 GDP 2004 according to Eurostat: EUR 2,178 billion (at respective prices), http://europa.eu.int/comm/eurostat
326 BIP 2003 according Eurostat: EUR 1,301 billion (at respective prices), http://europa.eu.int/comm/eurostat/; double GDP calculated since the Italian amnesties were effective over two years

3. Success factors

"Amnesty bargains in closing down sale"

Now that the two "major" amnesties in Germany and Italy have been described, a number of internationally valid success factors can be recorded. Empirical investigations – a good overview is provided by Torgler/Schaltegger (2003)[327] – prove that tax amnesties are more successful under consideration of certain circumstances. The effect of an amnesty is all the greater the:

- shorter the notice is (a premature announcement encourages evasion in order to profit during the amnesty period);
- higher the announced number of inspections after expiry of the amnesty period is (amnesty as an "opportunity" against inevitable discovery);
- smaller the imposed penalties are (financial incentive to accept);
- higher the penalties after the amnesty period are (deterrent in the event of non-acceptance);

---

[327] See *Benno Torgler/Christoph Schaltegger*, "Tax Amnesty and Political Participation", 2003 annual conference of the Swiss Society of Economics and Statistics (SGVS) in Bern

- more credible the government makes the "last chance" (no further amnesty in sight);
- more attractive the tax legislation is (permanent incentive for tax honesty after the amnesty);
- higher the general tax morale among taxpayers is (improvement through image campaigns by the government and attractive tax rates with intensive checks at the same time possible).

A further point – which is admittedly more difficult to influence – would be the attempt to effect herding behaviour. Like the exponential growth of mobile phone operators bordering on market saturation, positive herding behaviour can be assumed among tax evaders as well. In the case of mobile telephony the incentive for herding behaviour arises above a certain market share threshold, through network-internal special tariffs for example; in the case of a tax amnesty, with increasing probability of checks in the case of personal non-declaration and an increasing number of overall declarations, there may be a run on the amnesty.

4. Amnesty in Russia?

No definitive conclusions can be drawn for Russia from the amnesty experiences of other countries so far. Even from the amnesties carried out in Russia itself (1993, 1996, 1997), only contingent conclusions on a renewed amnesty settlement can be drawn as there have been many further changes in the basic legal and economic conditions.

The effect of a statutory amnesty is based on several – highly country-specific – pillars. The current tax burden, the applicable tax offence and procedural law, criminal prosecution intensity and the tax morale prevailing in the population are considerably responsible for the success of a call to honesty. Concerning tax morale a survey among 504 Russian small businesses brought to light the predominant problem:[328]

---

[328] See *Jakob Fruchtmann/Heiko Pleines*, The Russian Tax System [German], study by the University of Bremen concerning Russian tax practice and tax morale in Russia, discussion paper from the Financial Sciences Institution of the University of Hamburg, p.41-56, 2001

- Just under half admitted to little or no tax knowledge.
- One third faulted the incomprehensibility of the laws.
- 70 % view taxes as necessary, but at the same time tax evasion not as a crime, but only as a minor misdemeanour.

In addition to the lack of clarity in legislation itself, the exorbitantly high tax rates until the first major tax reform in 2001 had a negative effect on tax morale. These rates were in the range of 55 to 60 % and originated from Soviet times, something which for state-owned operations – taxes were de facto paid by companies only – represented mere redistribution from one pocket into the other and was therefore no problem. However, with privatisation, paying taxes also brought a change of ownership on the capital and the prohibitively high rates encouraged tax evasion. The 2001 reform modernised the system fundamentally and aligned it with Western standards. Nonetheless, there is a continued absence of a Russian "tax culture", and the most streamlined laws are not much use without equally streamlined administration.

After the 2001 tax reform, which considerably cut the number and amount of taxes and strongly curtailed the sovereignty of Russian regions in tax legislation, not much was left remaining of the old obsolete system. Internationally, extremely attractive tax rates were implemented until 2005, among them a flat-rate income tax of 13 % and profit tax of 24 %, though work still needs to be done on public perception and efficient execution.

Certainly, links must first be forged with tax evaders before the new tax system, which eliminates former defects and makes evasion less attractive, can be used.

4.1. Capital amnesty

Under the prevailing conditions, an amnesty on capital in Russia – apart from the currently still poor tax morale – would be deemed to be a great success. The high tax rates of the post-Communist era could be "forgotten" via the amnesty; internationally speaking, current taxes are located in the lower range. In interplay with an obligation to invest in Russian values and therefore a strengthening of the Russian economy, impetus for the market would be foreseeable.

The proportion of foreign flight capital which would be transferred back to Russia through an amnesty can be estimated only roughly. Estimates by the Russian Association of Industrialists and Entrepreneurs, which has already submitted its amnesty proposals to the Russian government, speak of potential returns in the billions of US dollar range and correspondingly high tax revenues. Alfa Bank estimates the potential return to be 10 to 20 billion US dollars.[329] A comprehensible order of magnitude, if one considers that billions were sent abroad out of the reach of taxes (or even – evasively) since the early 1990s and continue to be so. At 15 billion US dollars[330] the most current estimate by Pavel Voronin from the Duma Committee for Budget and Taxes is in a similar order of magnitude.

At the same, Russia's modernised tax system would promise more clarity in future tax issues. Black capital abroad could be freed up again for lucrative investments in Russia. Even foreign investors would have an incentive to join amnestied entrepreneurs economically and establish new partnerships, since the shadows of a dubious past – the sword of Damocles for many Russian companies – would no longer be able to damage a business relationship.

On the other hand there is the question – which frequently comes under intensive discussion in matters of amnesty in Western states too – of to what extent the official "forgetting" of crimes is morally defensible. Hitherto honest taxpayers would be at a considerable disadvantage compared with self-confessed tax offenders – particularly in the case of Russia with its formerly high tax rates. Unlawful behaviour could even be reinforced according to the motto, "the next amnesty will surely come". Correspondingly, an amnesty undermines the tax morale of honest taxpayers, who are left empty-handed.

---

329 See *Alfa Bank*, Inside and Upside: Monthly No.42, www.alfabank.com
330 See "Russia's economy can gain 15 billion US dollars from an amnesty on capital", economic news from Russia of 29th June 2005, www.russland.ru

4.2. Personal amnesty

The question of a personal amnesty can be answered only by weighing up possible economic advantages with prevailing society notions of morale. The predictable advantages are obvious. For many entrepreneurs it would present the opportunity to "make a clean start" and draw the line under past events. Uncertainties concerning possible misdemeanours in the privatisation phase and the highly incomplete legislation of the subsequent period would be pushed out of the way.

For Russia, in the long term, a personal amnesty for tax misdemeanours in the past decade would presumably be fertile ground for future economic growth. The legal certainty created would additionally encourage international investors and would put Russia back en route to being an attractive economic location.

In the short term an amnesty would bring incomprehension among the population and leave the Russian government, which in argumentative terms would be on the losing side against the accusation that "the great get away with it, while the little people are penalised", with much explaining to do. Viewed as a whole the Russian state would limit its attack opportunities to former state capital within the context of investigations (cf. Yukos affair), legitimise the formerly proverbial privatisation "at any price" and would consequently deprive itself of opportunities to legally avenge illegally acquired state property.

4.3. Realistic and economic appraisal

Considered realistically it has to be assumed that there is no question of a comprehensive personal amnesty in the immediate future, since the government would jeopardise its image in the eyes of the Russian population. Furthermore, a not unproblematic selection of personally amnestied individuals would need to be made, leaving many questions open in any case.

As before, the Russian government cannot take much pleasure in a personal amnesty; reports from the court of audit on aspects of the privatisation phase stress this clearly. The fault is deemed to lie solely with current owners and not with the then privatising state apparatus. Transaction reversal is even being demanded in the case of (inevitable) discovery of breaches of the law then applying.[331] In its monthly report on the market situation in February 2004, Alfa Bank published an outlook on capital amnesty according to which it said it was expecting a far-reaching amnesty as "thanks" from the economic minister if the composition of decision makers remained the same following the presidential elections in March 2004. This prognosis could hold according to the current state of things – even if a little belatedly. Thus in January 2005 the officially reconfirmed Minister of Economy German Grev still viewed general amnesties as the wrong method and set his focus on further tax reforms.[332] Like Grev, albeit in a toned-down form, Christof Ruehl, Chief Economist of the World Bank, was backing harsh anti-trust and anti-monopoly laws for taming the influence of the oligarchs as early as 1993.[333] Since the second half-year of 2005, however, the Russian government has adopted significantly more gentle tones with regard to a potential capital amnesty.

A pure amnesty on capital – i.e. without bypassing future checks on asset accumulation – is currently not only conceivable but also even highly probable. This confirms earlier statements, for example by Arkady Dvorkovitch, Deputy Minister for Economic Development and Trade, with, *"Amnesty for capital is expected to be passed in Russia in coming years [...] the question here is when exactly, and how"*[334]. Experts close to the government such as Andrei Sharanov, from the same ministry, were increasingly speaking out – in addition to entrepreneurs – for an amnesty soon, something which was definitely beneficial for the actual planning now.[335]

According to the latest reports from Russian news agencies a capital amnesty is predicted from 1st July 2006 for crimes before 1st January 2005. In the process the amnesty – as discussions

---

331 See "Privatisation the Russian Way", [Privatisierung russischer Art], Frankfurter Allgemeine Zeitung of 16th December 2004
332 See "Economy Demands Tax Amnesty" [Wirtschaft fordert Steueramnestie], Neue Zürcher Zeitung 31st January 2005
333 See "Interview with Christof Ruehl", Nizhny Novgorod of 16th September 2003, www.worldbank.org.ru
334 "Amnesty for illegally exported capital can be passed in Russia", economic news from Russia of 10th February 2004, http://wirtschaft.russlandonline.ru
335 See "Climate without Control", Kommersant of 8th February 2005

currently stand – is to apply for natural persons and principally bring income from clandestine employment to taxation. With the shadow economy's share in GDP at more than 40 %, as currently assumed by the Russian interior ministry, this goal is definitely comprehensible.[336] The tax rate on the declaration is to be between 9 % and 13 %, in which connection the original intention of forced depositing of funds at a Russian bank was abandoned again. A binding asset repatriation from abroad is no longer under consideration, thus also providing perspectives for fixed-assessment (black) funds, for example in the case of real estate.

The legal reflection is not yet completely worked out. Although prosecutions on the basis of tax law are ruled out, experts are of the opinion that the Russian judiciary could strike via other criminal laws if the declared capital is not a simple sum of black money arising from a normal work relationship. Logically speaking, talk therefore cannot be of a watertight offer and a redressing of uncertainty, since the "major evaders" certainly do not feel themselves addressed by this.[337]

The whole settlement still seems to be not fully worked out. If Russia is only concerned with the reintegration of minor taxpayers for the future expansion of the tax bases, then legal planning of this type can be sufficient. Without the involvement of legal persons and without more comprehensive earnings amnesty opportunities, though, the 2006 Russian amnesty will unfortunately fail to meet the more long-sighted goal of legal certainty.

Straightforward tax evaders who have generated their assets on a fixed legal basis could thereby be attracted back to Russia and their capital could flow as a financial injection into the sickly market which, after the latest capital flows in the course of the Zukos investigations (5.5 billion US dollars in the first half-year of

---

[336] See Russia: "Catastrophic scale of the shadow economy", economic news from Russia of 4th October 2005, www.russland.ru

[337] See, for example, "Amnesty of capital in Russia – a political matter" of 11th August 2005, "Government hopes for a positive reaction to capital amnesty" of 11th August 2005, "Russia agrees on the basic features of a tax amnesty" of 12th August 2005, "Amnestied capital may remain abroad" of 13th October 2005 or "Tax amnesty in Russia postponed by half a year" of 24th November 2005, economic news from Russia, www.russland.ru

2004[338]) and the incessant annual capital flight in the two-figure billions range, is showing a strong need for equilibrium. Solely the positive balance of trade due to the high commodities prices in 2004 allows the negative effects of capital flight to appear somewhat less tangible at the moment. However, as soon as market prices fall again and the balance of trade dwindles, a brisk recall action and the attraction of new investors will enjoy full priority.

From the economic viewpoint a personal amnesty – despite moral misgivings – would be the most sensible choice for Russia's longer-term development. An offer by the Russian government to oligarchs to buy themselves freedom from future investigations with substantial sums would kill two birds with one stone. Deficiencies from the Yeltsin privatisation phase could be partially compensated for at least financially at correspondingly high rates, and at the same time a friendly investment climate would be created in Russia by the resulting legal certainty – both for persons granted amnesty and for their international partners.

The present show trials, complete with convictions with high media impact of former economic captains such as Mikhail Khordokovsky, may indeed appease the hunger for justice a little. However, they only reinforce the hunger for legal certainty without really raising the prospect of a solution with a promising future for the insecure Russian economy.

4.4. Recommendation

Though no immediate recommendations for the present can be deduced from the Russian amnesties in the past – all basic conditions are too divergent – they shall nonetheless be mentioned briefly in terms of their form, in order to delimit the following recommendations from earlier attempts.

The first amnesty in 1993 was subsequently cancelled again in 1995, which is why it will not be considered in more detail. The second amnesty in 1996 was valid from January until April 1996 and referred to the enabling of deferment of tax arrears and tax

---

338 See news report from "Der Standard" of 7th July 2004, still higher flows can be assumed since this report. In addition the value of the Russian capital fell due to slumps in securities

exemptions with the simultaneous announcement of reinforced tax checks. Tax exemptions were partially the result of the substitution of monetary payments for goods payments, in which case the delivered products went to the state at overinflated prices. Just under a year later there was another amnesty period from March until June 1997, which again primarily dealt with tax arrears and their treatment (penalty interest etc.). Empirically speaking no sustainably significantly increase in income could be proven through the amnesties in 1996 and 1997.[339]

Under consideration of the success factors empirically proven in the specialist literature and the current situation in Russia following the formulation of important tax reforms, it can be noted that a tax amnesty in Russia in compliance with the rules for success could lead to a long-term economic bonus. The increased legal certainty and the stability-promoting effect should be stressed in the process.

"Now or never – cough up!"

---

339 See *James Alm et al*, "Tax Amnesties and Tax Collections in the Russian Federation", p.10, 2001

A general capital amnesty would be urgently required following the tax reforms for simplifying and increasing the attractiveness of the Russian tax legislation, in order to forge links into honesty with many "opportunistic evaders" – induced by prohibitively high tax rates, sluggish administration and negotiability of individual conditions at the regional level – from the former tax system. In the process, generous offers in terms of easily manageable tax back payments must be combined with the announcement and publicly traceable implementation of tightened penal standards in the event of non-acceptance and subsequent discovery of tax offenders.

The question of the oligarchs can apparently be clarified by personal amnesties which would only be applicable for selected groups of persons – in full awareness that such a selection could never be conclusively justified and implied massive criticism. Ceasing ongoing processes and a personal amnesty for misdemeanours in the context of the privatisation phase of the Russian economy would need to be characterised by considerably higher penalty rates than the residual amnesty. In the process, the aftertaste of "ransoming" would have to be accepted in the sense of a more long-sighted judgement of the situation. In addition to higher penalty rates an obligatory reinvestment of assets bunkered abroad on Russian state territory would be a further domestic boost, though the reinvestment can only be guaranteed via the sale of time-bound state loans or established projects. Other variations in the sense of simple capital remittances etc. would be exposed "without protection" to a recurring outflow from Russia. As a return service by the Russian state the cessation of criminal prosecution – oligarchs residing abroad are also endangered by extradition agreements – should offer sufficient incentives for accepting the amnesty.

An alternative to the limited personal amnesty of selected privatisation profiteers would be an alteration of corresponding laws. In respect of the still vaguely completed privatisation phase it would be desirable, for example, to have the appeal timeframe arising from privatisations reduced. This variation would offer an extremely elegant privatisation amnesty by a circuitous route without requiring an explicit limitation to oligarchs via personal amnesty. The population's dissatisfaction concerning exemption from punishment would more likely be restrained by the change in legislation since the term "amnesty" would not be pronounced directly.

However, all the indicated accompanying measures can only ultimately promise success if the mutual mistrust between state and citizen in Russia can turn into a permanent relationship of trust. Only on the basis of a credible and above all permanent government offer can an amnesty, and subsequently a tax settlement, be implemented to the satisfaction of all. In parallel with the implementation of the reformed tax laws it is necessary to convey transparency and credibly eliminate past insufficiencies – for example, unequal tax treatment under identical original conditions and implied placing of tax debtors in a position of uncertainty. In the process the question of acquired private property (untouchable by the state) is of crucial importance for the principle of trust for leading privatisation profiteers.

B.
Russia's Tax Situation
–
An Outline of Reforms

Russia's Tax Situation – An Outline of Reforms

> "The hardest thing in the world to understand is income tax"
> *Albert Einstein (1879-1955)*

Until the reform in 2001 Russia's tax system was barely transparent, even for specialists. In addition to incomprehensibility, other insufficiencies which delimited the Russian from modern Western systems took their toll:

- Extremely high overall burden at 55-60 % of GDP (for comparison: EU at approx. 41 %);
- Progressive demonetisation in the 1990s;
- Tax burden as "matter of negotiation";
- Additional burdens due to donations to civil servants etc.

Restructuring of the tax landscape was tackled when Putin took over the presidency in 2000. Owing to the broad backing of the president by the media and the Duma, as well as the lack of opposition parties, the government's reform plan was able to be implemented practically without structural influences from outside. The most important goals of the reform were the improvement of investment conditions in Russia, the repatriation of companies from the shadow economy to the legal arena, the simplification and standardisation of tax laws, the further monetisation of tax payment and the centralisation of revenues.

The centralisation of revenues was intended to limit tax federalism. Owing to the freedom of regions to pass their own taxes and to put the very generally maintained national tax laws of 1991/92 into concrete terms locally, the result was sometimes contradictory legal situations and an impenetrable confusion of various local taxes. The legislation became considerably more transparent with the abolition of numerous tax types and central codification. After the reform, the regional tax administration delivers up the majority of payments to the state, whereby the significance of regional taxes and, associated with this, of tax competition within the state is minimised.

Internationally speaking, the tax rates are in the lower range following the reform. The low income tax rates in particular (flat tax of 13 %) and the reduced corporate earnings tax (to 24 %) are designed to attract investors and consequently help the Russian state to a higher volume of contributions. Social contributions which were previously levied individually are now subject to a digressive tax rate between 35 % and 2 % and were brought together in a standardised social tax. In addition, by reducing the tax burden the reform aimed at a "level playing field", meaning that individual scopes for negotiation and tax privileges were largely abolished. The saying, "everyone is equal in the eyes of the law" finally found certain relevance in terms of tax.

This new structure predominantly implied an improvement for the oligarchs as representatives of the leaders of the Russian economy. The low tax rates leave companies a bigger reservoir of liquidity and the national codification of individual tax laws, which largely replaced the merely general basic conditions on further interpretation in regional tax administrations, takes care of increased legal certainty.

However, it must not be overlooked – particularly from the point of view of regionally influential major companies – that the new legislation against the tax evasion that was possible in many cases in the past due to clever exploitation of regional differences and existing legal loopholes could even lead to a higher tax for some of those affected. For smaller companies that previously operated in the market unregistered and paid no taxes, the reform provides the opportunity for a "disguised amnesty", since the low tax rates provide an incentive to step out of the shadow economy arena.

Initial effects were already evident in the first year after coming into force in increased tax revenues from income tax and customs duties. Advanced reforms could be linked to the sources of assets even more strongly in the future. In Russian industry in particular, which is dominated by oil, gas and steel companies, a higher taxation of commodity pumping quotas, for example, would be conceivable. In addition to the easier reviewability of the pumping volume compared with corporate results there would be the secondary symptom that company relocations abroad could no longer be used as an evasive manoeuvre.

Russia's Tax Situation – An Outline of Reforms

"No idea where the profits are – but the oil's spurting out of here. Fill her up!"

Crude oil pumping tax was at the USA level, announced government head Mikhail Kasyanov in February 2004, but siphoning off an additional part of oil companies' enormous profits at high market prices above 25.00 US dollars / barrel was still being considered.[340] Stricter licence conditions concerning raw materials extraction could, for their part, lead to additional revenues for Russia. An increase in export duties on oil was considered as early as 2004 as the next stage in the tax reform, which would have brought in an estimated additional 3.47 billion US dollars depending on the market price at a price of 30.00 US dollars /

---

340 See "Kasyanov views crude oil tax as appropriate", economic news from Russia of 16th January 2004, http://wirtschaft.russlandonline.ru

barrel. The specific duties were finally also increased with the breathtaking rise in crude oil prices in 2004 and 2005, lastly on 1st October 2005 to 179.9 US dollars / tonne[341].

Overall, the current tax legislation in Russia can be assessed thoroughly positively. Samuel DiPiazza, head of the renowned auditing company PriceWaterhouseCoopers (PWC), even described the income tax not long ago as *"tax paradise on earth"* and credited the Russian state with having created a *"competitive tax system"*[342].

The Deputy Minister for Finance of the Russian Federation, Sergei Shatalov, envisages further tax reductions in coming years. The government is reportedly making efforts to reduce the tax burden by 1 % annually; currently it is at just 30 % of GDP.[343]

Pronounced weak points can be found less in the legislation itself than in execution by regional civil servants, of whom comprehensive inspection by the national tax ministry appears unrealistic. The old concepts of the negotiability of the tax burden and the good terms with local authorities will only disappear with a change in mentality over the course of time. It consequently applies that, despite overwhelmingly positive reaction to the Russian tax reforms of recent years, efficiency on paper does still not necessarily imply everyday improvements.

Only when the Russian state is able to exercise its rights, but also its obligations in respect of taxpayers to their satisfaction, will willingness to pay taxes increase. Many entrepreneurs, for example, still prefer to entrust criminal organisations with the protection of their property and pay protection money, which consequently represents an alternative tax in a certain respect. Russia's arid tax steppe will need to be irrigated intensively in future in order to correspond to, or approach, the ideal of many westwardly flourishing cultural landscapes.

---

341 See "Russia raises crude oil duty on 1st October to 179.9 US dollars per tonne", economic news from Russia of 1st October 2005, http://wirtschaft.russlandonline.ru
342 "Russia creates a competitive tax system", economic news from Russia of 21st July 2004, http://wirtschaft.russlandonline.ru
343 See "The tax reform in Russia is nearing completion", economic news from Russia of 22nd April 2004, http://wirtschaft.russlandonline.ru

C.
Tax Chaos: Optimisation, not Maximisation

Brief Commentary
by
DDr. Vladislav V. Mudrych

DDr. Vladislav V. MUDRYCH

DDr. V. Mudrych, who grew up in Moscow, joined Hypo Investment Bank (Liechtenstein) AG in 2002. After his studies in legal sciences at Moscow International University there followed the acquisition of two post-graduate doctorates at the renowned universities of Zurich (Ph.D. 1998) and Oxford (D.Phil. 2001). His most important publications[344] are used as academic teaching materials, predominantly in Russia. He has been a member of the HIB team in Vaduz for three years; he built up the "Eastern European Department" and is its head.

With the strategic regionalisation of customer markets Hypo Investment Bank (Liechtenstein) AG is consistently pursuing the line of global "customer proximity" in interplay with comprehensive specialist competence in asset matters. With DDr. V. Mudrych's commitment as a leading figure in the Eastern European business orientation, Hypo Investment Bank (Liechtenstein) AG has gained both a special contact partner for customers from the East and a highly esteemed expert in Russian tax matters.

---

[344] "Russian Contract Law", Moscow 2000 / "Russian Tax Law – Liability in Tax Law", Moscow 2001 / "Russian Insurance Law", Moscow 2002

Tax Chaos: Optimisation, not Maximisation

The fundamental problems of the present Russian tax system following the reforms of recent years are visualised through three trenchant examples of particular succinctness:

Firstly:
The tax reforms lay, to put it simply, under the motto, "tax reductions instead of tax privileges". The tax tariffs were therefore reduced to internationally highly competitive rates, without, however, using the reforms for a purposeful formal adaptation as well. The chance to devote oneself to industrial policy modernisation as well by simplifying contribution regulations was unfortunately largely missed. The tax-related, respectively, statutory promotion/strengthening of Russia's industries of the future continues to be lacking. The Russian legislation is attempting to achieve short-term income maximisation rather than long-term economic optimisation. For me, that is the wrong way to an economic policy with a promising future. Owing to the lack of intrastate incentives the Russian economy is more dependent upon the (world) economy than would be necessary.

In the absence of the tax system's regulatory function through differentiated consideration of individual economic branches, Russia degenerates into a "raw materials producer". The customs tariffs are additionally making their contribution to inhibiting domestic production. It would be better to promote production development at home through low import duties and make up for the eluded duty revenues in the subsequent period via improved producer yields in other areas. Additionally, the opportunities for tax credits/deferments on the part of the tax authorities established in the course of the tax reform have so far not been accepted in practice. The best example was the oil concern Yukos, on which an horrendous short-term tax claim was imposed instead of a tax payment in instalments to keep the overall concern afloat while at the same time settling the Russian tax debt. This claim could not be settled without the sale (and subsequent relapse into state control) of parts of Yukos. The short-term revenues and regaining of control by Russian oil production were, in this case, held in higher political esteem than an economically more sensible solution complete with the maintenance of a positive investment climate for foreign financial backers in Russia.

Secondly:
The second fundamental problem of the Russian tax system exists in the still variable interpretation of laws. Unclear formulations lead to disputes between taxpayers and tax authorities, in which process it often applies to the detriment of taxpayers that: "The state is always right". The result of these differences of opinion is then innumerable processes which often refer to petty matters and keep Russian justice from more important things. Last year, the highest constitutional court even had to make decisions in the simplest of tax areas. In the process this involved, for example, dates of tax revisions, value added tax reimbursements or value added taxes on advance payments – all of them things that would never land up at the highest constitutional court with a legally certain legislation.

Thirdly:
As a final point I would like to briefly address the prerogative of tax authorities over taxpayers' interests. I have already mentioned the ambiguity of the laws. In addition to this is the fact that tax authorities are sometimes even in the position to pass regulations. These, for their part, then partially contradict valid legal regulations. Even past court decisions are sometimes ignored by these new regulations. However, objection against an incorrect tax notification or a regulation contradicting the legal code is not always easy for the ordinary citizen and also harbours certain procedural risks. The problem reaches right down to the smallest wheels in the executive – for example, among customers officers, who claim autonomous duties on existing goods declarations at their discretion. However, in this extreme example the "little customs officer" alone cannot be enlisted as a scapegoat; the question is rather why such a thing is the practice in officialdom at all and tolerated by the higher plane in each case.

As further reforms I would principally see a further tightening of criminal law with regard to abolition of many smaller regional taxes. A tax system must, in my opinion, be an overall work similar to a menu with several courses. A small number of cooks who understand their work and create complementary courses are more preferable to me than many cooks who together spoil the broth!

In the detailed criticism of taxes I see no major problems in income tax for natural persons; in the counterpart for legal persons, however, more freedoms would have to be created or, respectively, legally existing freedoms also granted. Here I am thinking of tax credits, tax-related investment incentives and, above all, the right to an independent tax calculation and payment, so that accounting is simplified. The current profits tax is causing extremely high calculation complexity and, for many companies, is simply too complicated or difficult to estimate. There is potential for improvement, for example, in the definition of "economic motivation" in the case of operating expenditure, so that a clear comparison of operating revenues and operating expenditure can already be deduced from the legal text.

In my opinion, there are no problems with wealth tax. In the case of value added tax, on the other hand, the abolition of value added tax on advance payments would be desirable, likewise unbureaucratic implementation of value added tax repayment to exporters. Currently, such a reimbursement must be claimed for months – sometimes even before the court – before the exporter receives his right. A reduction of value added tax could also have a positive effect on certain imports. Here I am thinking above all of imports that are important to Russia, such as technology components, which can help Russian companies in their international competitiveness.

In the case of customs duties I would, as already mentioned, encourage technology imports and additionally strengthen Russia's economy through cheaper raw materials imports. Currently, though the importation of finished products is already more expensive than the importation of raw materials, the difference is not, however, big enough to stimulate increased domestic production.

It is difficult to offer functioning solutions in the case of the discussion surrounding tax reductions by means of false transfer prices between companies. Tax oases within Russia were already limited so that it was made difficult, at least within the country's borders, to show profits – sometimes through false transfer prices, but also by means of other tricks – in low-tax regions. In the transnational area, with the oft-mentioned profit movement to states such as Cyprus, it is rarely possible to push forward legal regulations. Nevertheless, more efficient control would counteract common methods of capital or profit movement for the reduction of the tax burden in Russia. Worth considering in the process would principally be a strict tolerance limit for import/export deviations from internationally market-standard prices. This would be feasible to a certain extent at least in the case of goods; in the case of services, rates that are too high or too low are more difficult to prove. Additionally, services such as consultancy or similar are inherently not tangible and examinable.

The whole discussion surrounding methods of tax evasion is somewhat laborious, since the hunted is generally one step ahead of the hunter. From my viewpoint, therefore, it is much more rewarding and also significantly easier to actively eliminate the causes of tax evasion than passively only combat the consequences and showily convict a number of tax evaders caught in the act. In the absence of grounds – i.e. with a competitive, transparently attractive tax system – there would also be significantly fewer cases of contribution reductions and, at the final count, the Russian state would certainly be left with an increase in revenue.

D.
Examples Concerning Capital Flight and Tax Evasion

"Russian lesson: investment = journey round the world"

A number of selected brief examples of current capital migration variants[345], most of which simultaneously signify evasion of payments, to provide a brief glimpse of the methodology. We deal mostly with transaction details that are difficult to trace for authorities, such as pricing or the question of whether goods deliveries/services were only fabricated or really did happen.

---

345 See *L. Grigoryev/A. Kosarev*, "Capital Flight: Scale and Nature", Bureau of economic analysis, 2000 or *Vladislav V. Mudrych*, "Russian Tax Law", p. 576-628, 2001

- Underinvoicing on importation:
  Only half of the goods' value is indicated on importation and taxed. The rest of the value migrates to the foreign partner via a specially founded Russian bogus firm.

- Self-payment:
  Patents or trademarks are registered abroad, whereupon the Russian company then transfers high licence fees "to itself".

- Self-payment:
  A consultancy firm founded abroad legitimises high payments to its own consultants abroad (front man role). In the process, it can rarely be checked, particularly in the case of transnational service provision and payment, whether the sums are adequate or overdrawn.

- Overinvoicing on importation:
  Raw materials from abroad are delivered to the Russian producer at widely excessive prices (supplier can be a self-founded company), whereupon the finished products are exported without tax payment. The profit thereby remains abroad.

- Underinvoicing on exportation:
  Exports are sold far under value to the foreign partner company. Finished products can also be exposed disguised as raw materials – the "finishing" in the partner company is limited to petty details. In the process, the exported capital is limited to the difference between the production costs and the true market value, in which process the sales value must not deviate exorbitantly from the market value for reasons of potential raising of suspicion.

- Fictitious import/export agreements:
  Russian products are exported, in which process recipient and debtor are two different companies. The debtor does not pay.

- "Useless" advance payments:
A big advance payment (approximately 30 % of the value) is transferred abroad. The arriving delivery is worthless or does not arrive first at all.

- Interest fraud:
A foreign creditor demands higher interest than is justified by the risk premium.

- Fictitious credit agreements:
They are paid back transnationally. In reality, however, a loan was never claimed.

- Movement of profits to tax oases:
The problem of offshore centres as tax havens concerns Russian authorities in that offshore firms registered by Russian companies take away profits and can pay tax on them more favourably than at home. Only a legal regulation to prevent intercompany profit transfer to subsidiaries based in tax oases could restrict this much-utilised "tax avoidance". The most-chosen offshore centres are those with which Russia has a double taxation agreement (e.g. Cyprus).

The Russian state is not to be envied – on the one hand, the problem of weakly pronounced tax morale in Russia, on the other hand, rarely available effective ways to raise it. The borders are porous – not least because customs officials are sometimes still able to make their own "tax laws" or, in this case, the floodgates are opened for contribution evasion/tax evasion.

The small number of examples make it clear how urgent a comprehensive reform – away from the former structures, towards a modern tax legislation and state services to the citizen – is in order to reduce the incentive to capital flight. Only when capital no longer *wants* to flee, respectively, it is no longer greatly *worth it*, will the situation improve. That it involves, in the process, not only technical reforms of the regulatory body, but rather accompanying reforms of execution and, to a particular extent, a reform of the state – citizen trust basis "in the minds of each and every one", has already been emphasised many times.

Closing Remarks

"Suspicion of Money Laundering" has presented the reader with an abundance of information. In the foreground, in addition to the accurate portrayal of legal standards – both in the international and national context – with regard to money laundering prevention, as already touched on in the introduction, stood the "somewhat different glimpse into the Liechtensteinian banking business".

"Pros" from banking circles take an interest in the theoretical side of the due diligence check or, respectively, according to which standards this must be carried out in compliance with the law from the bank point of view. "Laymen", on other hand, are appealed to more by the simplified practice-oriented approach to this topic. Hypo Investment Bank (Liechtenstein) AG extended due respect to both of these diametrically opposed interests and linked precise theory with simple practice.

The constructed case study[346] led the reader into everyday questions of practice in the banking business and briefly and concisely answered how the present facts would be legally judged. Additionally, the statistics[347] from the money laundering reporting offices demonstrated the cost-benefit ratio of the complex process of "due diligence", which on paper, unfortunately, turned out to be thoroughly disappointing.

Through the presented complicated test standards Hypo Investment Bank (Liechtenstein) AG attempted to make the reader aware of what great effort in terms of administration, associated with high costs, burdens even small banks. Due diligence and streamlined administration are not reconcilable with each other so far – only the future will show whether simpler and equally efficient processes can be developed in order to separate "contaminated" from "clean" money.

Currently, the tightrope between customer interest (uncomplicated serious business relationship) and bank interest (safeguarding of

---

346 See p.271
347 See p.313

reputation, illumination of contract partners' backgrounds) is still feasible but, as regulation density rises, is increasingly becoming – especially for small institutions – a problem that is swallowing up important resources.

Annexe – Further Sources of Information

A concluding directory of legal sources for individual acts, regulations, directives etc. has deliberately been bypassed, since the publication moves in several legal areas that are subject to constant changes. Sources for the legislature underlying the publication can be found in the texts at the relevant points.

The only reference made here is to the future "mother" of anti-money laundering legal norms – the third EU money laundering directive "2005/60/EC of the European Parliament and Council of 26th October 2005 on the prevention of the use of the financial systems for the purpose of money laundering and terrorist financing"[348].

Numerous legal source directories from the jurisdictions concerned in this publication can be found online. The following sources are worth a look for the interested reader:

European Union (EU): Public legal data base
http://europa.eu.int/eur-lex

EU: Public documents (including legal documents)
http://europa.eu.int/documents/index_de.htm

Principality of Liechtenstein: Current legal source directory
http://www.recht.li

Austria: Federal legal information system
http://www.ris.bka.gv.at

Germany: Legal information system of the Federal Ministry for Justice
http://bundesrecht.juris.de

Switzerland: Compilation of Swiss federal law
http://www.admin.ch/ch/d/sr/sr.html

---

348 To be found at http://europa.eu.int/eur-lex

ANNEXE

Selected international organisations and associations in the fight against money laundry

Anti-money laundering – German information portal
http://www.antigeldwaesche.de

APG ... Asia/Pacific Group on Money Laundering
http://www.apgml.org

BIS ... Bank for International Settlements
http://www.bis.org

CFATF ... Caribbean Financial Action Task Force
http://www.cfatf.org

Commonwealth Secretariat
http://www.thecommonwealth.org

Eastern and South Africa Anti-Money Laundering Group
http://www.esaamlg.org

EBRD ... European Bank for Reconstruction and Development
http://www.ebrd.com

EGMONT Group
http://www.egmontgroup.org

European Council (e.g. "Moneyval" committee)
http://www.coe.int

European Commission
http://europa.eu.int

European Central Bank
http://www.ecb.int

European Parliament
http://www.europarl.eu.int

EUROPOL
http://www.europol.eu.int

FATF ... Financial Action Task Force on Money Laundering
http://www.fatf-gafi.org

GAFISUD ... Financial Action Task Force of South America ...
http://www.gafisud.org

INTERPOL
http://www.interpol.int

IMF ... International Monetary Fund
http://www.imf.org

IMoLIN ... International Money Laundering Information Network
http://www.imolin.org

OGBS ... Offshore group of Banking Supervisors
http://www.ogbs.net

IOSCO ... International Organization of Securities Commissions
http://www.iosco.org

MENAFATF ... Middle East and North Africa Financial Action Task Force
http://www.menafatf.org

OECD ... Organisation for Economic Co-operation and Development
http:// www.oecd.org

Organizations of American States (OAS) (e.g. Inter-American Drug Abuse Control Commission)
http://www.oas.org

Council of the European Union
http://ue.eu.int

ANNEXE

Transparency International
http://www.transparency.org

United Nations Crime and Justice Information Network
http://www.uncjin.org

United Nations Global Programme Against Money Laundering
http://www.unodc.org/unodc/money_laundering.html

United Nations Office for Drug Control and Crime Prevention
http://www.unodc.org

World Bank Group
http://www.worldbank.org, or
http://www.amlcft.org

Wolfsberg Group
http://www.wolfsberg-principles.com

World Customs Organisation (WCO)
http://www.wcoomd.org